MW00778633

BARCELONA, CITY OF MARGINS

Barcelona, City of Margins

OLGA SENDRA FERRER

UNIVERSITY OF TORONTO PRESS
Toronto Buffalo London

© University of Toronto Press 2022
Toronto Buffalo London
utorontopress.com
Printed in the U.S.A.

ISBN 978-1-4875-0848-7 (cloth)   ISBN 978-1-4875-3835-4 (EPUB)
                                   ISBN 978-1-4875-3834-7 (PDF)

Toronto Iberic

Library and Archives Canada Cataloguing in Publication

Title: Barcelona, city of margins / Olga Sendra Ferrer.
Names: Sendra Ferrer, Olga, author.
Series: Toronto Iberic ; 70.
Description: Series statement: Toronto Iberic ; 70 | Includes bibliographical
    references and index.
Identifiers: Canadiana (print) 2021033438X | Canadiana (ebook) 20210334428 |
    ISBN 9781487508487 (cloth) | ISBN 9781487538354 (EPUB) |
    ISBN 9781487538347 (PDF)
Subjects: LCSH: Literature and photography – Spain – Barcelona – History –
    20th century. | LCSH: Photography – Social aspects – Spain – Barcelona –
    History – 20th century. | LCSH: Public spaces – Spain – Barcelona – History –
    20th century. | LCSH: City and town life in literature. | LCSH: Public spaces
    in literature. | LCSH: Barcelona (Spain) – In literature.
Classification: LCC PQ6073.C56 S46 2022 | DDC 860.9/355 – dc23

We wish to acknowledge the land on which the University of Toronto Press operates.
This land is the traditional territory of the Wendat, the Anishnaabeg, the Haudenosaunee,
the Métis, and the Mississaugas of the Credit First Nation.

This book has been supported by a grant from the Thomas and Catherine McMahon
Fund at Wesleyan University.

University of Toronto Press acknowledges the financial support of the Government of
Canada, the Canada Council for the Arts, and the Ontario Arts Council, an agency of the
Government of Ontario, for its publishing activities.

Canada Council   Conseil des Arts
for the Arts   du Canada

ONTARIO ARTS COUNCIL
CONSEIL DES ARTS DE L'ONTARIO
an Ontario government agency
un organisme du gouvernement de l'Ontario

Funded by the   Financé par le
Government   gouvernement
of Canada   du Canada   Canadä

To Matthew

Contents

Illustrations

Acknowledgments

When does a book start to take shape? I am trying to find the point of origin, but I could go back as far as when I was six years old and stole that book from school (please, nobody translate this sentence for my parents!). There are obviously many small moments that make us go in one direction or another, but, in this case, and for the sake of keeping the reader on task, I should start with the ones that really matter, the ones that are inextricably bound up in the pages that you are holding right now.

Hence, when I think about writing, Jordi Marí and Elvira Vilches are the first people to come to mind. They were my first professors in the United States and taught me everything I believe was essential to make my way here, to this place, to these pages. Thank you both; I feel very lucky to have had you as teachers, mentors, and now friends. Since then, I have been fortunate enough to find others who taught me the ropes and who have contributed to my development as a scholar including Angel Loureiro and Antonio Monegal; my colleagues at the Department of Romance Languages and Literatures at Wesleyan University; and two other colleagues whom I deeply admire, who have unknowingly become mentors to me: Robert A. Davidson and H. Rosi Song.

Many institutions have helped me to complete this book by providing funds, photographs, and texts. Many thanks to the Thomas and Catherine McMahon Memorial Fund for making this book possible. I would like to thank the staff at the Museu Nacional d'Art de Catalunya for providing Joan Colom's images and for helping me locate many others. Thanks also to the Museu d'Art Contemporani de Barcelona, the Col·legi d'Arquitectes de Catalunya, and the Arxiu Fotogràfic de Barcelona for giving me access to the photographs for this book. I also thank *Catalan Review* and the *Journal of Catalan Studies* for permission to reprint sections of chapters 3 and 4. And, finally, to the anonymous reviewers of this book, whose generosity in dedicating their time and attention to evaluating and commenting on my manuscript was invaluable.

Photographers and writers themselves or, in many cases, their families have been essential to the completion of this book by granting permission for their images and work to be included: Colita, Laura Terré, Carme and Montserrat Colom, and María Candel. Thank you for sharing your work and for helping me to complete this project; I could not have done it without your generosity.

I would be remiss if I did not acknowledge all of those friends who helped me put together the million pieces that compose this book. You – article-seekers, exhibition-goers, book-finders, catalogue-hunters, forced museum-visitors, gentle readers, photographer-introducers, or just listeners – this book is for all of you: my dearest Montse Marsal, Xavier Garcia, Louise Neary, Elena Peregrina, Carme Uceda, Xènia Sendra Ferrer, Viviana Centeno, Óscar Sendra Ferrer, and Consuelo Bautista. And always to my parents, Albert Sendra y Encarna Ferrer, who always knew that I could.

My biggest debt is to my husband Matthew, who read every single version of this work and is always there to remind me what a life together means. To my daughter, Greta, who reminds me every day that life is all about moments.

A Note on Translations

Unless otherwise indicated, all bracketed translations are mine.

BARCELONA, CITY OF MARGINS

Coming into Presence: Margin and Dissent in the Barcelona of Francoism

In this book, I seek rupture, disjuncture, dissent. In order to discern a cogent view of Barcelona from among the multitude of essays, photographs, novels, and poems that have been produced about this city to date, it is necessary to forgo static chronologies and instead establish a new perspective that reconceptualizes the relationship between aesthetic and day-to-day experience through a new lens that can show us where to find the origins of Barcelona as it is understood today – as a global city subject to a process of modernization principally predicated upon its urbanistic structure. To do so, this book seizes upon moments when a disjuncture of/in space occurs: at these times and places, the structures that organize the city are called into question and, by extension, the city's inhabitants come to find themselves in a new physical and social space. In the currently available bibliography, there is a tendency to conflate this questioning of the material and social space of Barcelona with the city's democratic period, whether before or after Franco's dictatorship. This is due to the fact that it is in democratic periods that political, cultural, and social systems permit – in the case of Barcelona – the large-scale renovation of the city on the one hand, and, on the other, the levelling of open, direct, and therefore visible critiques of city government and the adoption of a (neo)capitalist economic system that has proven itself to be a quintessential piece in the construction of the global city.[1] Employing here the distinction between the constructed material environment and its social usage by its inhabitants,[2] urbanistic and urban renewal are therefore inextricably linked with political, social, and cultural renewal. As evident as that may be, here I will argue that it is in fact dictatorship-era Barcelona that offers us the most salient example of how the material city facilitates the creation and development of a system of critique that then lays the foundation for the democratic city to come. In a totalitarian system, where the possibilities for change beyond the narrow scope of the regime's political discourse are practically non-existent, Francoism's engagement with the material construction of Barcelona opens the door to dissent and, correspondingly, the political, social, and cultural renewal of the city. In this juncture we find a crucial connection between two key periods in Barcelona's material and social history: in its fervour to reshape the city, the dictatorship destroys physical space, the redevelopment of which will spur an urban, grassroots movement that in turn will set the pillars for a conceptual system that will spawn not just the democratic city itself, but also the underpinnings of a critical-analytical system vital to our understanding of contemporary Barcelona.

To register the dismemberment of physical, social, and even political space in Barcelona under the Francoist dictatorship, we must readjust our vantage point to seek out moments that allow us to observe fluctuations in public life in which daily experience reconfigures itself into a public space for dissidence that, in turn, restructures the social fabric. A classic example of this phenomenon is Jaime Gil de Biedma's walk through Montjuïc in "Barcelona ja no és bona" (1966). In terms of physical space, bodies are inevitably restrained by and disappear under the imposition of cement; they are physically tied to the city's materiality, geography, and discursivity, and they permeate its symbols and history. Consequently, in its movement made manifest through the act of walking, the body performs the physical space of that which is considered city or part of the city. To put it another way, in the body's practice, symbols that are deemed essential in the conceptualization of the city are revealed: here Montjuïc, as one of the geographical, social, and historical referents that demarcate the built city, assumes a bourgeois social personification through the act of strolling. Gil de Biedma's body, imbued in social power relations and institutional forms, configures the urban body of the Barcelona of the dictatorship, whose power structure is affirmed through the visual field, through what everyone can see, through the declaration of the social and urbanistic boundaries of the city, which to some extent is a natural boundary, but also a space of/under control. This same visuality, however, by employing the same elements that constitute the conceptuality of the city, makes critique possible. Using the very language of the regime, Gil de Biedma constructs a new narrative. His body, like the body of Montjuïc, becomes a point of intersection, joining past and present, memory and presence: he infuses the landscape with the patina of decadence that likewise characterizes his social class, but he also reveals the hidden presence of the bodies of those newly arrived to the city, in the process contrasting the bourgeois act of strolling through a place supposedly reserved for exclusive leisure with the quiet desperation of those whose only choice is to live there and hope to go unseen.[3]

Accordingly, this space – Montjuïc, Gil de Biedma, his poem – represents a departure from the norm: through the inscription of his body in the order of the text, the author lays out another space, one that supplants familiarity with estrangement. On the one hand, we have the familiar story: Unamuno's *intrahistoria* that reinscribes the body in the history of the city, perhaps best characterized by the filth and neglect of that bourgeois scene and the indifference towards this essential referent that becomes a *mise en abyme* of Barcelona. On the other hand, we have a viewpoint registered from the outside, from the other side, from the perspective of the forgotten that lies beyond the reigning physical, social, and cultural order; because no one looks in that direction, because the "fosos quemados por los fusilamientos" (Gil de Biedma, "Barcelona" 87) [moats lit on fire by executions] are ignored, we hearken to the voices that break the alleged harmony of Gil de Biedma's leisurely stroll, and, consequently, of that supposedly unmovable order, now a "despedazado anfiteatro" (88) [demolished amphitheater] or "fábula del tiempo" (85) [fable of the past], not just because of its bourgeois history, but also because of its oppressive present. On this guided tour, Gil de Biedma leads us along by our senses – sight but also hearing – to the other side: we can jump the rails that restrict and direct our movements, instead dismantling, questioning, and reconstructing them with the potentiality of elements not accounted for in the discourses and practices of the city government, still swayed by the interests of a bourgeoisie that is also in pieces.

By choosing one of the most prominent lookout points over Barcelona, Gil de Biedma distances himself from and reimagines a setting that serves for the crafting of a narrative that, in turn, acknowledges and embraces the noise that destabilizes Francoism's false harmony: the din of the voices that come from beyond, simultaneously inside and outside, as an essential component of the city, albeit one that is marginalized and excluded, reinforcing the notion of a presence that we can hear but not see. He offers us a multisensorial perspective that seeks to underscore the limitation of the visual guide imposed upon the city and to develop a new perspective that dismantles the regime's parameters of economic success.[4] Gil de Biedma himself becomes a margin, a figure that breaks the binaries of space and place, of city and the urban, and adopts a dialectical position. Hence, the place, that which we believe permanent, is fragmented and dispersed, dismantled as it is displaced "in a challenging mobility that does not respect places" (Certeau 130), heralding new narratives and concomitantly revealing the potentiality of a space that transgresses established boundaries. And that transgression becomes dissidence.

Thus, echoing the words of Manuel Delgado ("La ciudad" 140–1), this poem posits a strategic moment to acknowledge the everyday relationships between individuals who are socially homogenized by the urbanistic graph of the city, and Gil de Biedma encourages the possibility of a new structuring environment, which is to say, one capable of unleashing determined social relationships theretofore unimagined. Hence, drawn out from "the long poem of walking," as Michel de Certeau calls it, Gil de Biedma alters the panoptical view of urbanistic form, and the body becomes the point of contact and conflict between different components of the city, which facilitates the re-emergence of elements excluded from the urbanistic project:

> The long poem of walking manipulates spatial organization, no matter how panoptic they may be: it is neither foreign to them (it can take place only within them) nor in conformity with them (it does not receive its identity from them). It creates shadows and ambiguities within them. It inserts is multitudinous references and citations into them (social models, cultural mores, personal factors). Within them it is itself the effect of successive encounters and occasions that constantly alter it and make it the other's blazon: in other words, it is like a peddler, carrying something surprising, transverse or attractive compared with the usual choice. (Certeau 101)

Here de Certeau is talking about what Delgado called the urban, the "bajo continuo" [basso continuo], the "murmullo" [murmur] that punctuates the movements of pedestrians, "ballets imprevisibles y cambiantes" [unpredictable and changing ballet], referring to Jane Jacobs' famous image (*El animal* 128). As de Certeau notes (129–30), it is the opposition between seeing ("the knowledge of an order of places") and acting ("spatializing actions"), between established order and the use of that order. The body, in motion, creates its own rhetoric, which is not necessarily descriptive but rather narrative, productive; this motion in turn makes transgression possible, transforming a passer-by into a "social delinquent."

The margins of Barcelona come from this "delinquency," and while on the one hand it acknowledges the order that distributes, positions, and classifies bodies using a distanced gaze and the redistribution of space, on the other it identifies mobile and changing spatial matrices capable of transgressing said order. It is not just urban, although it can come from there; the margin is movement that can become, as we will see, dissent. Through this dialectic we seek to emphasize the diversity at the core of the urban space of Barcelona, and the way in which this diversity modifies the conception of a space that attempts to control difference and otherness through urban planning and its concomitant and purportedly unique and stable cartography.

Hence, in this book, I seek to renegotiate from the margin the visual paradigms that define the Barcelona of Francisco Franco's dictatorship. I am seeking further evidence of the epistemological displacement that we see in Gil de Biedma and that will allow us to glimpse the possibility of a new order, a democratic order. I am seeking voices that interrupt and subvert, voices that use their own otherness to disquiet the harmonious facade of the dictatorship's physical, social, and cultural structures and indicate other possibilities, confronting our gazes and breaking the canon of what we consider representative. In order to do so, I intend to employ examples that take matters a step further than Gil de Biedma, examples in which action directly affects the urban and urbanistic discourses and practices of Barcelona.

To that end, I examine the creation of a space of dissent during the Franco dictatorship in literature and photography through the (re) construction of urban and urbanistic space. I read this new space as a moment of an "urban turn," when most cities in Spain, and most importantly Barcelona, undergo a transformation due to mass migration to urban centres. This changing panorama implies a material change in the physiognomy of cities that allows the creation of interstices of dissent, giving shape to a public space that will be the foundation of the democratic city. The urban turn, therefore, allows us to visualize and trace those interstices in the work of writers (Francisco Candel) and photographers (Joan Colom and Colita) in whose artistic creations the use of urban surroundings sets a new engagement with the changing urban environment while articulating a radical perspective that questions and ruptures the political and social order imposed by the dictatorship.

Margins

Under the panopticon of the urbanistic bubble, Gil de Biedma's body helps us to perceive a hum, a constant buzzing that announces the autonomous insularity of those who do not fit into the city's visual urbanistic schematization. But this disturbance also crosses time and space and creates an independent movement that interrupts the relationships between supposedly stable elements. Between the codes that he displaces and dismantles, Gil de Biedma creates a transparent caesura, an interstitial fracture rather than a marginalized one, that allows us to see disruption and possibilities, new orders and directions. It is the murmur of another story, another city, another structure. And it is Gil de Biedma as margin, through his meandering and strolling body, who sees and hears, makes visible and heard, separates and connects: with his voice he (re)constructs the narrative structure of spatial syntax, the interplay between space and place, city and urban, and geometric and anthropological space. Precisely in the coexistence of these multiple identities in space, the order of things is destabilized.

The margin, then, is an essential category to locate this space of dissent. To speak of margins is to speak of things that are outside and inside simultaneously, which in their liminality, complicate and undermine the fictitious wholeness of place. The margin is the disrupting power of noisy everyday ugliness. It is the opposite of structure; it is what gets left out and counts only as otherness. And, thus, the margins unsettle our stable conception of the city and become potential spaces of presence. In the context of the city, we read the margin in the tradition of landscape studies as initiated by Henri Lefebvre and Michel de Certeau and expanded upon in Spain through the work of relevant figures such as Manuel Delgado. In this line of thought, and keeping in mind the image of Gil de Biedma's walk, think of the margin as constant extraterritoriality, whether in the centre or at the outskirts of what is defined as city or place. Therefore, the margin is not physically limited to the suburbs; neither is it limited to any particular heterotopic place, although it does maintain a direct connection to both. It is constant movement that simultaneously criss-crosses the city and, in certain moments, marks and renders visible what is overlooked or ignored and, hence, outside. Through this action of making visible the invisible or the consciously ignored, the margin critiques the status quo and makes possible a new social but also urban and urbanistic template. These movements are marginal because they step off of established pathways to create new ones.

Here we find an important connection to Manuel Delgado's "sociedades movedizas" [moveable societies], given that the margin is, in part, that other structure that underscores "la dislocación y el extrañamiento" (*Sociedades* 12) [dislocation and estrangement]. These structures, Delgado's urban or the not-city, or de Certeau's space – different terms used to refer to a space of countless possibilities that opens the door to voices excluded from urbanism – is the space of/for social action, since it is there that the city's infrastructure is organized and disorganized (Delgado, *Sociedades* 65–70). However, the margin does not necessarily imply physical movement, given that it is not exclusively personified by the movement of bodies in the street or in oppositional public protest – although, as we will see, it does maintain a connection to urbanistic planning. Indeed, the margin is not solely a matter of momentary physical occupation of space and does not assume a form comprised exclusively of the physical interstices produced in the urban framework (cracks, gaps, holes, intervals, intersections, etc.), although, of course, it is also found in these more obvious spaces for disruption. It is characterized by how these frameworks are produced on a social and cultural level that does not necessarily have a visual materiality (again, in the shape of protests or mobilizations), but which are organized thanks to the urbanistic inequality of space. They are interstices, pauses, that occur on different levels and are transmitted in different forms – words, images, noises.

Yes, the margin can be understood as Delgado's transversal spaces, since they "cruzan, intersectan otros espacios devenidos territorios" (*El animal* 36) [cross, intersect other spaces turned territories] and in this regard "space" as de Certeau designates it (117–29). The margin is threshold, boundary, the pure possibility that place offers for transformation, or practiced places to use Lefebvre's term for spatial practice, but it differs from these spaces in that its temporality and constant motion leave behind a sediment, a trace that, like deposits in a river, modifies the city's structure and becomes, as de Certeau would have it, place (91–108): it alters structure, improving or damaging it. The "stories" conceived by de Certeau leave a trace; they are a code that is born and vanishes, but they are not innocent or inconsequential as a result of their transience. The margin, like the pounding of feet, further erodes the well-worn path and marks new routes, which is how it becomes noise and creates a distortion that can change perspectives. In Gil de Biedma's poem, the poetic voice is margin, because it is through its subjectivity that the possibility of a new order, a new history based on the story it tells, is revealed. More importantly, however, Gil de Biedma hears the voices of "estos chavas nacidos en el Sur" (87) [these guys born in the south] who are also margin, as their subaltern status allows them to appear autonomously, in spite of structure's efforts to conceal them.[5] They become an instantaneous society and, borrowing Delgado's concept, create "proto-estructuras" (*El animal* 12) [proto-structures] that fossilize and develop in the prolific social tissue that will, as Manuel Castells puts it in his classic study *The City and the Grassroots* (1983), render obsolete the political institutions of Francoism. Using Delgado's words once more, "aturden el orden del mundo al tiempo que lo fundan" (*El animal* 117) [they disturb the order of the world while at the same time establishing it]. Here we see the formation of a collective in order to show how everyday life can be comprised of goals and structures that, given the right conditions, can signal political discord.

What the margin is not, here, is marginalization: the margin that we seek is not characterized by isolation but rather dialogue with and critiques of presumably stable power structures whose origin lies in the bipartite divisions that characterize the setting and social space of the Barcelona of the dictatorship. The margin opens up social and urban configurability by making room for new voices that interrupt the ruling discourses and practices of the time. Nevertheless, we should acknowledge that, in spite of this rift, certain parameters are upheld necessarily in this context: on a base level in their approach to the city's environs, structures of knowledge applied from the margin resemble and repeat the urban and urbanistic structures employed from the centre. If, as de Certeau does (32–3), we turn to Ferdinand de Saussure's parameter of the distinction between language (langue) and speech (parole), the margin elaborates its own speech, in its own specific voice that is predetermined by the system of representation.[6] The margin defines otherness in opposition to dominant practices and discourses not in order to portray itself as a "dislocation" but rather, taking up that same language, to create an identity of its own that is recognizable within those established parameters. Maintaining these parameters fulfils multiple objectives: first, language is made recognizable and can function within the constraints of censorship; second, and more importantly, a critique can be levelled against place; and finally, traces of the prevailing social and cultural discourses and practices of artists that move within the margin can be located and identified, which is important because in spite of the critique that they are making, involuntary traces of those discourses and practices – for example, class or gender – still mark their identity. In other words, if culture affects perception (Tuan 162), we should be aware of what discourses and practices it creates and uses so we can understand the criteria for the selection of what to show or not show. Therefore, the margin, "el marginal" [the marginal] as Manuel Delgado calls it (El animal 114–15), is not on the edge of society but rather at the heart of its activity; it lies at its very centre. These are strangers or outsiders who move in and out of the light and shadows, crossing thresholds and revealing a transversal space that crosses and diverges; they confirm the existence of the social system while simultaneously interrupting and defying it, filling it with noise, as it were, like the voices of "estos chavas nacidos en el Sur" that interrupt Gil de Biedma's – and Barcelona's – reflection and narrative construction. The margin uncovers new experiences that envision new frameworks for perception that diverge from those imposed, in this case, by the Francoist regime through urban materiality.

With that in mind, the rhythms of the city that Henri Lefebvre describes are part of the margin; that is, they offer the possibility of dialectic encounters that make up and can modify the material city. They are an essential part of the daily life that the artists analysed here depict as the basis for a new city. Of particular interest is how these rhythms are both present and absent, or as Lefebvre notes, how they "present themselves without being present" (*Writings* 223). Their multiple appearances and temporalities, orchestrated repetition, and especially the oppositions that they induce are key features, because together they open a space for encounter and negotiation, and the creation of nonlinear time and history, as Lefebvre explains in *Rhythmanalisis* (27). In other words, in the margin we uncover the interdisciplinarity beneath material space, that is, the variety of practices and discourses that make it up; in this discovery we can also see how urban space is defined not only from an urbanistic or official perspective, but also by the conjugation of rhythms, including those that are expressed and visible – that give the city a recognizable form – and those that are not. Similar to Lefebvre, and as we have seen in Gil de Biedma's walk, Amin and Thrift refer to this nonlinear construction of the city with their concept of the "footprint," that is, "the present crossed by influences from the past," the "simultaneity of trajectories composed of the practices and thoughts of [for example] those travelling" (22–3). Concordantly, the city stops being organized and subdivided by established patterns of mobility; it is a multitudinous city, connected and separate at the same time, a palimpsest negotiated by the sketches and imaginary that are built up around it. This approach is vitally important for how it recasts urban mythologies: it can create new myths that define the city and its inhabitants, and it can also dismantle pre-existing ones. Space and narration are superimposed; physical space cannot be understood without the narratives that shape it, which is another way of approaching the human conception of space that we saw in Lefebvre. The concept of margin asserts this amalgam of sometimes contrary movements, and in the process recovers that which is forgotten or hidden in occasionally undesired forms and embraces precisely the existence of multiplicity, light and shadow. In its make-up, the margin accentuates certain rhythms by making them visible and in doing so incorporating them into the formal structure of the city, a structure that has been inescapably modified by that marginal movement and can therefore no longer be what it once was. This modification concerns not just urban rhythms, but also how these rhythms are inserted into a narrative that can change perspectives.

Like the voices in Gil de Biedma's poem, the margin is what is there, even if we decide to ignore or eliminate it; the margin remains insistently present and winds up taking the city, changing its physiognomy as the ephemeral is made structure and so challenges and registers complaint with certain social and material policies of the dictatorship's governance. It is true that Gil de Biedma's utopia never materializes, at least not in the economic and class-based form that he envisioned in terms of his Marxist principles; however, it does reverberate in terms of space: the noise of the immigrant voices is also the noise of the slums that disturb the visual harmony of Barcelona, a city that was undergoing a process of a supposed beautification meant to create investment and attract foreign tourists.[7] This noise makes its mark on the system and winds up becoming the basis for an identity that was overlooked and would go on to lay the foundation for one of democracy's most important social structures: its neighbourhood associations. This noise, which is caused by the margin, is what precedes visualization and allows us to change how we look at and understand Barcelona. It is a metaphor that allows us to describe that which has not yet come to be; it is the representation of that which has not yet been said.

Hence, the margin, as glimpsed in Gil de Biedma's poem, stands out for two reasons. First, for how the author writes a new narrative of history that, instead of continuing an illusory line shaped by an evolutionary vision, heeds the complexity and circularity of movements and, by using the noise of voices ignored by the system, creates a new space – a new order that emphasizes new rhythms, new ways or new possibilities of being outside what is considered straight. Second, the margin stands out for its emphasis on the voices, on noise as a disturbance, which breaks with the order and purity of its opposite, the harmony of the structural shape of the city. Hence, the margin becomes a source of power that is worth listening to or looking at since it indicates the limits of a territory and the way to make oneself heard within it. The interruption or disturbance intrinsic to the margin creates a disorientation that introduces new coordinates, multiplies angles, and selects improbable points of view. That is to say, it rewrites history from its hidden corners; it seizes history in its absence rather than its imposed presence, becoming a transgression that destabilizes rhythms. Michel Foucault states that "transgression carries the limit right to the limit of its being; transgression forces the limit to face the fact of its imminent disappearance, to find itself in what it excludes" ("Preface" 34). Hence, the margin, incorporating all those parts that are discarded because they do not belong to the harmonious whole, takes on presence and agency. These new structures and these margins do not dismantle limitations; instead, they expose and transgress them in order to make possible, for the first time, a zone of existence.[8] This gesture of interruption is unlimited – since, as Foucault says, no limitation can contain or restrain transgression ("Preface" 35) – and principally designates the existence of other ways of doing and being in the world. Continuity and interruption open a space for continuous movement in which structure acquires meaning(s) through the encounter between bodies, of whatever type they may be.

The idea of looking into a period of time from the perspective of the margins, from that which has been deemed different – because the margins are defined as such by a code that is considered the norm and, hence, ignored, repressed, or assimilated – is the path this analysis seeks to follow. I will trace a narrative that breaks with what is considered "tradition," that lies outside of institutional power, and that grants visibility to dissidence, emphasizing the dialectic nature of any type of organization.

Hence, in this book, I seek those structures, narratives, stories, spaces, and delinquencies that make noise, that make us question the harmony of the spatial structure of the city. The search for margins, then, will be the guiding principle of my reconstruction of the Barcelona of the dictatorship. This framework that will allow me to approach the city's social and material structure from a new perspective, that of photographers and writers who show how, with a simple shift in position, the singular and monolithic construction imposed by a centre/periphery dynamic can be dismantled by the dissent that it generates and which directly affects the urban/urbanistic landscape.

Structures of Dissent

The concept of margin renders visible elements, perspectives, and moments that escape the physical structure of the city and the social order that it imposes. It beseeches us to focus our attention on moments when noise can be heard; it reveals the other's existence and materializes opposition that responds to the institutional domination produced through urban space and the zoning, characterization, and social division that arise within it. To locate these kinds of structures entails an active reading that makes daily activities, like Gil de Biedma's walk or the din of the voices of the slums' inhabitants, not disappear in their temporality, a characteristic that Delgado, Lefebvre, and de Certeau all point out as an essential element of the urban and its repetition; instead, these activities leave cracks in the city, underscoring the presence of latent tension that becomes a conscious moment of comparison, which can give way to critique and, then, the potential for dissent.

However, when speaking of dissent, we should not think exclusively of directly confrontational acts of protest or resistance. That is to say, it is not solely a direct challenge issued to power or the legitimacy of the government, although both protest and resistance are indeed acts of dis-sidence (Roberts 654–5; Hollander and Einwohner 533–54); dissidence can also take the form of "less political, less organised and less conscious acts of defiance against perceived grievances" (Roberts 655). By dissent we understand, then, oppositional manoeuvres, to borrow the concept put forth by Ross Chambers (1–18), or as Roberts explains by turning to David Harvey and Michel de Certeau, "everyday micro-struggles within specific locales in which ordinary people use resources at hand to make small 'tactical' raids upon the different ways in which our lives are gov-erned" (655). To dissent is, in its most traditional sense, to differ in senti-ment, to disagree with the methods, goals, and so on of a political party or, in this case, a dictatorial regime, a disagreement that arises between individuals, groups, and contexts, and "rather than acts of resistance helps us to underscore … the lack of organization and the conscious acts of defiance" (654). Dissent discovers the structure of power and reveals its image, spelling out how it affects daily life, not in order to change the essential structure of power, but to change the effect that it has on those who live under its rule: with dissent we are in the presence of a change "that is not radical or even forceful, and indeed mostly passes unnoticed, but that functions as a critical agency in liberal democracies as well as in situations revolutionary or totalitarian" (Chambers 1). Rather than a rev-olution, it is the acceptance of opposition to a dominant practice, which in turn grants presence, voice, and agency, but without breaking the sys-tem or turning it into a diametrically opposed structure.

Like the oppositional practices that Chambers examines, this dis-sent, although it can be characterized as an involuntary response to dehumanizing practices, is "consciously planned" (9), because it seeks change or restructuring, but it is not a disruption of the distribution of power's political and social components. Following Jacques Rancière when he speaks about the political character of aesthetics, dissent ena-bles the creation of a structure that "re-frames the world of a common experience as the world of a shared impersonal experience. In this way, it aims to help create the fabric of a common experience in which new modes of constructing common objects and new possibilities of sub-jective enunciation may be developed" (141–2). That is to say, through dissent a social fabric predicated upon day-to-day life takes shape and goes on to be considered common and impersonal, which leads to a structure that connects different individual parts and forms a collectiv-ity that becomes a cohesive social group, which in turn leads to a voice and identity; here unity comes from spatial identity.

As Manuel Castells explains when speaking about the creation of neighbourhood associations in the 1970s, "the neighbourhood became an organizational base where most struggles, though triggered by a particular problem, gave rise during the mobilization to neighbourhood associations aimed at dealing with all matters of everyday life" (*City* 215). Although my book focuses on a historical moment that precedes the rise of neighbourhood associations, Castells's example serves to show how organization arises from an individual difficulty that becomes a shared experience and, from there, a complaint and critique of the system, but does not necessarily assume the form of direct and violent opposition to the system of power. We articulate a form of dissent that criticizes from a common base and becomes structure itself in how it gives shape to a group and identity and goes on to grant visibility, presence, and, consequently, the reconstitution of space.

Dissent is therefore related to specific, local concerns affecting the population's experience of day-to-day life. It engages images of daily life that indirectly defy and diminish the social structures that affect the lives of those who inhabit them. Although they are in sync with the possibilities offered by the material nature of cities, "these transverse tactics," Michel de Certeau tells us, "do not obey the law of the place, for they are not defined or identified by it. In this respect, they are not any more localizable than the technocratic (and scriptural) strategies that seek to create places of inconformity with abstract models" (29). Hence, and following once again John Michael Roberts (654–5), our focus on dissent rather than acts of resistance helps us to underscore, on the one hand, the lack of emphasis on the political nature of these actions – although late during the years of the Transition they will indeed become highly politicized – and, on the other, the lack of organization and conscious acts of defiance. Focusing on urbanistic concerns rather than directly challenging the reigning power of the dictatorship enabled expression in an atmosphere of censorship, such as was the case under Franco.

Therefore, urbanistic concerns spawn structures of dissent that become organized around spatial practices formulated in response to a common complaint. We do not have demonstrations, understood here as coordinated physical movement in the streets, nor is the street the principal place of expression of dissent; rather, we are in the presence of a "dispositivo de reificación de identidades habitualmente negadas en la vida pública" (Delgado, *Sociedades* 171) [mechanism for the reification of identities that are habitually rejected in public life], which cements the "derecho democrático a expresar libremente la opinión, derecho personal ejercido colectivamente" (172) [democratic right to freely express one's opinion, an individual right exercised collectively] through different forms, texts, and spaces. That is, in place of "la acción política en la calle" [political action in the street] that "constituye una modalidad democrática directa y radical" (177) [constitutes a direct and radical democratic modality], we are in the presence of a practice that reactivates the public sphere, the space for the presentation of individuality, with the usurpation of neither spaces nor power, but where those affected feel legitimized to speak for themselves without institutional mediators. Dissenters subvert the system from within, without abandoning it or its laws, but they introduce ambiguity that sets the pillars for a democratic system by structuring a public space for visibility and expression. It is a structure that organizes deviation, bringing it to a meeting point, but as part of the established social structure. It is dissent because it is a disturbance, a displacement, a noise that causes a ripple effect, like a stone hitting the water. It does not seek out conflict, but it finds a homogenization of the subaltern condition that becomes an unforeseen opposition in the indissolubility of socio-physical relationships between unanticipated and potential protagonists. In this way, the margin personifies fluidity, the movement put into play by the potentiality in structures of dissent that generates a new culture, a new way of acting in the face of the urbanistic and social prescriptions of the dictatorship.

In this context, the margin and its establishment in structures of dissent allows us to see the steps that precede what Francisco Fernández de Alba describes as "collective experiences," such as neighbourhood associations or cooperatives, that enable citizen participation in the democratization of the country (8). These groups built an alternative public sphere out of the drive to improve political, ethical, and material circumstances (8), but we can already see the prior establishment of these concerns in the marginal structures of dissent under the dictatorship. As Fernández de Alba explains, these are not secret or underground movements (9), but rather moments of visibility, of the formation of identities based on a right to the city, giving form to a public sphere predicated upon an inherent collectivity in the experience of daily life that makes the immediate environment its vehicle for transmission. In likewise fashion, the margin transforms a text or photograph into a space of and for a plurality of perspectives that, as Hannah Arendt explains in *The Human Condition*, will continue to agree on similarities and differences. Instead of the street, where democratic rights are claimed by opposing the administrative powers that be (Delgado, *Sociedades* 172), the texts analysed here in this book become the public space of and for appearance. Optics – the gaze and the act of seeing and being seen – are subverted without being altogether cast aside because visibility continues to be the fundamental language of the city (although it will be challenged as the sole register for this purpose). The margin reveals, therefore, the randomness of the regime, whose limits are not clear, definitive, or stable, by means of the subtlety of dissent that conceptualizes the city by employing different methods of appropriation.

With this theoretical approach, the objective of this book is the (re)construction of Barcelona through its margins during the dictatorship. Barcelona was chosen principally for how the city was already representative of the creation of urban social movements in the 1960s (McNeill 118–25). As Donald McNeill explains, although social mobilization is normally illustrated by turning to the case of Madrid due to its exemplary nature in Castells' classic study, in Barcelona the extent of mobilization was even more surprising. This claim is all the more justified in light of how this mobilization could already be perceived in the 1950s, when it began to manifest organically through the writings of Francisco Candel and the urban photography of Joan Colom and Colita. Simultaneously, we see how photography, one of the forgotten arts when we speak about Barcelona, begins to constitute an essential piece of the urban turn, reclaiming, once again, a perspective missing from the urban (re)constitution of Barcelona.[9]

Chapter Description

The following study, therefore, dives into this rift along the margins, paradoxical spaces that fracture the restrictive centre/periphery hierarchy, cracked open by Francisco Candel's writing and the photographs of Joan Colom and Colita. The selection of these three artists is not random; they are linked by a genealogical undercurrent that runs through the theme of marginal spaces. Candel inaugurated a narration from within the margin, a new perspective that exploded in narrative and photography following the 1957 publication of *Donde la ciudad cambia su nombre* [Where the city changes its name], but moreover, these artists are also the first ones to do what they do: make noise, create dissent. In the work of these creators, the previously non-narrated and non-photographed city emerges, shaping a popular architecture that will later engender new perspectives to reveal the interconnectedness of society and its cultural spaces. Their connection, therefore, does not lie in how they narrate from beyond the limits, but what they reveal about the informal city into which they plunge: they bring to light marginal discourses and practices, other ways of understanding the city, its construction, and what it produces. They create a fissure, not just a critique; they make a dent not only in the way we perceive the city but in the status quo itself. This book, then, seeks out and makes these fractures identifiable, as they displace the gaze and portray a culturally specific visuality or different "scopic regimes" – to borrow from the film critic Christian Metz – that question the static structure imposed by the absolute space of Francoism. The view present in the narratives and photographs analysed in this book is best characterized as disruption; it is noise, and it is crucial in three important ways that I develop in the next four chapters.

In chapter 1, "A Change of Pace: The Spatial Dimensions of the Franco Dictatorship," the book opens with our approach to the study of Barcelona from the concept of "urban turn," where I will make the case for the construction and expansion of cities as a key component of the elaboration of a national Spanish identity, the result of a reorientation of economic policy towards European and North American capitalism. This urbanistic inversion will be accompanied by a discursive turn in the regime's identity-based raison d'être that will allow for the possibility of legitimate critique and airing of grievances, justified within the regime's legal parameters, and which will begin to define the contours of a future democratic society. Here, the marginal writer/photographer becomes the interstice that allows the creation of dissent in an urban context that is characterized by the attempt to create a harmonious city. The noise of the margins is, thus, the cacophony that brings ambiguity, compromise, and change to the new discursivity and practices of the urban identity of Francoism.

Chapter 2, "Breaking the Silence: The Cultural Mobilization of Francisco Candel," begins this exploration of dissent and the marginal with the work that Francisco Candel published during the years of the Franco dictatorship. Because his work evolves with the changing social panorama of Barcelona, which is a very relevant characteristic of his writing given his dialectic approach to the city, it is very important to limit the scope of our enquiry to his work during the 1950s and 1960s, which takes place specifically in the suburbs of Barcelona, where his gaze consequently sees the city from the margins and as marginal. This approach allows him to create, in an ironic turn of the figure of the flâneur, a multisensorial perception of urban space that breaks with the monocular view of the Francoist city being imposed over the suburbs in the form of *polígonos de viviendas* [public housing]. From this rupture, he creates a new identity of the suburbs that reconstructs the understanding of the Barcelona being built at this moment and, simultaneously, shapes a democratic space by splitting said identity in a choral voice that makes his own voice disappear in the form of a *cronista* [chronicler]. His democratization of the narrative voice and constant references to and denunciations of the precarious space of the suburbs, establish a democratic city based on a grassroots movement that establishes a direct relationship with the neighbourhood associations that will be the cradle of the social movements that will shape democratic change in Spain. Candel's works represent the initial phase in the reconstruction of the city because of the way in which they make the suburbs visible and show the possibility of a democratic space in the otherwise authoritarian space of the dictatorial regime.

In chapter 3, "The Quiet Revolution of Photography: The Barcelona of Joan Colom," marginal visuality expands to the lens of Joan Colom's camera that, following in Candel's footsteps, plunges into the "immoral" space of the Raval to conceive a city whose material base depends precisely on its multiplicity, on the difference that the construction of a socially and culturally homogeneous Barcelona was designed to eliminate. With his wanderings through everyday life in the Raval, he heralds the possibility of a new urban order and a notion of a democratic public space, which breaks with the rectilinear design that the regime sought to impose through the fragmentation of the city. In his exhibition "La Calle, ca 1958–1961" [The street], Colom seeks to emphasize a mobile city in which the movements of bodies take precedence over the material environment. And this emphasis on movement, which emerges as a formal path to break away from the predominance of photographic *costumbrismo* or *paisajismo*, evolves into a critique of the structures imposed from the formal city and, consequently, of the material and social structures of the regime. Of course, he is not the only one capturing the movements of the city; many of his generational peers jump into the streets in search of urban flows. However, by breaking down the social walls imposed upon the Raval, he breaks free from their structure, steps off of clearly delineated paths, and dives into a new social order where the chaos of everyday life is what shapes space.

The last chapter, "A Female City: Colita and the Conceptualization of Barcelona," brings us to the work of Colita. If the language of the city objectifies the female body, even more so when these bodies are in the margins, Colita objectifies the language of the city and the photography of her predecessors – some of whom were her teachers – through irony to create a new space where women take the street. They are no longer women "of the street" or just women "in the street," but women with agency, with a place in the street. Echoing the contradictions that we will see during the years of the Transition under what is known as the "destape" – literally, "undressing," a period when the opening of the regime took shape in part under an erotic imaginary that in turn exploited the female body – Colita's Barcelona reshapes physical and social space by making the body act. In other words, the body does not seek to submit itself to the meaning imposed by space, but to scar urban space with its presence and its movements. Thus, if in the previous chapters we see a modification of the social patterns of the city in search of a democratic space, in Colita's work we find an acceptance of the possibility of democracy and the construction of a social space where a feminist discourse is starting to take shape under the dictatorship. However, it is important to consider that this new order is not separate from the city; Colita's is not a city exclusively of women nor is it a parenthesis to the changes generated by male dissent (hence the strike through the word "female" in this chapter's title). It is part of a complex texture built up in the urban fabric, where lived daily urban experience is also female.

The body of work under consideration here forms a genealogy that allows us to use this urban turn to see an epistemological change in how the city is perceived and, consequently, in how we perceive urbanism as a humanistic tool. The work of these artists creates a new grammar that transcends prescribed limits and insinuates possible new structures. These artists herald in a formidable subversion, one leading to a radically new organization never before theorized. They are artists that, from the margins, make noise, seek subversion, and breach the structure, cracking open and expanding what is accepted as canon, coming into presence.

Chapter One

A Change of Pace: The Spatial Dimensions of the Franco Dictatorship

Our approach to margins is going to be framed in a very specific period of time, from 1950 to 1970 under the Franco dictatorship, and it is going to be shaped by space, specifically the Barcelona of that period of time. These two decades are a key period for understanding how the social and the cultural mobility of the time were already announcing the democratic changes to come. In fact, what these decades produce, I argue, is a new epistemology centred on the urban form that simultaneously changes the physical and the social image of Barcelona. Space is key in this development, given that it is what allows the creation of dissent. When translated into space, dissent is dirt (Davidov 24), slums, and shantytowns that hamper the official city's attempts to unify its inhabitantants' experience into a single harmonious state. In this context, the city is, as postulated by the geographer Yi-Fu Tuan, a place, a quintessential centre of meaning, a symbol, an ideal of human community (173). "Centre of meaning," "symbol," and "ideal" are the concepts that enable us to characterize the city as a narration, as a fiction – just as Hayden White posited[1] – through which culture employs architecture and urbanism in its search for visibility in a physical sense: selection and representation. Here we find Henri Lefebvre's abstract space, which presents the city as homogeneous, but only in appearance, even though this appearance might be one of its most important characteristics. Using a visual register, this abstract space punctuates homogeneity as "its goal, its orientation, its lens" (*Production* 287–8). Space then, like the body in Gil de Biedma's poem, "creates a culture's image: a physically present human environment that expresses the characteristic rhythmic functional patterns which constitute a culture" (Langer 96). In this context, space depends on and imposes an experience, with the city being the centre of meaning, "the sense of self," Tuan tells us, "whether individual or collective," from which identity grows out of the exercise of power (175). This power is rendered visible by the social body and spatial relations mobilized and maintained by the conditions set up by a determined mode of production or political system. And here is where the margin comes into play, as it reveals a layout of relationships of power that include, but are not limited to, a mode of production.[2] These power relations exalt, as Michel de Certeau would say, a "scopic and gnostic drive" such that "the fiction of knowledge is related to this lust to be a viewpoint and nothing more" (92), but seen from this viewpoint, the margin draws attention to those uncontemplated areas of the city that would otherwise go unnoticed. And in this process, the social and material structure of the city is questioned, defied, and tweaked. It becomes dissent.

Through the dialogue between literature and photography on/of the urban space of the margin during the years of the dictatorship, this book traces the search for an – until then – absent Barcelona that will form the pillars of a new way to understand the city socially and physically. To that end, I will examine the opening of a space of dissent during the Franco dictatorship through the (re)construction of urban space. I propose the reading of this new space as a moment of an "urban turn," when the changing panorama of urban centres implies a material change in the physiognomy of cities that allows the creation of interstices of dissent, giving shape to a public space that will be the foundation of a democratic city.[3]

Urban Turn

Dissent and urban space conjoin in the making of modern citizens in cities, as James Holston and Arjun Appadurai announce in their introduction to *Cities and Citizenship*. When we consider the role of cities in the construction of democracy during the Franco dictatorship, however, there is an important twist in this approach. As Holston explains, "for most of the modern era, the nation and not the city has been the principal domain of citizenship" (*Cities* vii). And so it is confirmed by the approach taken by the Franco regime in the construction of Spain, which sought the formation of a Spanish state under the principles of nationhood, which subordinated and coordinated identity – of religion, estate, family, gender, ethnicity, and region – using its framework of a uniform body of law offered by an authority, that of Franco himself, that creates uniqueness, unity, and identity. In this context, the resulting idea of Spanishness, with its corresponding privileges, eroded local identities under the weight and prevalence of a Spanish nation. The Francoist motto, "Una, grande y libre" [One nation, great and free], expressed the regime's nation building process that sought to replace and dismantle the possibility of other identities and opposition of any kind. However, as Holston and Appadurai affirm, "cities have been and still remain the strategic arena for the development of citizenship ... Their crowds catalyze processes that decisively expand and erode the rules, meanings, and practices of citizenship" (2); this could not be truer in the context at hand, but – and here is the twist – with a stronger emphasis on urbanistic space and the material form that contains those rules, meanings, and practices. In other words, it is the urbanistic form of the space of the city that materializes and opens the door to dissent. That is, the urbanistic practices of the dictatorship open the door to critique: specifically, abusive urbanism, the material structure imposed on the city's inhabitants, affects their daily experience and gives birth to discontent, identity, and, later, resistance. This connection is essential given that the "complaint" or "discontent" is not squelched by censorship because it is perceived as politically neutral, precisely because it is a consequence of abusive urbanism and unmet basic needs rather than a direct political affront to the regime.

As Manuel Castells explains when talking about the creation of neighbourhood associations, urbanism is related to the politics of everyday life and, consequently, complaints about living conditions enjoyed the sympathy and support of most sectors of society (*City* 215–16). The social process that we will see forming in these cultural products "offers a striking illustration of the interplay between grassroots protest and housing policy" (94), exemplifying what Manuel Delgado states when explaining that "las morfologías urbanas tienen un papel activo en el desarrollo del uso insolente de los espacios urbanos" [urban morphologies play an active role in the development of the insolent use of urban spaces] given that they incorporate an urban space that is where conflict occurs ("La ciudad" 137–8).[4] That is, urbanism is socialized. It is seen as a public service that provides relatively uniform living conditions firmly under the government's control. However, the precarious conditions of these dwellings, for example, make their inhabitants painfully aware of the problems that come from the government's application of its policies and, therefore, of what residents have in common, creating a rallying point for a collective sense of self rooted precisely in dissent, in the critique of and challenge to urbanistic structure first and, later, the social and cultural structure of the regime. This dissent will become protest in the final years of the dictatorship and under the Transition, a watershed period when these critiques found legitimacy and took the guise of direct political protest against the government.

Urbanism is not dissent or "urban practice," to use Manuel Delgado's definition of social movements (*Sociedades* 11 and *El Animal* 12), but rather the spark that ignites the formation of a collective discontent that leads to mobilization.[5] In the words of David Harvey, "conflicts arise not merely out of admittedly diverse subjective appreciations, but because different objective material qualities of time and space are deemed relevant to social life in different situations" (*Condition* 205). For this reason, in a context where "any movement was bound to be in confrontation with the state by virtue of their very existence" (Castells, *City* 215–16), the critique that comes from the living conditions imposed by urbanism on day-to-day existence offers an escape, pause, or interstice that first becomes dissent, and later becomes an agent of social change (given that it is not a critique of the political system, at least not at first glance or not directly, but rather of the model of urbanistic development that cannot manage to respond to a series of social needs). Consequently, what is challenged is not the system of power but the logic of the model of urbanistic development that, because it is tied to the development of a Francoist national identity, ends up becoming a critique of the social and political system. It is in this sense that the city becomes, echoing the words of Holston and Appadurai (*Cities* vii), the place where raw materials come together not just in the construction of the nation, but also in the constitution of the social and cultural process, given that, as Lefebvre explains, space "is permeated with social relations; it is not only supported by social relations but it is also producing and produced by social relations" (*Production* 286). This permeated state makes space always political in how it expresses power relations that are challenged through their physical materiality.

The concept of urban turn seeks to underscore precisely the predominance of urban materiality in the construction of social and political discourses and practices during Francoism, but most importantly how this change in perspective allows for the creation of dissent using the supposed neutrality of urbanistic discourse. In other words, the power of the cities to change social structures takes two different forms in the context of the Franco dictatorship: (1) the official discourse and practices of the regime, which simultaneously allow for (2) the construction of an urban practice of dissent that will eventually take the form of social and political protest. In the 1950s, the discourse of the regime shifts from the acceptance of its autarchic, rural life–centred rhetoric as the root of the truer Spain during the 1940s to an urban discourse that emphasizes the value of urban life, pressured of course by the thousands of Spaniards migrating from the country to the cities, which brought a crisis to housing and urban infrastructure and culminated in a change in the use and perception of urbanism itself.[6] In its roots, space continues to be an expression of a fascist conceptual, imaginary, and, later, material space, especially emphasized during the formation and establishment of the regime during the 1930s and 1940s, as explained by Nil Santiáñez in *Topographies of Fascism*; however, the regime's subsequent search for a modern image on the international stage adopts a concept of urbanism that presents itself as a neutral tool to modernize cities. In other words, the monumentalization of the city that happened as a response to the imposition of a totalitarian regime – the construction of monuments to national figures, the naming of streets after decorated figures in the regime, or the shaping of a Francoist architecture – gives way to the creation of a city that seeks instead a modern image as a consequence of a change in the patterns of population and in international relationships.[7]

This rhetorical turn arises in response to an overwhelming spatial reality: the countryside was incapable of sustaining the Spanish population due to a lack of investment in its development, which consequently unleashed the mass exodus towards urban centres that came to be seen as the only viable way out of the nation's economic stagnation. We can see this rhetorical shift in the justifications that officials issued to explain the reasons for migration, in which the city stops being the source of evil and becomes the centre of progress.[8] From statements that emphasize the economic development of the country – for example, "Estos problemas son comunes en todos los países desarrollados … un mal endémico a todas las ciudades del mundo, especialmente las industralizadas" (Porcioles 96) [These problems are common in all developed countries … an endemic evil in all of the world's cities, especially the industrialized ones] or "el problema viene forzado por las razones positivas de nuestro franco desarrollo" (Porcioles qtd. in Hall 75) [the problem is forced by the positive aspects of our frank development] – to others that seek to sing the praises of the regime – "sois propietarios [de estas viviendas] porque Franco así lo ha dispuesto" (José Solís Ruiz qtd. in Hall 75) [you are the owners of these dwellings because Franco has willed it so] – the state denies the principal reason behind migratory movement: the overwhelming poverty of the countryside, and hence the failure of Franco's utopia to craft a new discourse to highlight the modernization of its cities on a growing international stage, beginning with the Pactos de Madrid in 1953 and continuing with the new alliances that emerged from Spain's entry into the United Nations in 1955.

Cities become the focus of a new discourse centred on the development of a material reality, the consumerism of future capitalism.[9] In this regard, 1957 becomes a key year: due to the heightened number of migrants – in the 1950s Catalonia received some 400,000 migrants, half of which settled in Barcelona (Ferrer, "Barraques" 63) – migration could no longer be ignored. The year 1957 marked a dramatic increase in this process of migration and forced the acknowledgment of not just the role of cities in economic development but also the housing shortage exacerbated by the disproportional increase in the number of constantly arriving inhabitants. This is also the year that technocratic ministers, "hábiles economistas que emprenden urgentes planes de desarrollo" (Fontcuberta, "De la posguerra" 414) [capable economists that undertake urgent development plans], enter into government service, which indicates a reorientation in the discourse and practice of the dictatorship.[10] In this general time frame, several key events and institutions herald the emerging prominence of urban concerns: the creation of a Ministerio de la Vivienda [Ministry of Housing], which reorganized the state's central administration of housing and assimilated the Instituto Nacional de la Vivienda [National Institute of Housing]; the celebration of the Semana del Suburbio [Week of the Suburb], the "primera manifestación de la conciencia ciudadana so-bre la parte más visible del problema de la vivienda" (Tatjer 52) [first manifestation of the citizenry's consciousness of the most visible part of the housing problem], which was organized by the Church and predicated upon the development of the image of an idealized city where barraquismo [shantytowns] had no place; the beginning of the mayoralty of Josep Maria de Porcioles (1957–73), the principal expo-nent of a new Francoist political economy that came to rely on the real estate and banking sector;[11] and the presentation of the Grupo R, which brought about the official beginning of architectural renova-tion movements in Catalonia. Together, these events represent the first steps towards an urban discourse and practice that will respond to the optics of a functionalist urbanism that was strongly imbued with a sanitizing and modernizing character, and thus perceived shanty-towns as a social hindrance that disturbed the tightly controlled or-ganization of the planned city.

To that end, we need go no further than the words of Porcioles him-self, who referred to suburban shantytowns as an "endemic evil." Therefore, it comes as no surprise that they are all united by a com-mon interest in proposals to eradicate substandard housing and slums through the large-scale application and construction of tightly regu-lated residential zoning (Tatjer 52). At this juncture, the myth promul-gated in the early years of Franco of two Spains, one rural and the other urban, assumes a new form, the myth of two cities:

Franco, el capitán de la Liberación militar, dio también la consigna para la batalla contra la miseria: "Que en el plazo más corto, que yo desearía que fuese el de mi próxima visita, hayan desparecido por completo esas barracas, que desdicen de la grandeza de Barcelona y del civismo y la laboriosidad de sus hijos ..." Cada etapa, en esta importantísima y necesaria realización del Paseo Marítimo, señala una nueva frontera entre los dos mundos de la ciudad, en beneficio de aquel que quisiéramos definitivamente triunfante. ("La liberación" 35)

The captain of military liberation, Franco also gave the signal to battle poverty: "In the short term, preferably by my next visit, I want those slums torn down, because they contradict Barcelona's grandeur and the civility and industriousness of its children ..." Each stage in this important and necessary completion of the Promenade marks a new boundary between the two worlds of the city, in benefit of the one we wish to see decisively triumph.

The poverty to be combatted is urbanistic in nature and should be confronted not by a change to the economic system so as to assimilate those residents, but by the force and weight of bricks and other building materials, in this example, the cement of Barcelona's seaside promenade. Here we see, together with the modernizing discourse of official pronouncements on the existence of slums, a discourse and practice that oversimplify urban relationships by strictly differentiating between official and unofficial development.

This split is a product of the rationalism that emerged from the nineteenth-century bourgeois city (the city of social and urban order that would come to be aligned with the order imposed by Franco's state), which preserves the city's urbanistic grid and also scorns all that which is not yet city or is disorder, such as is the case with the suburbs and slums. This tension between centrality and marginality, as explained by Miquel Fernández González, transforms urbanism into a technique for social intervention, even though it is perceived as "un instrumento científico, neutro e incuestionable al servicio del gobierno de la ciudad" (31) [a neutral and unquestionable scientific instrument at the service of the city]. This conceptualization of a neutral urbanism is reinforced through an emphasis on the act of looking with a distant gaze that organizes space and distributes its inhabitants from far off, and which consequently produces a loss of materiality in bodies and relationships. We find an example of this way of looking in Manuel Vázquez Montalbán's *Barcelones*, where the author describes the Catalonian capital as seen from el Tibidabo in the following manner:

Des d'aquest mirador es podia llegir la ciutat a vista d'ocell, fer-ne la lectura del passat i de la seva textura actual. Barcelona. Barcelona, no. Barcelones. Tantes com arqueologies supervivents. Tantes ciutats en una, encara que, a simple vista, des d'aquest mirador definitiu, predomini la imatge d'aquesta retícula burgesa que ha quadriculat fonamentalment l'ànima i el cos d'aquesta ciutat. (33)

The bird's eye view from el Tibidabo allows one to read the city's past and present. Not one Barcelona but many. There are as many cities contained in one as there are surviving architectural styles. Many cities in one, although at first glance, from this definitive viewpoint, the image of the bourgeois reticle that has drawn the grid on the body and soul of this city overpowers all else.

Although in his description Vázquez Montalbán uncovers the contrast, clash, and coexistence of the inhabitable and inhabited cities that give form to the metropolis, invoking a heterogeneous Barcelona that will be the base of the city as it is understood – and which will be the productive part of space emphasized here – he highlights the influence of one pervasive perspective: all of these cities are framed by the "bourgeois reticle," which is to say, the singularity of the straight line, the expression of power that gave rise to the grid that is essentially the body and soul of Barcelona. Through the resulting simplification and division of urban space, both this view from above and the bourgeois reticle from the distance, throw into sharp relief the nineteenth-century city that has moulded the physical construction of Barcelona up to the present.

In a similar fashion, in his description of the view from the Eiffel Tower, Roland Barthes understands that viewing the city from above implies converting "el hormigueo de los hombres en paisaje, [añadir] al mito urbano, a menudo sombrío, una dimension romántica, una armonía, un alivio" ("Torre Eiffel" 61) [the human swarm into landscape, adding to the often-somber myth a romantic dimension, a harmony, a relief]. It makes the city legible by allowing things to be seen in their basic structure; in short, Barthes explains, "separa y armoniza" (62) [it separates and harmonizes].[12] This rationalization or, if you will, reduction, of the complexity of urban space is reminiscent of the consequences of the grid designed by Ildefons Cerdà (1858). Although in his design of the Eixample he sought to confront inequalities that continued to structure urban life, the neutrality of the grid wound up contradicting his social-utopian intention (Fraser, *Henri* 87). That is to say, the application of a systematic, geometrical, and rational order conceived of the city as an entity that was immobile, fragmented, and compartmentalized into a manageable whole, and rejected the "archipiélago de microestructuras fugaces y cambiantes" (*El animal* 182) [archipielago of fleeting and changing microstructures] that in reality comprise the urban.[13] Cerdà's grid is the epitome of rational order, of a viewpoint that peers from above, from a distance, and belongs to both urban planners and government representatives that functionally inscribe a physical and social order on an otherwise abstract space.

The straight line represents the imposition of urbanistic practices that read the city from a singular perspective imposed by a class-based discourse that, in spite of the diverse political forms that it can take, always reads the chaotic and allegedly troublesome parts of the city as problematic, unhygienic, and in need of reforms that would make them disappear materially, socially, and culturally. The neutrality of the Cartesian perspectivism seen in these projects, the creation of an isotropic, homogeneous, and continuous space that is both social and material, lies underneath the reorganization of the nation and the regime's social body, but so too do the social movements that oppose them.

Two seminal works on the discursive construction of Francoism, one by Nil Santiáñez and the other by Aurora G. Morcillo, lay out the ideological make-up of the regime in two different historical moments: the years prior to and during the Civil War in the case of the former, and the changes resulting from the economic liberalization of the 1950s in the case of the latter. In their analyses we can see how concepts such as absolute space or organic democracy trace their origins to the urbanistic trends in vogue since the end of the nineteenth century in order to form a "space of truth," (Lefebvre, *Production* 236) that, as Santiáñez explains, rearticulates the nation and social body under the dictatorship guided by the organizing principle of organicism and the structuring of the citizenry as an integral "people's community" (16). We see the same principle in the idea of organic democracy that describes Franco's authoritarian model as an order authorized by the divine and in which every individual has a predetermined and immutable role (Morcillo 17).[14] In both cases, we find the presentation of an absolute space where social reorganizing is made possible by a set of hierarchical and static relations that eliminate antagonisms and replace the autonomy and dynamism of the subject by immersing it in a fixed concept of community that shapes individual behaviour and controls flow (Santiáñez 23).

Indeed, the dictatorship's tendency to seek this sort of absolute space of singular truth, the equivalent of Lefebvre's abstract space, reveals the Foucauldian structure of power/knowledge that creates the individual according to a practical model of spatial distribution that centralizes, classifies, and organizes individuals by placing them in discernable groups, as happens with the application of "planes parciales," piecemeal plans that are the result of a capitalistic approach to development.[15] This political, social, and material space is perceived as natural, based on a foundational model in which individual perspective is extrapolated into a broader view of the world as an organic totality that halts movement, as if we were dealing with David Harvey's "preexisting, immovable, continuous, and unchanging framework ... within which distinctive objects can be clearly identified and events and processes accurately described" (*Cosmopolitanism* 34), which in turn allows Santiáñez to show the radical modification carried out by the regime.[16]

Considering Francoism in these terms hearkens back to Barthes and de Certeau and the distant panoptical viewpoint that emphasizes the predominance of the visual field in the constitution of urban space as an underlying principle of urbanism; here the supposed neutrality, streamlining, and reduction of complexity provided by the distant gaze that makes for that foundational perception ties this moment of creation by the regime to an idea of almost divine perception, with all of the connotations of ineffability, omnipresence, and ubiquity that such a characterization implies. Connection to urbanistic practices is essential in the constitution of this social and discursive paradigm: like the distant gaze of the urbanist, we see a geometric space that, in theory, eliminates the presence of the subject that it creates or represents. This physical distancing in turn produces an emotional distancing that grants this alleged neutrality, and consequently other possible viewpoints that could be considered in the construction of an object, be it a city or a political system, are eliminated. Therefore, the symbology of the city takes a new turn: the visual pre-eminence and evocative power of its architecture reduces its social complexity and in doing so results in a space that is, again, not just neutral but neutralizing; corporal identity, whether urban or social, is overlooked and eliminated by the imposition of forms that adapt to the discourse of power.

Consequently, with the urban turn, two crucial changes take place. First, there is a shift in the direction of Francoism's national organizing discourse, in which the city becomes the source of the nation's identity and modernization. Second, if the city is to be the origin of national identity, it should be reconfigured according to the organizing dictates of nineteenth-century urbanism, a neutral tool that, in principle, seeks to solve a problem – here the slums that stifle the development of the modern city. This discourse of urbanistic renewal becomes embedded in the construction of identity and the development of the economy.

A Spain of "Property Owners, Not Proletarians"

Within the flux of these parameters, the Francoist utopia of a homogeneous and unified Spain represented through the Castilian countryside undergoes a necessary update in response to this new urban cartography that requires that the construction of community pass through new urban development that is influenced by the capitalism of Spain's allies, and is as much a product of the requirements of an economic system based on foreign investment and tourism as it is of the changes brought about by a migratory population.[17] Real estate development was an important part of the response to this new set of relations, shifting from a Plan General de Ordenación Urbana (1941) [General Proposal for Urban Planning] that sought to advance the state's "engrandecimiento" [aggrandizement] and "fachada imperial" [imperial facade] to a series of general and regional proposals whose objective was to facilitate the exploitation of land, as speculation became a key component of planning.[18] In 1959, José Luis Arrese, the minister of housing, told the real estate agents that were honouring him the following:

> La misión que de una manera concreta está encomendada a vuestro quehacer diario, es la de intervenir en la transacción de la propiedad inmobiliaria; pero para ello, para que haya transacción, es preciso que primero haya propiedad; y mirad por dónde, repito, os vamos a necesitar cada vez más, porque cada vez más claramente y sin torceduras vamos a fomentar la propiedad privada ... No queremos, y lo consideramos un mal, aunque a veces sea un mal necesario, que la construcción derive de un modo colectivo hacia el arrendamiento ... [L]a fórmula ideal, la cristiana, la revolucionaria desde el punto de vista de nuestra propia revolución, es la fórmula estable y armoniosa de la propiedad ... Queremos un país de propietarios, no de proletarios. ("No queremos" 42)

The mission concretely entrusted to your daily labour is intervening in the transaction of real estate; but so that there can be a transaction, there must be property; and, look, I repeat, we are going to need you more and more, because more and more clearly and without distortion we are going to encourage private property ... We do not want, and we consider it an evil, although at times a necessary one, construction that comes from a collective mode of renting ... [T]he ideal formula, one that is Christian and revolutionary from the point of view of our revolution, is the stable and harmonious formula of property ... We want a country of property owners, not proletarians.

On the one hand, Arrese's words were responding to the regime's political and economic need to geographically redistribute the most disadvantaged sectors of the population. The regime's drive to solve the housing problem culminated in the creation of a Ministry of Housing, from whose helm Arrese perceived the situation as a matter of public order (Naredo 18),[19] taking up the Falangist rhetoric of the day and also taking us back to nineteenth-century urbanism's discourse of sanitization, both used to sanction the control and social intervention being leveraged against the working class, as is made explicit in the passage's closing phrase: "a country of property owners, not proletarians." On the other hand, this distancing from what was considered the origin of the Marxist revolution begins to show the outline of an identity politics that sought to promote housing as a primary part of ownership, "reforzando así las políticas extremadamente conservadoras y de control social del régimen" (Aricó) [thus reinforcing the extremely conservative and socially restrictive politics of the regime]. A squalor perceived to be economic, moral, and social comes to characterize the slums, a notion that we also see applied to other neighbourhoods, such as the Raval, even as the urban physical margins that hem in the slums simultaneously become integral to the urbanistic expansion of the city, both physically and economically. In spite of the fact that they contributed to the creation of urban capital in hard times, both in terms of fixed capital through the construction of informal dwellings that housed thousands for decades and human capital through the development of complex social networks (Roca i Albert 14), the slums were continually subjected to paternalistic revisions and remodeling, first through a rationalism that imitated the modern urbanism of the Republic, and later through the repressive attitude towards informal settlements whose first stage (1939–57) would later give way to the construction of large housing zones located at the outskirts of Barcelona proper (Larrea and Tatjer 18).

As Ton Salvadó and Josep M. Miró explain, the problem of housing, "entendida como la preocupación burguesa de ocuparse del alojamiento obrero" (140) ["understood as the bourgeois preoccupation with worker housing"], was framed by the administration as a question of zoning. The Plan Comarcal [Regional Plan] of 1953 "és el primer intent ... de codificar les relacions entre tipologies arquitectòniques i formes d'ordenació urbana" (Ferrer, "El Pla" 132) [is the first intent ... to codify the relationships between architectural typologies and forms of urban order]. In principle, this codification was not very different from the reforms that would come years later. However, the Plan "no tan sols analitza les quantitats de població sinó que les classifica en categories socials, a fi de poder assignar, posteriorment, tipus de població, sobre àrees del territori" (Salvadó and Miró 144) [not only analyses population numbers but classifies them into social categories, in order to then be able to assign population types to areas of territory]. Conceptually, these residential zones were staked out in terms of geography and their relation to the city; that is to say, they became part of the city through their location, dimension, and connection to transportation and service infrastructure. The overall plan, the layout of the buildings, and the presence of public space were key features of their conceptualization; they became part of the city because they prioritized housing and the consequences of the type of buildings erected. However, "no hi va haver cap idea ni cap voluntat política d'entendre l'habitatge en un altre marc que l'estrictament quantitatiu" (Ferrer qtd. in Salvadó and Miró 140) [there was no political will or desire to see the problem of housing in any context other than the strictly quantitative] and, consequently, concerns about location and the urbanization of public space and its features were set aside or forgotten. Moreover, the buildings themselves, which were often the only thing actually built, frequently had critical defects, and the criteria for awarding public contracts to private companies was nebulous at best, as all kinds of civil servants had their hands out and evident attempts to influence the process abounded.

The dominance of the bourgeois grid in city planning is predicated upon both the aforementioned physical make-up of urban margins and the establishment of a legal framework to carry out the proposed changes. The legality for reforms was based on the regime's reinstatement of a law first enacted in 1934, the Ley de Vagos y Maleantes [Law on Vagrants and Criminals], which stipulated the detection and detainment of "los individuos peligrosos y violentos" (Ealham, *La lucha* 139) [dangerous and violent individuals] in order to "detener la avalancha del desorden" [halt the avalanche of disorder]; with this law the regime took possession of urban space and redefined it ideologically by establishing the protection of "gente razonable" [reasonable people] as a key priority of what can best be described as a bourgeois morality. Additionally, through the criminalization of the construction of slums, the regime's legal framework brought into focus their extraterritoriality and the divide between the planned and the informal city, divisions propped up by the formation of an order that conceived of the city as a hierarchical space that codified freedoms and restrictions and also as a whole that required officials to uphold certain discursive and practical structures deemed necessary, natural, and therefore unquestionable.[20] As a final step, the criminalization of prostitution became a significant law enforcement tool that reveals a lot about the uses of space in the city. As Morcillo explains (29–126), politically the regime maintained an attitude of tolerance towards prostitution in the 1940s.[21] However, with the ideological realignment of the regime in the aftermath of the Second World War, predicated upon the legal establishment of Catholic values more aligned with European and North American morality, brothels officially closed their doors in 1956.[22] In spite of this prohibition, the Barrio Chino continued to engage in prostitution clandestinely behind the facade of furnished apartments, hostels, and boarding houses. The increase in underground prostitution underscored the immoral and dangerous character of the neighbourhood, and also its legal extra-territoriality. Here marginal spaces are perceived as threats to the city because they challenge the meaning of the spatial structure of place by breaking its laws, which in turn justifies their elimination and the relocation of their inhabitants to new urban structures where they can be kept apart and controlled. To legitimize the city, immigration and its social and material manifestations must be delegitimized; all the while, the continuity of urbanistic laws and forms between the Republic and the dictatorship reveals the neutral and dispassionate characterization of urbanism.[23]

Arrese's speech on the need to create property owners and not pro-letarians arises from the emphasis put on creating a legal framework that seeks above all else to avert the social instability represented by political discourse inextricably connected to the material form of urban space. Thus, the material nature of the city modifies the dictatorship's discourse and practice and presides over the creation and organization of a population whose identity undergoes an "urbanization of con-sciousness," as Richardson explains (10), borrowing Harvey's concept in which inhabitants accept and adopt the city's order and encoded meanings as if they were a product of urbanism's supposed neutrality, which understands space in a city as something natural (Harvey, *Urban* 240). The city's materiality also opens space for a dialectics that results from the imposition of structure, characterization, and discrimination based precisely on the myth of two cities, one whose simplicity and contrast gives rise to dissent.

Margin: Urbanism and Dissent

It is in the supposed neutrality of urbanism that the second aspect of this urban turn becomes manifest. Under the simulacrum of the order of the Franco regime, under the totalitarianism of absolute space, difference seemed to disappear; noise seemed to be silenced. However, this disappearance or erasure had the opposite effect: the creation of a cartography of difference that established the foundation of a movement of dissent that takes shape, first, in literature and photography and, later, in neighbourhood associations.

The city's strategies impose these spaces, while the tactics of dissent use and manipulate them and redirect them from their proposed uses, all the while presenting themselves, like urbanistic structure itself, as neutral. In this way, urban space becomes the axis of a socially organized structure that can become dissent; this makes sense if we heed the urban identities created by the urban turn, as disagreement comes precisely from the space created to distinguish and define them. In other words, spatial practice opens a space of its own in which to use the oppressive order of place or its language to construct its own expression, establishing a degree of plurality that in principle does not exist (Certeau 30). It is not that these urban identities reject power and its impositions; rather, they make it work in another register. In the context of the alleged neutrality of urbanism and actions taken by the city and state to preserve the physical and social order of urban space, the suburbs, that is, the physical and social margins they represent, including the Raval, introduce an element of instability through an apolitical channel of communication that simultaneously preserves and rejects the structure of the formal city and gives way to the possibility for new orders that can redefine the characterization of space and its inhabitants.

Within this critical approach, one of the changes that results from the perception and visibility of the margin and its subsequent clash with the formal order of the city is the creation of a civil identity that makes the city legible for those who inhabit it in the physical margins; this identity opposes Francoism not with discourses and practices that are necessarily political or as part of the bourgeois intelligentsia of the 1950s – or at least not exclusively – but rather, as an alternative force that emanates from a critique that seeks solidarity and dialogue precisely in an environment that suppresses them. Consequently, dissent is constituted in the physical margins of the city, whether in the suburbs or the Raval, because they offer an alternative view of the structure imposed upon the city by the dictatorship on a physical but also social and cultural level, a structure whose materiality makes it impossible to ignore. This civil identity comes from this very contrast: in the same way that Manuel Vázquez Montalbán saw in the literature of the 1950s the beginnings of a democratic logic that evolved from within its system of communication (writer, editor, critic, reader) "en un forcejeo dialéctico constante con las reglas de permisividad o de intolerancia que el régimen establecía" (*La literatura* 72) [in a constant dialectic struggle with the rules of permissiveness or intolerance that the regime established], in the context of the margin that we are laying out here, the urban structure of Barcelona personifies this same dialectic struggle that opposes those same rules of permissiveness and intolerance, but based on a physical and urban structure that extends to questions of class and enables the construction of a socially based marginal movement capable of critiquing the status quo. By focusing on an external landscape – urban and urbanistic – that is different from "la colección de cromos oficiales de la ciudad franquista" (74) [the collection of official postcards of the Francoist city], we see the construction of a new city with an urban and urbanistic landscape that incorporates and contours the physical margin instead of hiding it away and destroying it. We also see a channel for communication rife with new possibilities and dynamics that comes from the clash with structures proposed by Francoism, which promote social exclusion.

This social and material critique makes those structures visible in a way that would be otherwise impossible since, although they must necessarily negotiate with censorship, they move within the same social parameters and linguistic code used by official organizations and bodies. In the words of Vázquez Montalbán (88), we are dealing with an adaptation of the abilities of the gaze to discern non-linguistic artistic forms that can link the internal discourse of the aesthetic tradition with tendencies, such as photography and urbanism, that continue to advance in spite of the cultural blockade in the country.[24] This approach announces a broader receiving audience and simultaneously presents itself as an alternative to the regime's limited access to cultural materials. If, as Vázquez Montalbán claims, "la literatura, las artes, la cultura Noble, con mayúscula, tal y como la habíamos considerado tradicionalmente había perdido su hegemonía como instrumento orientador, si es que alguna vez lo había tenido" (86) [literature, the arts, and uppercase Noble culture as traditionally considered lost their hegemony as a guiding instrument, if they ever had it], the photography and literature of this period, with a documentary bent and connected to the graphic journalism of magazines such as *Serra d'Or* or the *Gaceta Ilustrada*, offers a new means of communication that substitutes the elites' "mirada distanciadora sobre la sociedad" (87) [distancing gaze above society], a viewpoint that we have seen applied to the practice of urbanism by that far-away gaze the flattens the identity of bodies.

This approach characterizes the literary and photographic production that we will analyse here, initiating the shift in direction announced by Josep Maria Castellet in *La hora del lector* towards different artistic tendencies applied to the construction of society.[25] However, this aesthetic configures an artistic gaze centred on the formation of a collective sense of identity based not on memory – at least, not entirely – but rather on the present, making its critique not that of the antagonist that the dictatorship sought to suppress, but rather one concerned with the construction and formation of the immediate physical and social environment. That said, it is important to insist that this platform will be used by determined political parties that will play a fundamental role in the transition to democracy,[26] hence the importance of these authors and artists. In this sense, we are closely following the theory laid out by Vázquez Montalbán, who affirms the following:

> El proyecto de ciudad democrática fraguó de una manera mucho más espontánea, aunque activado por las vanguardias clandestinas y por la frustración asumida por una persona medianamente inteligente en la España de los años cincuenta y sesenta, al percibir el desfase entre sus necesidades culturales y las satisfacciones que recibía. Esa mecánica entre necesidad y satisfacción en cultura es mucho más determinante que las consignas y las élites, es la que hizo que aquella sociedad, muchos sin saberlo, se movilizara hacia el proyecto democrático. (*La literatura* 79)

> The plans for the democratic city were hatched in a much more spontaneous way, although stimulated by the clandestine avant-gardes and the frustration felt by any reasonably intelligent person in Spain in the 1950s and 1960s upon perceiving the gap between their cultural needs and the satisfaction with which they were met. This mechanics of need and satisfaction in terms of culture is much more decisive than slogans or elites; it is what made that society, many without even realizing it, move towards the democratic project.

That is to say, the quest to balance need and fulfilment is what led to the development of different fronts to socially and culturally oppose Francoism. In this regard, for positive reasons – for example, the visualization of an until-then suppressed identity – as well as for negative ones – the justification, separation, and alienation of the physical margins with respect to the centre, culturally and socially speaking – the city that is built from the margins lays the foundation for the democratic city.

Shaping Democracy through the Margins

The type of democracy forged under the dictatorship is more closely aligned with the concept of dissent applied here in this analysis than with a political party structure. For example, Manuel Vázquez Montalbán talks about a democratic city and project from a vantage point that allows him to see how they lead to the Transition, which translates above all into political freedom; his concept of "democratic city" embodies the idea of a democratic culture and society made up of student movements, strikes, social rebellion, organizing, and political parties (see *La literatura*). Although it is accurate to state, as I already have, that this social identity can be found, for example, at the heart of neighbourhood associations and urban movements, which were essential forces in the restoration of democracy due to the role they played in reviving political parties banned by the dictatorship,[27] what most interests us in this analysis here is the relationship between this social identity and urbanistic space, and how this interaction comes from a democratic notion of what a city is.

This democratic notion references, on the one hand, an acknowledgment of the juxtaposition of difference, as Doreen Massey affirms when describing how the spatiality of the city gives rise to "dense networks of interaction" ("On Space" 160); on the other, these networks of interaction emphasize the multiplicity and irreducibility of the city, substituting the binaries commonly used to describe cities with the concept of a mobility that interferes with the stability of place (Amin and Thrift 3). This conception of the urban underscores its potentiality, "a set of potentials which contain unpredictable elements as a result of the co-evolution of problems and solutions" (Amin and Thrift 4). The dialectic relationship that enables this potentiality becomes democratic when new organizations and spaces to make politics spring from its core, as Giorgio Agamben professes in *Potentialities*. Consequently, the definition of democracy applied herein more closely aligns with the concept laid out in Amin and Thrift's new urbanism project than with what we find in Vázquez Montalbán: based on this potentiality, its consideration of difference, and the acceptance of multiplicity and diversity of activities, classes, temporality, and spatiality, the root nature of this democracy "lies in the democratization of the terms of engagement. Such a democratization must include the active encouragement of

subjectivities, for it seems to us that politics is increasingly being meas-
ured through performative display" (Amin and Thrift 131). Amin and
Thrift emphasize in politics and the democratic project the creation of a
civil identity that seeks civic empowerment and enables the creation of
a public space of negotiation between citizens and institutional power
that we find reflected in the work of both writers and photographers.

Here we see echoes of the ubiquitous principle that guides Jane
Jacobs' conception of the urban: "the need of cities for a most intricate and close-grained diversity of uses that give each other constant
mutual support, both economically and socially" (14). Democracy in
this case is predicated upon the reactivation of *communitas*, as Manuel
Delgado explains (channeling Victor Turner), and is not a pristine state
of society to which we long to return "sino una dimensión siempre
presente y periódicamente activada, cuya latencia y disponibilidad el
marginal recibe el encargo de evocar en todo momento a través de las
aparentemente extrañas formas de sociedad que protagoniza con otro
como él" (*El animal* 116) [but rather an ever-present and periodically
activated dimension, whose latency and availability the marginal are
charged with evoking at all times through the apparently strange forms
of society where together with others they are protagonists]. The urbanistic projects applied to the margins of the city during the dictatorship
were characterized by anonymity, impersonality, and a paternalistic
attitude that blocked and cancelled out social actions, thus producing
the negation of a sense of civic democracy. A further complication was
the dictatorship's essential lack of a representative democracy, and also
here specifically the implementation of a new politics that, as Naredo
explains, prioritized property in order to avert social instability, make
"gente de orden" (18) [orderly people], and assure the conformism of
the population when there are no other avenues for negotiation. In this
context, direct democracy founded on civic activism becomes the only
way to procure an expansion of basic rights (such as access to housing
or education) and to establish communication between the inhabitants
of the suburbs and government representatives. It should be noted that
although the regime promoted home ownership as a core tenet of social stability, it created a paradoxical environment in which inflation
and soaring prices coincided with regulations that decreed rent freezes
to protect the security of renters, which only wound up exacerbating
the shortfalls of social life (Naredo 18). These concerns accentuated the
need for a democracy that, using viable and allowable practices in the
context of dictatorship, was inserted into a system associated with charity, networks of family and friends, and community volunteerism. We
are talking about a grassroots democracy that allows us to see how city

and identity become entwined and debunk the notion of a fundamental neutrality in urban planning and reforms.

The functional approach to the city perceives environment as determinant of living conditions, which bolsters the implementation of a program of sanitization as the best form of redress for social problems rooted in a material poverty that in turn leads to moral and social deterioration; consequently, it obstructs the perception of space and its organization, shape, and meaning as fundamentally social in nature. If the city and its spaces are perceived as responding to functional needs, spatial order seems to be governed by laws that are natural, mechanical, or organic, and only social insofar as they cover the needs of individuals that inhabit the city (Deutsche, "Uneven" 107). This functional space is what makes for the perception of urbanism as politically neutral, since it is ostensibly just utilitarian (109). However, this material space incorporates political and class interests, and in the same way that it shapes the margin, the Raval, and the suburbs – all uncharted spaces, albeit ones that are imbued with the discourse of the city that characterizes them – it also offers potentiality. From an urbanistic point of view, since their beginnings (but in large part due to the many reforms undertaken over the years) these two areas have been construed as heterotopias, which, on the one hand excludes them from the formal city – coinciding with the bourgeois city – but which on the other, although they are in constant dialogue with the structure of the very place that effectively marginalizes them, through their very chaos grants them certain freedom in the discourses and practices at work within them. This ambiguous disposition, this state of being both in and outside of place, is what produces a margin that challenges urbanistic plans and the social discourses that they impose and constructs a kaleidoscopic, dynamic, and therefore transgressive cartography.

This spatial antagonism and the controversial appropriations of urbanistic space that create dissent set in motion the dialectic opposition in Lefebvre's tripartite division, which results from the opposition between abstract and social space and the subsequent enunciation of the presence and breakdown of the power structures that materialize in spatial structures. The all-encompassing space of the dictatorship assails a social space composed of the conceptual triad of spatial practice, representations of space, and representational spaces, which correspond to the three ways of being and seizing space in the domains of "the perceived," "the conceived," and "the lived" (*Production* 33–40). We have already seen this dialectical interplay with the urban turn: spatial practices and migration lead to a reappraisal of the representations of space and the representational spaces of Francoism, such that this dialectic relationship is the point of contact that makes space fluid and contra-dictory through the actions of its users, undermining the regime's tight grip on the control of space and enabling competing ways of construct-ing and using space to different ends. In spite of presenting a structure of knowledge that appears stable and fixed, whether in the material form of place or the systemization of a theoretical approach, the im-possibility of clearly and definitively separating the component parts of this supposed stability presents an interstice for change-enabling ac-tion. It is in these interstices where the uncontrollable movement of the users of place, the margin, is formed.

It is true that a more contemporary form of urbanism, such as the version presented by Amin and Thrift (7–26), aims to comment on not just the human element that we have emphasized in the construction of the margin by focusing on the body – which is also found, as we have pointed out, at the centre of the urban theories of Jane Jacobs, Michel de Certeau, or Henri Lefebvre – but also the "trans-human" and the "in-organic" ("from rats to sewers"). Moreover, this urbanism simultane-ously expresses both the limits established by a technological structure that regulates urban rhythms, which are never totally free, as well as the lack thereof, evinced by the lack of borders that results from global circulation and communication.[28] Nevertheless, due to the authoritar-ian historical context that confronts us, we are interested in examining the construction of the Barcelona of this period as the basis for a form of urbanism that was taking shape then and was a first step towards what Jacobs, de Certeau, and Lefebvre would later describe as an urbanism of everyday life. Here we will find a new urbanism that, unshackling itself from the social discourse and practice of the dictatorship and the physical structure imposed by urban planners of that time, seeks out "common, ordinary things" that promote the vitality of the city (Jacobs 3–4). It is through bodies and their relationship to the material city that we find questioning and dissent, and consequently the possibility of a new identity that goes beyond the limitations imposed by the far-off gaze and makes the suburbs' and slums' inhabitants into agents of change. The margin offers a new way to understand and see the city, but first we need to find, reconfigure, and make visible the city's base structure if we are to criticize it. By presenting the margin as a multiple, dialectical process, we anticipate what Amin and Thrift among others denominate "moments of encounter," in which places "are best thought of not so much as enduring sites … not so much as presents, fixed in space and time, but as variable events; twists and fluxes of interrelation" (30). These moments of encounter in our context here have an effect on place: they comment on it and (re)construct it using its kaleidoscopic movement, which reveals the mythologies and stereotypes of the total, complete, and static city that exists in the temporal pause that characterizes the city as place.

The dialectics of the margin, then, in order to dismantle the mythologies of the prosperous capitalist city and carve out a more socially just city, strives to revise the remotely created images that affect those areas that are more chaotic or difficult to define physically, socially, and culturally because they do not precisely conform to the established pattern of the dictatorship or the bourgeoise. The margin comes from urban rhythm and movement and is itself pure movement in the sense that it emphasizes fluidity, porosity, and contact between physical, urban, and social bodies. Physical interstices are relevant because they allow us to directly observe the clash, contact, and separation of the built city and the chaos that it seems on the brink of unleashing, but the margin breaks through that boundary in search of what we could call a new aesthetic that looks to uncover a new topography of place. These artists do not stop at this boundary, but rather they are the boundary itself. They insert themselves into these spaces that are considered out of bounds and (re)construct the other using the matrix of elements that place – the physical and social order that distributes relations of coexistence (Certeau 117) – uses to exclude and obscure. It is the figure of the artist who shows the porosity between them and us, our mutual dependence, and the existence of movements beyond this duality that can remend urbanistic structuring.

Both literature and photography in this context make the city manifest through the collective imagination that shapes its physical and social margins, while simultaneously dismantling them using the same contrivance: a material environment under construction – found at the heart of urbanistic debates of that time – that can be used to extol the idea of city as process. The margin breaks through and, in doing so, defies the physical structure of the city and demonstrates how said structure leads to stereotypes that disavow and obscure the multiple realities that inhabit and constitute the physical boundaries of the city; in other words, the margin appropriates the city in order to bring to light its hidden contradictions, as Deutsche described when speaking about the function of art in public space ("Uneven" 128).[29] Instead of smoothly inserting physical margins into the orderly and calm city surface, like urbanistic plans propose to do, the margin disturbs the city's supposedly coherent image, which is obtained by neutralizing and hiding everything that is formally and socially chaotic; the margin legitimizes this chaos, showing it as another valid possibility, orderly in its difference, counteracting the practical and discursive campaign against physical margins. In this way, the bourgeois grid that dominates the heart and soul of the city caves in, confirming what Lefebvre and de Certeau announced: the city is not just under the control of those who plan and build it, but also those who use and appropriate it as they go about their daily lives.

Finally, we should consider that, although the margin makes these new identities visible and they in turn act upon and modify the concept of what is understood as city generally or Barcelona specifically, these social and urbanistic changes were not radical in these spaces; that is to say, we do not witness the collapse of the dictatorship or the fall of the capitalistic system that carried out the urban reforms of the 1950s and 1960s. Nevertheless, here I will indicate how, by shifting the perspective from which we approach this place and considering the role of the physical margin, we can discern a dominant culture and class, and grant some degree of power and agency to the otherness buried under the norms of the centre, the bourgeoisie, and the dictatorship, initiating dissent that will end up becoming protest and, eventually, change.

The margin allows us to identify, then, a series of movements undertaken by photographers and writers who, to repeat Delgado's words, "upset the order of the world as they set it up" (*El animal* 117). Their works construct a public space that establishes an involuntary social element, "the intricate, almost unconscious, network of voluntary controls and standards among the people themselves," as described by Jacobs (32), who defines them as community and citizenship, finding in this concept the democratic tone that eluded the dictatorship. It is true that contact in public space is ephemeral and its fleeting nature the very essence of the urban; however, in the context of the margin constructed by these authors, random movement becomes the basis for an identity that, although apparently chaotic or lacking in structure, becomes the basis for a formative space. With this assertion, we depart from theories that define public space as utopian places of tolerance, sociability, and respect for law and order, and therefore we are not claiming a utopian definition of public space based on consensus and peaceful coexistence. Rather, we are defining a public space that acknowledges the legitimacy of the debate over what is and is not legitimate (Deutsche, *Agorafobia* 8), which leads to conceiving of society as a space that can be contested rather than as something fixed or permanent (Laclau and Moffe 122), an approach that we saw in Lefebvre, de Certeau, and Delgado that picks up on the dialectic relationship from the other side. Consequently, we see the conflation of public space and democratic space, as we find room for negotiation in the destabilization and lack of moorings caused by this shift. That is, from the moment that we question the existence of a singular idea at the core of everything social, we open the possibility for debate and for potentially establishing other social and material structures. If we apply this conceptualization of the social to physical space, we can see how through the margin the questioning of a city and its materiality activates a space for dialogue that interrupts the dominant paradigm and posits other ways of being and living in an urbanistic environment. This is the function of the margin; this is the breach.

Chapter Two

Breaking the Silence: The Cultural Mobilization of Francisco Candel

As mentioned in the previous chapter, 1957 saw a multitude of urbanistic actions carried out through official channels, including by the regime – with the creation of the Ministry of Housing and the initiation of a series of partial plans coming from the new political establishment – and also by the Church – with pointed actions meant to fix the problem of the slums, culminating in the conference of the Semana del Suburbio [Week of the Suburb], which, in spite of its precariousness, such as the defence of an ideal image-based city, was the first opposition to the partial plans. These actions were symptomatic of a widespread environment in which suburbs and slums were beginning to become visible and, due to their heightened visibility, became the subject of critiques that could for the first time be expressed publicly. These critiques were rooted in the attempts to reform the city in the 1950s, which in the context of the previous decade's standstill in urban growth gave absolute authority to private over public interests, destroying neighbourhoods and the life that defined them. Josep M. Huertas Clavería and Jaume Fabre explain this disappearance of neighbourhoods with two key elements: (1) the destruction of associative life, carried out by decree from the moment Franco's troops occupied the city, and (2) the physical destruction of neighbourhoods through the enactment of policies that gave priority to private transport and the construction of broad arterial roads, both of which reveal an express desire to destroy the communities of resistance that could potentially arise in these neighbourhoods in deference to the oligarchic interests of automobile factories and real estate speculators (353). The capitalist city that had supplanted the Francoist utopia of a rural Spain became the guiding force for urban reform that sought to homogenize the population in consonance with a new idea of nation based on economic progress. Consequently, we see the development of a policy of urban exploitation begin to take shape in the partial plans derived from the Regional Plan of 1953; these plans permitted the development of residential zones characterized by isolation and a lack of infrastructure, which demonstrated that the housing problem was only understood from a quantitative perspective that sought to eradicate the presence of slums and their inhabitants in favour of an image of the ideal city for sale to an international public and for the economic benefit of a new capitalist oligarchy. The absolute space of Francoism, then, goes on to project its interests in the exploitation of the urban domain.

As a result of the termination of the international embargo that would lead to expanded industrial growth thanks to an influx of foreign capital, the Regional Plan was created in 1953 as a first step in classifying and regulating land, controls not previously applied in Barcelona, which was still under the authority of the Plan Cerdà of 1860 and the Plan de Enlaces of 1917 (Ferrer, "El Pla" 132). The emphasis of these antiquated plans was on the material rather than social form of the city, which was perceived as an object reduced to a series of streets, avenues, and buildings, and which did not consider the daily life of its users in its decisions. The Regional Plan encouraged growth in what would later be counties and the garden cities of the metropolitan area that surrounded Barcelona with green belts dedicated mainly to agriculture and housing units, emphasizing the idea of a polycentric city.[1] Each one of these zones was developed according to a series of partial plans that attempted to physically organize the city to make up for the shortcomings and gaps in the Regional Plan, which had not accounted for rapid increases in industry and population. The speed and precariousness with which these plans were executed opened the door to a series of speculative processes that would come to characterize the dictatorship's urbanism. Together with the resultant corruption of rampant speculation, the urbanistic practice of this time was based above all on the question of social-urban image and characterized by an emphasis on the beautification and ennoblement of the material spaces. The slums that were created to house the large migratory waves that overran Barcelona did not fit with the image of an ideal city that was opening up to the outside world, which plunged the Regional Plan into a discourse of eradicating slums that had been taking shape since 1949 in institutions such as the Servicio de Represión del Barraquismo [Service for the Repression of Slums], created by Barcelona's city hall and focused on eradicating entire slums as the most important urban action to improve the city (Salvadó and Miró 138). The search for a solution to the housing problem lead to the appearance of housing complexes such as Eduardo Aunós, a much smaller scale complex than what would be produced under the dictatorship, which in 1936 was already described as "aquells barris de barraques titulats Cases Barates" (Torres Clavé 82) [those neighbourhoods of slums called the Cheap Houses], which is indicative of an important shortcoming in subsidized housing.[2] In 1957, Porcioles decided to bypass the Regional Plan and create a series of developmental and social emergency plans that would allow reorganization of the legal and institutional framework of the construction industry and open the door for a series of partial plans to systematize the city.[3] Successive modifications of ordinances authorized an expansion of constructability through land reassessment, which meant the elimination of green areas, the construction of housing complexes in zones unsuitable for development, and the processing of these complexes without prior partial planning (Salvadó and Miró 144). The radical modern appearance of public housing offered a sharp contrast to the widespread lack of basic urbanization and was evidence of a "ciudad inacabada" (148) [unfinished city], which could be seen in their low quality of construction, deficiencies in urbanization and features, and isolation.[4]

Consequently, as Ivan Bordetas Jiménez explains (45–7), in the 1950s political measures pertaining to the urbanistic space of Barcelona were predicated upon two designs: first, the construction of the greatest number of housing units possible, even if it meant a lack of oversight regarding their location and quality and the possibility of corruption and nepotism in the regime's administration;[5] and second, the elimination of suburbs understood "com aquell espai en el qual no era possible trobar o reproduir els valors culturals, polítics i socials que el règim pretenia imposar" (Bordetas Jiménez 46) [as that space in which it was not possible to find or reproduce the cultural, political, and social values that the regime intended to impose]. In light of the connection between immigration, suburbs, and moral and social problems, the latter was also an ambition developed in the immediate postwar period by the Church, highly conservative and akin to the regime, in order to craft a popular discourse of the history and grandiosity of Spanish Catholicism; this ambition further reinforced the discourse of sanitization and the mechanisms of control over these areas, justifying their erasure. In the words of Fabre and Huertas Clavería, "al barri s'hi feien coses, al suburbi s'hi anava a fer apostolat" (354) [in the neighbourhood things got done, in the suburbs the Gospel was preached].[6] Both objectives were justified precisely by that distinction; the suburbs' chaos and supposed lack of morality allowed them to be perceived as a problem to be rectified or a tabula rasa to start from scratch. At this point, what Porcioles initiated in the early years of his term took definitive shape in the 1970s, when the eradication of suburbs became a reality in the form of a functional urbanism, "fortament impregnat d'un caràcter higienista i modernitzador" [heavily infused with a sanitizing and modernizing character] and charged with demolishing the slums and transferring their inhabitants to remote and poorly equipped housing complexes (Tatjer 54–8).

Material deficiencies were accompanied by social isolation and urban disorder that opened one of the first critical fronts possible under the dictatorship. That is, the material city opened the door to a critique of the regime decoupled from politics, a possibility due to overwhelming and incontrovertible evidence of shortcomings and flaws in the regime's policies. A prime example is the article "Elogi a la barraca" [Eulogy of the slum] by Oriol Bohigas,[7] whose publication coincided with the Semana del Suburbio and in which the author criticized the functional and sanitizing approach of measures meant to eliminate slums because of how they destroyed the social life of these areas by dispersing their inhabitants in low quality and poorly accessible housing complexes.[8] This article was followed by a wave of works that reflected on the city, especially in the 1960s,[9] as Vázquez Montalbán claims, thanks to the growth of neighbourhood associations characteristic of the later years of the dictatorship (*Barcelones* 251). However, when Porcioles assumed the mayorship in 1957, Barcelona did not have any social movements, and no one dared to criticize the actions of the government. And here is where Francisco Candel enters the picture.

"Providence Is Called Paco"[10]

Francisco Candel (1925–2007) would be the first to open the door to dissent in the form of literature and urban journalism, not only contributing the "primeras tentativas al primer periodismo de barrio" (Huertas Clavería, "Han roto" 7) [first attempts at neighbourhood journalism], but also using his work to create a sense of neighbourhood identity that fomented the establishment of neighbourhood associations and a base-level democracy that would be essential for the later transition to democracy in a political and social context that sought to dismantle that sort of horizontal solidarity.

Francisco Candel's work developed hand in hand with the area where he lived, the Zona Franca (Can Tunis, Casas Baratas, and el Port), an eminently immigrant neighbourhood where he arrived at two years of age from Casas Altas (País Valencià), and where he would live until his death. As Rosa Rull explains, this backdrop is readily identifiable in his books (123), in which he acts as an unofficial chronicler of these suburban areas throughought the most significant moments of Spain's history in the twentieth century (the period of immigration, the Republic, the Civil War, Francoism, the democratic struggle). His connection to this area of Barcelona led to his election in 1977 as a senator of the coalition Entensa dels Catalans, even though he was never affiliated with any political party in particular. These ties to his physical and social environment led to the fusion of his novelistic production and his journalistic work, especially insofar as the development of his notion of public space is concerned, and led him to collaborate with newspapers such as *Serra d'Or*, *Pueblo*, *El Correo Catalán*, *Tele/Expres*, and *Avui*, among many others. Candel described himself as "rebelde, inconformista y revolucionario" [rebellious, noncomformist, and revolutionary], characteristics that he believed essential in any novelist, because otherwise "vale más que, como decimos en Cataluña, 'plegues'" (qtd. in Tubau 9) [it would be better if, as we say in Catalán, you "give it up"].[11] This perception of his writing as an essential tool for social change makes his production dialectical in nature; devoid of idealizations of any sort, his critical approach configured Barcelona in terms of its contradictions and its geographical layout, with the author himself serving as the bridge between worlds separated by an invisible boundary that ineludibly divided the city's inhabitants.

In 1957, Candel published *Donde la ciudad cambia su nombre* [Where the city changes its name], "una de las grandes novelas de Barcelona … [donde] la burguesía no es la eterna protagonista" (Rull 124) [one of the great novels of Barcelona … [where] the bourgeoisie is not the eternal protagonist]. With this novel, Candel completely changed the social and physical panorama of Barcelona during the dictatorship and through his urban description realigned the relationship between space and daily life. In other words, Candel's suburban Barcelona generated democratic possibilities that came from and were inscribed in urbanistic space; the author emphasized the role of the city's inhabitants by granting them an agency that remade them into citizens, a concept that underscores the notion of belonging and the construction of a social system opposed to the political structures of Francoism, which characterized immigrants principally by the spatial, albeit temporary, illegality of their status. In his detailed description of social life in the suburbs, based on physical materiality and expressed through the direct voice of those who actually live there, Candel showed a vibrant city, not just the imposition of a structure or material form or the strict regulation implied therein. His is the first critical voice that comes from the suburbs, bringing out into the open a reality that until that moment was concealed and censored. By humanizing its inhabitants, he generated a

new perspective on the city and a new idea of what it could be: "A mí ...
em tocava explicar-ho ... perquè els barcelonins dels barris benestants
vinguessin al 'zoològic' per veure aquestes feres ... del suburbi, per
comprovar que no mossegaven" (Candel qtd. in Sinca 197) [I ... had to
explain it ... so that the residents of wealthy neighbourhoods would
come to the "zoo" to see these beasts ... from the suburbs, to check
that they did not bite"]; "el suburbio ya existía, pero no fue una realidad hasta que publiqué *Donde la ciudad cambia su nombre*" (Candel, "De
cuando" 22) [the suburb already existed, but it was not a reality until
I published *Where the City Changes Its Name*]. But Candel did not dema-
terialize the city – place continues to be essential to define and characterize its inhabitants; rather, he used it to renegotiate the terms used to
judge the suburbs and their inhabitants, and by extension the practices
and discourses of Francoism that were playing out at that time in the
urban/urbanistic domain.

For this reason, although Candel has always been read in connection with the assimilation of immigrants,[12] in his work this intention is
accompanied by a practice of dissent that is drawn from urban form,
which can be seen in *Donde la ciudad cambia su nombre* and will be more
prominent still in *Els altres catalans* (1964) [The other Catalans]. This
practice of dissent will also be inserted into the political discourse of
the city through the subsequent creation of neighbourhood associations. Candel's material critique becomes a complex question that deconstructs the symbolism imposed on the suburbs by challenging the
legitimacy of discourses and practices applied from the city, from the
absolute space of the state. To that end, this critique takes on the lack of
structure of new construction:

La celeritat [que] obeeix a la construcció del monobloc tipus rusc [als que es
traslladen] eixams de famílies que viuen en una altra banda de la ciutat on
oficialmente feien nosa ... Els arquitectes s'han tornat micos per poder ficar
més coses en menys espai ... Això de construir estatges a qualsevol lloc, uns
blocs damunt d'altres, és una cosa que l'urbanisme modern no veu o no vol
veure i que a la llarga serà de conseqüències fatals. (*Els altres* 208–9, 250–72)

The speed required to construct monobloc type beehives [to which they
transferred] swarms of families that lived on the other side of the city so
they didn't bother anyone officially ... The architects have become mon-
keys in order to fit things into less space ... Building housing complexes
in any random place, piling blocks on top of each other, is something that
modern urbanism does not see or refuses to see and in the long term will
have fatal consequences.

Candel's critique also points out the problems caused by speculation:

Si fos possible desemmascarar tots els tripijocs que l'estatge protegit i
econòmic, el construït per la iniciativa privada o amb ajuda pública ...
han fet possibles, seriem rics en trames i arguments, sobretot drames,
per a les nostres produccions novel·lístiques: desfalcs, traspassos il·le-
gals, utilització de materials defectuosos, contractistes enriquits, estafes,
personatges [importants] atrapats in fraganti, falses promeses, predilec-
cions, recomanacions, tota la variada i assortida gama de berganteria i la
picaresca justament dintre de les classes no picaresques ni bergants. (265)

If we could unmask all of the schemes made possible by state-provided
and affordable housing, whether private or publicly funded ... we would
be rich in plots and stories, especially dramas, for our novelistic production: embezzlement, illegal transfers, use of defective materials, get-rich-
quick contractors, scams, prominent personalities caught red-handed,
false promises, favoritism, biased recommendations, a whole gamut of
scoundrels and swindlers found precisely in the classes that are not scoundrels and swindlers.

For Candel, material and social reality are key pieces in the construction of a marginal, transgressive, and ultimately dissident rhetoric.

Candel himself is central to making this critique work: his voice,
wanderings, and actions craft it and enable a new way of conceiving
the identity of the suburbs. In the indetermination of Lefebvre's tripartite division and the impossibility of pinning down the separation of
the disparate elements that make up the constitution of the city and simultaneously reveal their interdependence and the possibility of showing place through space, in this interstice Candel emerges as the point
of contact between suburb and city and brings greater complexity to
the visibility of the material space of the city. This space depends on the
impersonal and neutralizing tendencies of modern urbanism, which
paralyze urban movement with the violence of the absolute space of
the dictatorship, but Candel manages to reactivate this movement. In
this regard, he establishes with his work a polyvalent city constituted
by "a dialectally interwoven matrix of human interactions" (Wegner
qtd. in Tally 118), which makes him the point of contact in the simplistic
division of the two cities, in a clash that reveals their dialectic nature.
Through his marginality, Candel elevates unforeseen and intangible instants and the action of the manifold agents that move throughout the
city, and draws attention to what in principle is invisible – whether urban or suburban – and forms the basis for the city's growth. Therefore,

by virtue of his being an outsider, distant yet inside and outside at the same time, he allows us to visualize how these uncalculated movements are articulated by and from place and crystallize in the collective urban imagination, while they simultaneously make manifest the presence and articulation of the difference and the plurality of collectivity, and how the two come together to form the social body that comprises Barcelona in this moment. The clash between the regime's officialism and the uncontrollable social movement set in motion by urbanistic practice helps the inhabitants of the suburbs recover the participation and agency dispelled by the supposed neutrality of Francoist urbanism, offering a new "landscape." Thus, Candel carves into the officiality of the urban landscape a new path where alternatives are possible. He forges a new public space where dissidence becomes the norm, recovering antagonisms and dynamics of the uncontrollable flow of individuals.

In order to do so, Candel focuses almost exclusively on "el suburbio [que] aún era suburbio, con todas las connotaciones, y no las áreas metropolitanas, con todos sus eufemismos" (Candel, "De cuando" 13) [the suburb that was still suburb, with all of its connotations, and not metropolitan areas, with all of their euphemisms]. We can see even in this phrase his critique of the oversimplification of the type of urbanism that suppresses and removes from consideration different kinds of urban experience as he sets up his biography and reformulates the image of Barcelona. In his marginality Candel does not just seek the reflection where boundaries are blurred, a literary slant that can be found in other authors such as Jaime Gil de Biedma in his poem "Barcelona ja no és bona," or even Juan Goytisolo in his novels *Fiestas* (1958) [Celebrations] or *Señas de identidad* (1966) [Marks of identity], both of whom allow others to be the ones to change the city; rather, Candel tries to utilize that contrast to make the other city visible, to show the other Barcelonas and put them in dialectic contact. To do so, to break away from the materiality that hinders any type of action, Candel grants agency to suburban voices from within the suburb itself, stressing the body and its activities, keeping with what could be called the Lefebvrian interaction of body-space-culture, so that fragmentation goes on to form a new urbanism in a dual sense. On the one hand, it is a critique of the fragmentation imposed on the suburb from the city, the oversimplified division that diminishes the complexity of the city and alienates through the visual language of abstract space, which makes the inhabitant of the suburb "es sent[i] exclós de la ciutat" [feel excluded from the city], or "suburbialitzat" [suburbanized], as Candel calls it in *Els altres*. On the other hand, this new urbanism proposes that this fragmentation caused by urban processes be visualized, which can lead to the acceptance of difference and an acknowledgment of its role in the construction of the city and its potential to formulate responses and encourage mobilization. For Candel, the city is not made up only of a Cartesian graph, liminality, or the static and disembodied way of viewing typical of absolute space, but rather he finds something else in the city's constitution – matter, time, subjectivity, memory, history, intra-history, present, past – and this spatial complexity, which characterizes space as both a product and a producer, which forms an active, mobile urban space through agency that subverts the reality imposed upon the suburbs.

With Candel, we find the beginnings of a transgression of the Cartesian gaze and the prevailing homogeneous notion of urbanistic space, and as a social consequence from there, a new conception of the spatial project through social and cultural concepts that expand upon material objectives by applying them to space as conceived and lived, showing the malleability of the supposed singularity of the regime's logic. Throughout his novels, essays, and articles, he moulds a project that, in "su denuncia de cierto estado de cosas" (*Dios* 36) [its denunciation of a certain state of affairs], probes the physical and social make-up of the suburbs (as we see in *Donde* and *Han matado un hombre, han roto un paisaje*), as well as their history (as in *Han matado*) and relationship to the city (as in *Els altres*). In this way, in a project logically developed by following the changes taking place in the suburbs, Candel does not just shape the other city, but rather through the description of the sometimes violent and depraved world of the suburbs he builds another city entirely, dismantling the Barcelona of "las buenas costumbres" [good habits] of the slogans of the "Paz de Franco" [Franco's Peace] or the mythical Barcelona of the local bourgeoisie. The outsider character of his works in the context of what was being produced in the city at that time, in both the field of literature as well as urbanism or national discourse, marked a departure from all three:

> Potser per això, o per aquesta primera aparença, quan en vaig tenir un exemplar a les mans em vaig quedar bastant desolat. Vaig tenir la sensació que havia pixat fora de test. El meu article ... em semblava una mica detonant, resultava un gep, una sinuositat més pronunciada que la resta. No era erudit, no tractava de la literatura o de l'art català, no evocava la historia del país, no n'esmentava els homes ... Per acabar-ho d'adobar va sortir una nota en un diari, si no recordo malament a *Solidaridad Nacional*, signada per Enrique Fafián. En aquest article es feien alguns retrets a la revista *La Jirafa*: l'acusaven d'haver-se tornat un cenacle i d'emprar formes que només arribaven a una minoria ínfima. (*Els altres* 31)[13]

Maybe because of this, or because of this first appearance, when I had a copy in my hands I was pretty devastated. I had the feeling that I had peed outside the pot. My article ... seemed like it clashed, it was a nuisance, a sinuosity more pronounced than the rest. It was not erudite, it was not about Catalan literature or art, it did not evoke the country's history, it made no mention of notable men ... To complicate matters further, a note signed by Enrique Fafián appeared in a newspaper, *Solidaridad Nacional* if memory serves me correctly. In this article he reproached the magazine *La Jirafa*: he accused it of having turned into a clique and employing forms that only reached a tiny minority.

His work breaks away from the simulacrum of false coherence that grips the ties that seek to bind language, culture, and history naturalistically and attempts to actively exclude everyday activities and day-to-day life. If we accept that the guiding intentions behind monumentalization are comparable to the objectives of absolute space, that is, "imponer lo lógico sobre lo heterológico, lo normalizado sobre lo heteronómico o sobre lo anómico" [the imposition of the logical over the heterological, the normalized over the heteronymic or the anomic], which like a monument "fetichiza el espacio, lo rescata de la acción subversiva del tiempo cotidiano, de la zapa a que se entregan sin descanso las prácticas ordinarias ... está siempre ahí, indiferente al paso del tiempo" (Delgado, *Memoria* 17) [fetishizes space, wrests it from the subversive action of everyday time, from the change to which ordinary practices are tirelessly subjected ... and is always there, indifferent to the passage of time], then the schism perceived by Candel goes beyond the publication of his article, as can be seen in Enrique Fabián's critique, since in Candel's conceptualization of the suburbs he surpasses the conceptualization of urban space and absorbs those elements that over time become fossilized as part of the origin of a mythical and unchanging identity.

Candel throws us off centre; he breaks away from established order in order to look from a different point of view. To do so, he focuses on the body and its actions, and, simultaneously, he treats space like a body, seeking its movement, that is, its language, representations, and the structures that give it meaning. In this shift, he breaks away from established parameters and finds an alternative way of visualizing and constructing the city by focusing on the interplay of what is visible and invisible and what is present and absent, which allows him to challenge the representational structure being developed at that time and reveal the connection between vision and the desire for power and control.[14] To a certain degree, this connection links his transgression to voyeurism, that is, peeking through the keyhole at intimate but also forbidden areas, guided by the desire to discover a world meant by officials to be hidden from view; here Candel's gaze upends officialdom's supposed urban and social harmony. His way of looking is voyeuristic because of how it displaces vision, intrudes, and is forbidden, all qualities that allow him to generate a new story, a new space. This intrusion proposes a narrative,[15] a material and physical body that in turn proposes new knowledge and a transgression of the dynamics of power through a meeting of gazes that upsets the dynamic between observer and observed. It is a clandestine gaze in which the presence and absence of the suburbs are essential because they uncover the hidden make-up of Barcelona and also the source of critiques and censorship of Candel's works, a censorship applied also to the suburbs themselves.[16]

Candel's Visibility

In 1965, the magazine *CAU* (*Construcción, Arquitectura y Urbanismo*) [Construction, Architecture, and Urbanism] published a monograph dedicated to the suburbs, opened by an article from Candel entitled "El Amazacotamiento" [Densification], in which he sought to buck the censorship that hid away the suburbs in order to include them in the urbanistic narrativity of Barcelona. His visualization of the suburbs was predicated upon their physical and architectural description accompanied by a historiographical narration of their origins, making them recognizable within a narrative that was itself recognizable from the place of the city. In his introduction to this issue of *CAU*, architect José E. Donato explains:

> La zona suburbial, objeto de este comentario, no constituye en modo alguno una entidad urbana ni en el espacio ni por su historia. Su heterogeneidad es evidente en relación a los llamados polígonos de vivienda, aunque en su desarrollo histórico y geográfico existen "inclusiones" urbanísticas que, predecesoras de las actuales, en la etapa de postguerra fueron promovidas por organismos de carácter más bien político que administrativo o técnico. Sin embargo, la mayor parte de su textura suburbial es de generación espontánea y en consecuencia se hace difícil su crítica en términos de diseño por faltarle un planteamiento previo y unitario que traduzca unos criterios urbanísticos que, buenos o malos, puedan ser objeto de análisis … En segundo lugar queremos señalar, antes de pasar al tema, la absoluta falta de estudios históricos sobre los suburbios de Barcelona … La historiografía local nada, o casi nada, nos dice del desarrollo

de unas zonas de la ciudad que, si bien son de reciente aparición, alcanzan hoy una extensión y un volumen demográfico tales que, sin su existencia, nuestra ciudad ni habría alcanzado su potencial económico ni consecuentemente su importancia política y cultural en el marco de nuestra región ni en el más amplio de todo el país ... Una injustificable visión selectiva de la historia ha dado como resultado que el fenómeno de mayor magnitud de la historia de nuestra ciudad, fundamental para la comprensión de la Barcelona actual, haya sido dejado de lado ... sólo a la Barcelona que acaba en el Ensanche le es permitido tener historia. (19)

The suburban zone, subject of this commentary, does not in any way constitute an urban entity either in space or history. Its heterogeneity is evident in relation to the so-called housing complexes, although in its geographical and historical development there are urbanistic "inclusions" that, preceding current ones, were promoted in the postwar period by organisms more political than administrative or technical in nature. However, the greater part of its suburban texture is spontaneously generated and thus hard to criticize in terms of design since it lacks prior and united planning that translates urbanistic criteria which, whether good or bad, could be the object of analysis ... In second place, we want to point out, before moving on to our topic, the absolute lack of historical studies on the suburbs of Barcelona ... Local historiography tells us nothing, or almost nothing, about the development of some zones of the city that, even though they have only recently appeared, have achieved today a size and demographic volume such that without their existence our city would have achieved neither its economic potential nor consequently its political and cultural importance in the scope of our region or the country more broadly ... An unjustifiable selective view of history has cast aside the greatest phenomenon in the history of our city, one which is crucial to our understanding of present-day Barcelona ... only the Barcelona that ends at the Eixample is allowed to have history.

Material form is what sets in motion a new narrative that recovers the presence of censored suburbs. Although Candel was already aware of this detail years earlier when he wrote *Donde la ciudad cambia su nombre*, his emphasis on the presence of bodies that inhabit those spaces is what gives form to a specular narrative that lays the basis not just for a critique of the place of the city, which was already common when Donato was writing, but also the basis for the construction of a specifically suburban identity. Where urbanistic narration seeks to "normalize" or "rationalize" the chaos that seems to characterize the suburbs by introducing them into the city's history, Candel satirizes that type of narration in order to show the opposite, the irrationality of the city's forms of place:

> La populosa barriada de las Casas Baratas o Eduardo Aunós, que suena mucho mejor, consta de ventiuna calles. Así (disimulen, por favor):

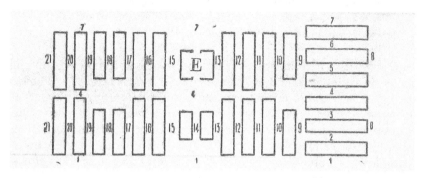

Figure 2.1   Francisco Candel, *Donde la ciudad cambia su nombre* (1957). © CEDRO.

> Medio aparrillada. Como un San Lorenzo del Escorial, pero menos. Antes estaban numeradas. Calle 1, calle 2, calle 3, calle 4, hasta 21. Sonaban a prisión o a Nueva York estos números. Ahora les han puesto nombres. Unos nombres catalanes, unos enrevesados nombres catalanes, más enrevesados aún para las estropajosas lenguas murcianas de sus moradores. Ahora los nombres son: calle Ulldecona, calle Pinatell, calle Cisquer, calle Pontils, Rojals … Ellos, sus moradores, dicen calle Urdecona, calle Pinatey, calle Sirqué, calle Pontís, Rochal, Traguirá, Arné, Asco, sin el acento, Motril, Rudón, etc. Algunas gitanas enturbian más las cosas. A la calle Tragurá la llaman: Trasgirá, desgrasiau, Trasgirá; ¿qué se ha creío er payo ejte? A la calle Ulldecona, Urdecoña, ¡cucha por Dios! Y así sucesivamente.
>
> La barriada, en total, con sus puertas y ventanas tan simétricas, tan iguales, semeja un queso Gruyère. (*Donde* 53).

The crowded neighbourhood of the Cheap Houses or Eduardo Aunós, which sounds much better, is made up of twenty-one streets. Like this (pretend, please): [see figure 2.1 above]

Kind of like a grill. Like a San Lorenzo del Escorial, but less so. Before they were numbered. First Street, Second, Third, Fourth, up to Twenty-first. Those numbers sounded like prison or New York. Now they have named them. Some Catalan names, some convoluted Catalan names, even more convoluted for the unclear Murcian tongues of their inhabitants. Now the names are Ulldecona Street, Pinatell Street, Cisquer Street,

Pontils Street, Rojals … They, their inhabitants, say Urdecona Street, Pinatey Street, Sirqué Street, Pontís Street, Rochal, Traguirá, Arné, Asco, without the accent, Motril, Rudón, etc.

Some gypsies make things even more politically incorrect. They call Tragurá Street "Trasgirá," you wretch, Trasgirá. What are they thinking? They call Ulldecona Street "Urdecoña." Dear God, listen. And so on.[17]

The neighbourhood, as a whole, with its symmetrical and identical doors and windows, looks like Gruyère cheese.

Candel uses this imagery to satirize the official discourse's unwillingness to understand how the neighbourhood's residents function and its desire to eliminate them through structural homogenization, order, and exclusion, making an ironic commentary on imposed structures reflected not just in his comparison but also in the simplicity of his sketch (figure 2.1) which, like the language of urbanism, eliminates all complexity, emphasizing the characteristic ignorance of said structures. The similarity between these margins and a prison, or New York City, recovers the image of the grid, the bourgeois reticle: order, clarity, but above all, exclusion, which taken together allow us to perceive how the suburbs are acted upon from the vantage point of the city with the application of a form of visibility that reduces and simplifies the suburbs and their marginality by imposing the tyranny of the straight line marking and limiting space. The grid makes the margin a place that is locatable, homogeneous and controllable, at least in principle, insofar as the bourgeois order of the formal city distributes the lower classes. Upon the chaos previously occupied by the slums it imposes numbered streets without end that are disorienting because, as Richard Sennett tells us, there is no point of reference to hold on to and locate oneself, only "a mindless geometric division" (55) that seeks the neutrality of the grid not because it is understood as a tabula rasa but rather because, as Sennett goes on to tell us, "it subdues those who must live in the space, disorienting their ability to see and to evaluate relationships. In that sense, the planning of neutral space is an act of dominating and subduing others" (60). In other words, the numbing effect of the grid flattens identity and specificity.

The neutrality of the numerical grid in this case is substituted by names with a Catalan origin that create a place-specific neutrality, evoking a sensation of inclusion that is undone by the distance that separates residents of these areas from the place of the city. However, as we can see in how the residents of the Casas Baratas adapt the street names, Candel picks up on the reconstruction of the signifier/signified relationship by reusing official discourse to create a new perspective on the peripheral neighbourhoods. The residents remake symbolism through everyday usage. Lived space invades conceived space and the conceptualized space of the margin through a dialectic relationship that reveals, in Lefebvrian terms, the tension between grand urbanistic blueprints and individual practices, creating a new meaning and explaining the daily uses of the suburban environment. He gives voice, not a voice projected by an all-seeing and all-knowing entity that looks from afar, but a personal voice that emerges from within, bestowing specificity and experience. And here we find an important contrast to Donato's description, which sought a formal rigour that overlooked, once again, those who lived in these structures. Lefebvre posits this same contradiction: "Is the city the sum of indices and facts, of variables and parameters, of correlations, this collection of facts, of descriptions, of fragmentary analyses, because it is fragmentary? These analytical divisions do no lack rigour, but as has already been said, rigour is uninhabitable" ("The Right" 94). Candel, for his part, is conscious of the alienation felt by residents of the suburbs, a place that "ha estat el seu corralet, el lloc on ha estat acorralat" (*Els altres* 206) [has been their corral, the place where they are corralled], and finds in that alienation the dialectic relationship between created space and imposed space, and his own language that redefines urban structure and the identity of its residents, reconciling the body's space with the material space imposed and at the same time privileging movement and the whole over staticity and division. In other words, he thinks about the city as an object to be reconstructed without overlooking the importance of its constituent parts, making way for the basis of a new urban identity that incorporates those different parts. To that end, Candel reformulates the uses of space to fashion a new urban identity based on community:

> A raíz de haber prohibido en el Barrio Chino y en los alrededores de Ataranzas la venta ambulante durante los domingos, sus vendedores sentaron sus reales en las Casas Baratas, barrio sin ley, o donde no alcanzaba la ley, si no esto no se explica. Sentaron sus reales a todo lo largo de la calle Tortosa, antes calle 4; de la calle Sovelles, antes calle 21, y a la entrada de esta barriada, en el camino del Prat Vermell. Así:

> ⌐____

> … Ahora es como un rastro en Madrid, pero menos, según unos; un poco más, tal vez, según otros; la gente le llama Mercadillo, a esta ristra de puestos y paradas; el Francisco Candel, poeta, escritor, visionario, soñador, loco, todo eso que se dice, le llama el Zoco, no sabemos bien por qué …

Entrando en las Casas Baratas por la parte de la parada del autobús –los domingos, claro–, empieza el Mercadillo, el Zoco, que dice el Francisco Candel. Hay una vieja tumbada, una vieja haraposa llena de bubas y roña, la abuela del Picaor; una vieja a quien los años y la miseria han puesto lo ojos blancos, descolorido el iris, ciegos. ¡Que Santa Lucía les conserve la vista!, salmodia, como los ciegos de romance, y la gente le echa calderilla o no le echa, según. (*Donde* 125)

Due to the prohibition of street vending in the Barrio Chino and around Ataranzas on Sundays, the vendors established themselves in the Casas Baratas, a lawless neighbourhood, or where the law did not reach, otherwise this cannot be explained. They set up all along Tortosa Street, previously Fourth Street; on Sovelles Street, previously Twenty-first, and at the entrance to the neighbourhood, on Prat Vermell road. Like this:

... Now it's like the flea market in Madrid, but smaller, according to some; a little larger, perhaps, according to others; people called this string of stands and booths the Little Market; Francisco Candel, poet, writer, visionary, dreamer, crazy person, whatever else they call him, calls it the Bazaar and we have no idea why ... Entering the Casas Baratas by the bus stop – on Sundays, of course – the Little Market, or Bazaar as Francisco Candel says, starts. There's an old lady lying down, an old lady dressed in rags and full of pustules and scabies, Picaor's grandmother; an old lady whose eyes have been turned white by the years and poverty, her irises faded, blind. May Saint Lucia preserve her eyesight! she chants, like the blind of ballads, and people toss her loose change, or not, as is their wont.

In his stroll through the Mercadillo, Candel, like a flâneur, begins with a geographical description that is then substituted by an experience that constitutes new guidelines: the name of the street is substituted by the bus stop and then by different zones that make up the market, starting with the beggars that "los domingos madrugan, a cual más, para coger los sitios más estratégicos" (126) [wake up early on Sundays, each earlier than the next, to grab the most strategic spots]. Zoning, which organizes the city and expels these inhabitants in order to normalize the spectacle of the street, is substituted by a new layout characterized by disorganization and lawlessness, a supposedly chaotic situation when viewed from the outside, but one whose order becomes apparent as a response to poverty and the culture of improvisation. This new and of course unofficial rezoning returns to the idea of the street as a public space that, although the law tries to control it, as we see in Candel's descriptions of police raids, winds up becoming a space for transgression in which those expelled from the city reclaim and reassume their place in a new order where what is out of place finds its place.

Just as he does with the structure of the Casas Baratas, Candel takes up the spectacle of commerce and the language of capitalism that steer urbanistic projects in order to criticize the colonization of daily life that will also be criticized by Guy Debord and Henri Lefebvre later: the appropriation of space, the imposition of profit-driven organization, social relations as an inherent part of property relations; in other words, exchange networks and the flow of products become the defining and determinant elements of space. But on this satirical stroll, Candel divulges the intimate relationship between space and the bodies that inhabit it and their reciprocal influence, and he imposes a need-based criterion for construction that dismantles the geometrical idea of the city and asserts "an urban reality for users and not for speculators" (Lefebvre, "The Right" 168). If, as Lefebvre claims, space is both norm and normalization, Candel reveals a space for subversion and appropriation: the French boulevard becomes a "bazaar" or "flea market," maintaining the bourgeois practice of accumulation, but with an ironic twist that shows us the reality of that capitalist system through its shortages and shortcomings, its exclusions and abuses. It should be noted, however, that Candel's portrayal is not only about emphasizing spatial practice, but rather showing a contest for space in a constant clash, and the idea of space as a dialectic practice defined by the complexity of the bodies that compose it. We should also be mindful of how the voices of those who use and inhabit space are those who define it. "La gente" [people], Candel among them, are the ones who give names, who characterize the use of space, a narrative trait that will define Candel's novels and be the basis for the creation of that identity and dissenting voice.

Physical space is immediately reclaimed by bodies – beginning with the writer's – that take it over and make the suburbs "transient," but at the same time concrete, tangible, and visible, showing how the strict place of the grid – which always lies at the base of actions, as the narrator reminds us by mentioning numbers and names – is subverted by the use that inhabitants make of it. To do just that, Candel takes up the tools of urbanism that rely on the hegemony of vision and inserts them in a multisensorial world that destroys linear perspective:

> Per observar, en canvi, només cal deixar-te anar, veure com passen les coses, practicar una mena de ganduleria estàtica. El que passa és que ...

Com ho diría? Mireu: quan bades amb alguna cosa, t'envolta el remolí del que observes i t'hi involucres. És como si fossis un lector, però no només mitjançant el sentit de la vista, sinó també del tacte. És aquest sistema Braille el que millor t'orienta; el tacte i el compromís que comporta. (*Els altres* 402).

In order to observe, on the other hand, all you have to do is loosen up, watch how things happen, practice a type of static idleness. What happens is ... How should I say it? Look: when you're spaced out, you're surrounded by the whirlwind of what you're observing and you become a part of what's happening. It's as if you were a reader, but not just using the sense of sight but also touch. That Braille system is the best way to orient yourself; touch and the commitment that accompanies it.

In this Baudelarian "static idleness," Candel defies the restraints of the visual field; that is, whereas Francoist urbanism depends on a monocular visual structure that ignores the experience of the body, Candel recaptures that experience and uses it to give meaning to the chaos in the whirlwind of everyday lived experience. This whirlwind of experience orients and gives meaning to the noise, finding rhythms underneath all of the chaos of the city. As Lefebvre will tell us, in order to capture the chaos, you have to allow yourself to be caught up in it (*Writings* 219). The distance of the urbanist's viewpoint is substituted with the proximity of the user. The numerical logic that oversees the streets and layout of the neighbourhood – and which Candel constantly emphasizes in his writing, as we have already pointed out, by mentioning the current street names and the numbers used to identify them before the war – a logic controlled by a monocular, disembodied, and static visual field, is substituted with a space ruled by affectual engagement with the world. It negates the presumed neutrality of the order imposed on the suburbs and gives them a sensory quality not through any imposed organization but through an immersive experience that accords them an uncontrollable collective disposition. Candel's approach widens the gaze and the space it perceives, and also produces a collectivity that joins togetherness and difference, thereby reconfiguring the urban cartography of Barcelona. By breaking with the visual forms of legibility imposed by urban design governed by speculation and social control, which no longer suggest much about subjective life or heal the wounds of those in need, Candel examines the actions of individuals who try to challenge an authority that, distinct from the collectivity of the suburb, imposes the rationalization of an absolute space through fragmentation and isolation. For Candel, just like for Lefebvre (*Writings* 219), to comprehend the meaning of the noise and the chaos, one should be inside and outside at the same time, although in this case, Lefebvre's distance vanishes in Candel's spatial immersion:

> [El doctor] sube a lo alto de la montaña de Montjuïc, donde el coche no llega, con lluvia, por el barro, con frío, con calor. Se mete en cuevas, en barracas, en la suciedad, en la miseria; se llena de piojos, a veces. De continuo se le ve por aquí. Incluso los domingos y las fiestas se deja caer por casa de algún enfermo que no tiene a nadie y sabe que se aburre. No va en plan de visita del médico. Va a hacerle compañía, a estarse un rato con él. El cura le ha dicho muchas veces:
>
> "Usted tiene que hacerse una casa aquí. Usted pertenece más a estos barrios que a Barcelona."
>
> Ya se la haría, ya. Pero no puede dejar su clientela de pago, su clientela rica, su clientela de la que algunos ya le han plantado porque iguales deferencias tiene para el pobre que para el adinerado. (*Donde* 62)

> [The doctor] climbs to the top of the mountain of Montjuïc, where his car cannot reach, under the rain, through the mud, in the cold, in the heat. He goes inside caves, in shanties, in the muck, in the misery; sometimes he gets lice all over him. He's constantly seen around here. Even on Sundays and holidays he drops in on sick people who don't have anybody else and know that he knows are bored. He doesn't go in his capacity as a doctor. He goes to keep them company, to be with them for a while. The priest has told him many times:
>
> "You should build a house here. You belong more in these neighbourhoods than in Barcelona."
>
> He would do it already, sure. But he can't leave his paying clientele, his rich clientele, his clientele that sometimes stands him up because he has the same deference for the poor as for the wealthy.

In spite of the fact that the doctor is from and lives in the place of the city – it is worth noting the distinction that he makes between "these neighbourhoods" and "Barcelona," again, inside and outside at the same time – in Montjuïc his walk is completely integrated into the informal city and draws attention to the lack of infrastructure and basic services. The holistic visualization of the urbanistic landscape is substituted with a view of a body that endures and transmits tactile and olfactory impressions that underscore the proximity of the space in which it circulates; we see the insertion of the body in an order that distances itself from the logic of the city. In doing so, Candel establishes the uniqueness of the suburb and its right to exist; he wants it to be acknowledged, which in turn expands the city towards its outskirts. To that end, he never describes the place of the formal city; he frees himself from the monumentalization of the city, and brings his characters to the outskirts, to describe from the inside not only the interior of the sub-urbs, but also the insides of a system of oppression. This interconnec-tion happens through the body, the body of the doctor, the body of the city, the body of the suburb: we have the positioning of a body and how it relates to the space that surrounds it, creating a new blueprint that is used to synchronize the actions that happen in space and to modify the perception of the place. Keeping in line once again with Lefebvre (*Production* 169), space is mapped out by the actions of the body, which is completed with a new genealogy and a new way of narrating, with which Candel seeks to reshape the city by offering new perspectives, new orientations in space.

If Candel's objective is to defy urbanism's monocular view, he will also have to counter the narrative totalitarianism of place, to which end he fosters a democratization of the narrative voice, seen in his works as the presence of multiple narrating bodies. His chronicler's voice spreads through the voices of the protagonists of his stories in two key ways: through the influence of oral storytelling, found in both *Donde* and *Els altres*, and in his articles, through his condition as rep-resentative, advocate, and loudspeaker to amplify the voices buried beneath the crushing order of the city because, as he puts it, "aquests veïns m'han cridat perquè parli damunt el paper" ("La vida" 71) [these neighbours have called on me to say it on paper]. In this plurality of voices and the constitution of narration and space by a choral structure, the suburbs interfere with the perception and construction of the city and shake loose the monocular view of the state because, as Lefebvre reminds us, "space does not consist in the projection of an intellectual representation, does not arise from a visible-readable real, but it is first of all heard (listened to) and enacted (through physical gestures and movements)" (*Production* 200). That is, similar to how urbanism's dis-tanced and all-encompassing viewpoint vanishes in the experience of the body and what is enacted, the mythical narrative of two cities van-ishes in the multiplicity of voices listened to and then transmitted by Candel in his narrative.

In *Donde*, each chapter tells the story of a different character, part of the larger narrative of the suburbs, a new element of the structure of Barcelona, and in their own way these characters each respond to the fictitious congruity of the bourgeois city. Candel's body circulates among them and is always present alongside them in his novels (as a character himself in *Donde*, as Gafas in *Han matado*, or examples from his own experience in *Els altres*); he walks among his characters and comes into contact and interacts with all kinds of realities, inserting himself into everyday spaces using all five senses. In this commingling, the suburbs transgress physical, social, and cultural boundaries – literal and symbolic city limits – which upsets urbanism's false equilibrium and fosters the dialectic clash of its parts through interaction, not separation and division. In this context, if visibility constitutes a cultural domain, where the quality of being visible is what dictates and controls the realm where identity is articulated, Candel takes this visual practice of papier-mâché urbanism, clearly demarcated technical urbanism that conceals and ignores the previsions of social evolution and privileges a flattened and absolute space of time, and he substitutes it with a scopic regime that reclaims the potentiality of space through an alternative way of looking, admitting its possibilities and accepting its difference by critiquing the flaws and shortcomings of the neutralizing urbanism practiced up to that point.

Disruptions

By placing emphasis on the body and choral voice of the suburbs, Candel breaks free from the mythology of the dual city and puts in its place the complex relationship of space/place. That is, he is aware of the dichotomous material separation between city and suburb, which is assumed as the only order possible by and from the city, a posture seen for example in Donato's introduction to the issue of *CAU* discussed above. But Candel also measures the separation between the physical form imposed by urbanism and the contradiction that becomes apparent once the unpredictable flow of bodies is set in motion, revealing relationships, clashes, and connections impossible to imagine from within the confines of the city's structure. In this regard, Candel shares and prefigures the perspective of Jane Jacobs, who in *The Death and Life of Great American Cities* (originally published in 1961) shows precisely how urban order imposed from above is defied from below, through the actions of its users. Like Jacobs, and as we have seen, also like Lefebvre, who uses his idea of urban rhythms to conceive of daily life in the city as a living process that plays out in spaces of representation, representational spaces, and spatial practices, Candel shows us through the actions and movements of suburban residents how multiple social variables are at play at any given time in any given space and are connected to an organic whole that does not respect the boundaries or conditions set by the urbanism of static geometrical structure. In the process, he neutralizes the isolation endured by the suburb and its inhabitants, thus criticizing the static paradigms of an urbanism that is based on speculation and perceives the city as a product to be sold to the highest bidder.

A good example of this critique can be found in *Han matado*, where Candel constructs a formal and social history of the suburbs, their history in spite of History, an intra-history that predates the urban structure of the dictatorship and is used to cement their presence despite the city's attempts to erase them from the map. He designates the suburbs, granting them visibility and a place in the city's history, and fashioning an identity that questions and defies the certainty of the stereotypes imposed on them by and from the city. This legitimization simultaneously produces the activation of a collective consciousness through a unifying voice, Candel's own, that comes from within the suburbs. His model of the city is predicated, therefore, on upholding these collectivities, and recognizing and preserving their identity instead of suppressing it.

> Sense tenir en compte per res l'humil veïnat que fa més temps que és allà que no les fàbriques, sense comptar-hi per res, han declarat zona industrial aquells terrenys, s'ha decretat que sigui així. I així ha d'ésser i muts i a la gàbia. Per què no construeixen fàbriques a les zones aristocràtiques i residencials i ens repartim la càrrega? Si ho fessin, no mancarien queixes als diaris, cartes al director a les respectives seccions, i la gent no pararia de fer mans i mànigues per tal d'aconseguir l'eliminació d'aquest projecte. (*Els altres* 220)

> Without considering at all the humble neighbourhood that has been there longer than the factories, without considering it at all, they have declared those plots an industrial zone, they have decreed it so. That's how it has to be, end of discussion. Why don't they build factories in aristocratic and residential areas, and we share the burden? If they did that, there would be endless complaints to the newspapers, letters to the directors of different offices, and people would do whatever it takes to put an end to this project.

Whether slums or housing complexes, the suburbs are a "humble neighbourhood" with all of the social and spatial connotations such a characterization entails; that is, this concept reconstructs the suburbs based on the complex network of social relationships tied to a space that is equivalent to the spaces of the city. This legitimization, as we see in the citation above, ties into the transgression of official urban models, a direct criticism that starts in *Donde*, is further elaborated in *Han matado*, and finds its maximum expression in the article "Los otros catalanes" published in *La Jirafa* (1958), which will become the book of the same name.[18]

Already in *Han matado* Candel subverts official parameters through his lengthy homage to the slums, entitled "Divagación, apología, lanza, glosa, lo que se quiera, en torno, sobre, por, de las barracas" [Digression, defense, lance, gloss, whatever, about, on, of the slums], which reads like a long parenthetical detour that bursts into the narration like the slums burst into the ideal structure of the city, and where he develops a detailed account of their history, social and material configuration, and development in order to show how "las barracas son una necesidad, fruto de una necesidad, pero no son necesarias" (226) [the slums are a necessity, the product of necessity, but are not necessary]. He reuses the architect's or urbanist's criteria – the gaze over geometric space ("he visto ..." [I have seen ...]), the use of materials ("las barracas de la Fontana eran de obra, con tejas ... las barracas de los Arbitrios, de madera, de cartón cuero ..." ["the Fontana slums were made of brick, with tiles ... the Arbitrios slums were made of wood and hardboard ..."]), dimensions ("bajitas, pequeñas, en lugares inverosímiles" [short, small, in unlikely places]) – but he always dresses these dwellings as spaces of life and experience:

> Los gitanos vivían más fuera de ellas que dentro: los gitanos de largas patillas y chalecos; las gitanas de sucios refajos; los churumbeles como su madre los parió ... ¡Cuánta poesía, ¿verdad?, y qué cotidiano milagro de vivir, comer, multiplicarse, subsistir, no perecer!, ¿eh? Por favor, honduras, no. Vamos a dejarlo, si os parece bien. Sí que nos parece bien. Pues dejado. (229)

> The gypsies lived more outside than inside them: gypsies with long sideburns and vests; gypsies with dirty underskirts; children as naked as the day their mother gave birth to them ... How poetic, right? And the daily miracle of living, eating, multiplying, subsisting, not perishing, huh? Please, no depth. We'll leave it at that, if it's okay with you. It's okay with us. Okay, done.

Daily life is considered "poetic" from an urbanistic point of view because of its irrelevance in how urbanism goes about its work and because of how it has been exoticized in the discourses of the regime, literature, and photography; it invades material space and deforms the simplicity of the city's "ojos colonizadores" [colonizing eyes]. In this way, he jumps from a horizontal view of the slums to Porcioles' vertical view, whose city "para bien o para mal, para bien, eso ya lo veremos, eso habrá que demostrarlo, empezaba a poner sus ojos de colonizador en aquellas tierras" (229) [for better or worse, we'll see if for better, that will have to be proven, begins to set its colonizing eyes upon those properties]. Through the use of this adjective, "colonizing," Candel shows how the city writes upon what it claims is a vacant space, negating the presence of the other. The city creates worlds with stone, hence the return to urbanism and wholesale construction over a supposed tabula rasa, and uses them to promote images centred on the interests of the city, ignoring the social nature of those who live in the margin.

In this new urban syntax, we again see the ironic twist that we saw in the flâneur's wanderings, always creating the reverse image of what is known. The importance of visual order highlights the separation of the suburbs, their rejection by the city, and the disconnection and simplicity of the argumentation of place:

> De tota manera, als que veuen aquest pisos – als del Patronat, a les dames pies, als visitadors de suburbi – se'ls eixampla el cor, i també la consciència. Per comparació amb abans, que vivien en barraques o rellogats, aquesta gent està de primera. Resolt – això pla, resolt! – resolt, diguem, el problema del barraquisme, es va creant el del monobloc. Es viu d'esquena a la ciutat, fora de la ciutat. Es un viure bigarrat, tipus rusc, tipus presó, amb sensació de poca intimitat, d'estar despullats dins aquests pisos. Tot se sent, tot es veu, es copsen totes les olors … Mossèn Jaume Cuspinera em diu: Els primers dies t'indignes. Vols protestar. Vols que se t'adaptin a tu, als teus mètodes, al teu silenci. Però després comprens que "ets tu que t'has d'adaptar a ells." (*Els altres* 267–8)

> In any case, the people who see these apartments – the people from the Board, pious ladies, visitors to the suburbs – their hearts expand, and their conscience, too. By comparison with before, when they lived in slums or sublets, these people are well off. Problem solved – piece of cake, solved! – the problem of the shanty towns, let's say, solved, we've got the new problem of the monobloc. They live with their backs to the city, outside the city. It's a disjointed way of living, like a beehive or prison, with a sensation of little privacy, like being naked inside these apartments. Everything can be seen, heard, and smelled … Father Jaume Cuspinera tells me: At first you are indignant. You want to complain. You want them to adapt to you, your ways, your silence. But then you understand that "you are the one who has to adapt to them."

The disconnect between residents and the structure assigned to them is a response to the disconnect between space and everyday life, both

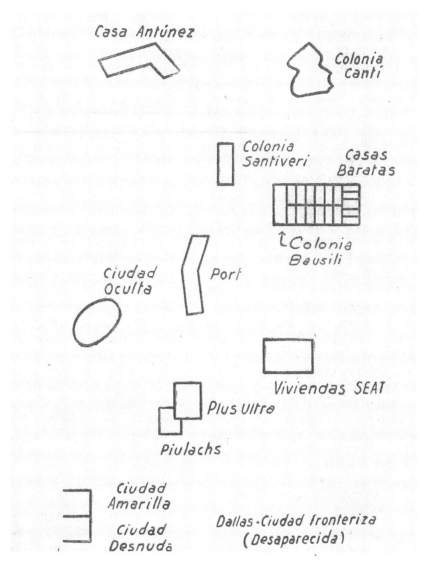

Figure 2.2 Francisco Candel, *Donde la ciudad cambia su nombre* (1957).
© CEDRO.

on an individual and urban level. The rhythms of daily life in the margin counteract the bourgeois way of looking. The bourgeoisie owns the land and imposes a structure, but residents' habits and uses interrupt

that structure. At the same time, the inadequacy of that structure ignores the complexity of daily life, as Candel materially demonstrates
(see figure 2.2).

The layout of this map (figure 2.2) of housing complexes, outside the
urban map of Barcelona, on a blank page, emphasizes precisely their
condition of being outside, compelling them to be a world apart that
lays plain the difference between the haves and have nots (see also *Els
altres* 292–3). In fact, years later Candel will say of these neighbourhoods "que no constan en los mapas o guías, y esto no solamente el año
de su inauguración, sino el siguiente y el otro. Y lo más increíble: no se
les advierte, para que los coloquen inmediatamente en sus planos, a los
bomberos, al 091 y a los servicios de urgencia" ("El amazacotamiento"
6) [that they do not figure on maps or guides, and not just the year they
were built, but the following and the next. And more incredible still:
no one tells firefighters, 911, or emergency response services so they
can immediately put them on their maps]. The visual vocabulary of
the buildings contradicts the form of the community where – to return
to Candel's hand drawn map – the lack of connection between their
constituent parts, their isolation, and the void in which they are erected
all stand out. The simplicity of the straight line scoffs at urbanistic
projects and, by extension, the dictatorship's identity project. The emphasis on the gaze, mainly through urban planers' distant viewpoint
and the concept of the whole that results from the single snapshot of
urbanistic blueprints, foregrounds the loss of memory and the elimination of the social networks that Candel had sought to recover since
Donde, his starting point to go on to establish a collectivity formed "no
per esperit gregari ni reaccionari, sinó, senzillament, per paisanatge"
(*Els altres* 153) [not out of a gregarious or reactionary spirit, but, simply,
compatriotism] with the purpose of welcoming and loaning money to
newcomers, and facilitating access to housing or a shanty that would
open the doors of the city to them.

This community represents a social conscience rooted in a process
of migration that breaks with the exclusionary practices of Francoism,
which included demolishing slums, forcibly returning newcomers
to their places of origin and detaining those to be expelled in the pa-
vilions of the old fairgrounds to await their expulsion from the city.
This heightened social awareness reveals the disconnect between the
dictatorship's local governments and the citizenry, and in doing so
denounces the cartographic production of space that, similar to the dictatorship's absolute space, attempts to capture, limit, and demarcate,
preventing connection and concealing combative visualization through
a homogenization that suppresses alterity. In this regard, Candel moves

at the fringe of legality. Similar to how with *Donde* he broke neighbours' unspoken but presumed contract of peaceful coexistence predicated upon respecting each other's privacy by directly describing the state's actions in the suburbs – questionable actions that everyone knew about but did not talk about, such as the destruction of slums or expropriation (see, for example, *Han matado* 278) – Candel broke the agreement between city and suburb in the absolute space imposed by a state that assumed the ineffability of its actions under the neutral form of the law.

This clash reinforced the presence of an absolute space through the "rule of nobody," by which we mean the relationship between bureaucracy and violence that Hannah Arendt talked about and which we have already seen applied to urbanistic discourse: "In a fully developed bureaucracy there is nobody left with whom one could argue, to whom one could present grievances, on whom the pressures of power could be exerted" (*On Violence* 81). In the context we are examining, this law confirms the space of truth that is not located in any one place because it is everywhere (Lefebvre, *Production* 240) and is represented in the performativity of words, that is, in what is said and the action it produces. Candel takes the same approach: describing and displaying these actions implies creating an image somewhere between what is invisible and what is legible in the intersection of power and knowledge, which violates the practice of the state through strategies of representation. That is, if the state seeks to conceal the suburbs in order to maintain a homogeneous and pacific social and urbanistic physiognomy based on materiality, then showing the destruction of the slums implies, on the one hand, an acknowledgment of their existence, and on the other, the corrupt practices that guide reforms and the life of the suburbs in general. But above all, it implies acknowledging the presence of their inhabitants and, moreover, criticizing state discourse and practices in regards to a spatial organization that ignores and actively excludes the inhabitants of the suburbs, once again, the human side of the "housing problem":

> *Un affaire silenciós.* A la Muntanya, a les Banderes, un centenar de barraques han estat amençades de demolició. No estan legalitzades – així anomenen les altres – perquè no tenen número o placa. Ja fa mesos que són fetes. A part del dret que tenien a edificar-les, per què van deixar que les fessin per enrunar-les ara? És absurd.
>
> Bé, l'amenaça d'enrunament és per al 21 d'aquest mes. (Aquestes notes són del 7 de setembre de 1962.) Els propietaris de les barraques poden escollir entre anar a Missions o tornar-se'n als seus pobles, viatges pagats.
>
> Ahir al matí es van presentar els del pico. La primera barraca que van enderrocar, l'home era dintre. (Ja hem dit que sempre actuen procurant

que els homes siguin fora, a la feina.) L'home va oposar resistència, i, men-
trestant, van avisar el señor rector el cual va anar a veure l'alcalde, el portà
al lloc de l'incident i, de moment, es va suspendre la demolició.

Per aquestes barraques, els seus habitants han abonat diverses quantitats que oscil.len entre les 5.000 i les 20.000 pessetes a diversos individus,
a uns pels terrenys, a uns altres pels materials de construcció, a uns altres
per les barraques ja fetes.

El rector ha recollit unes declaracions signades pels ocupants de les barraques dient qui els va vendre el terreny, la barraca o els materials, i quant
en van pagar. Aquest matí el rector m'ha ensenyat aquestes declaracions.
No he pogut observar-les amb deteniment. Seria interessant d'esbrinar qui
són aquests venedors, si ocupen càrrecs elevats i on ...

Però calgué animar aquells veïns a fi que reclamessin, i posar-los una
mica en peu de guerra; si no, els haurien asservits. (*Els altres* 246)[19]

A silent affair. In Muntanya, in Banderes, a hundred shanties have been
threatened with demolition. They are not legal – that's how the others are
designated – because they don't have a number or placard. They have been
finished for months. Apart from the right they had to build them, why did
they let them build them only to tear them down now? It's absurd.

Well, the threat of demolition is for the twenty-first of this month. (These
notes are from 7 September 1962.) The owners of the shanties can choose
between going to Misiones or returning to their towns with the trip paid.

Yesterday morning the pickax people showed up. The first shanty they
demolished, the guy was inside. (We have already said that they always
try to act when the men are away, at work.) The guy put up resistance, and,
meanwhile, they informed the rector, who went to see the mayor, took him
to the place in question, and he temporarily suspended the demolition.

In these shanties, residents have paid out various amounts ranging
from 5,000 to 20,000 pesetas to various individuals, to some for the land,
to others for materials, to others for already built shanties.

The rector has collected affidavits signed by the residents saying who
sold them the land, the shanty, or the materials, and how much they paid.
This morning the rector showed me those affidavits. I was not able to carefully read them. It would be interesting to find out who sold them, if they
hold higher offices and where ...

But those residents had to be encouraged to complain and go on a war
standing; if not, they would have trampled all over them.

Already with his title, Candel establishes the silence and darkness
enshrouding the reality of the residents of the slums, but with a rhetorical twist he seizes upon the moment to carefully describe their history,

how they came to be, and the roles played in this process by the state and city, thus making the suburbs visible within the city's order and showing how they are a product of its mechanism of creation and expansion, a speculative mechanism focused on capitalist development where the only thing that matters is profit.

The elimination of the suburbs and their humanity is expedited by the dissolution of the agency of their inhabitants: absolute space creates a system in which suburbs depend on the charity of the city, in this way eliminating all possibility to act. Needs can only be satisfied through the network of dependency established from and by the city:

> Però el que és certament greu no és la manca d'una cosa necessària, sinó la manca d'un criteri just per a mesurar equànimement la seva necessitat; un criteri just que els va ésser deformat a còpia de "donar" seguint només els dictats d'un cor malatís que no va pensar que a aquest "donar" segueix un "demanar" que deforma la dignitat humana ... I encara és més greu el fet que aquest "donar," amb el seu "demanar" deformador, no solament s'ha aplicat en l'aspecte material d'unes mongetes ... sinó també en unes influències, unes recomanacions, unes distincions, uns favors, diguem-ne, de tipus moral o almenys intangibles. (*Els altres* 296)

> But what is certainly grave is not the lack of a necessary thing, but rather the lack of fair criteria to measure their need impartially; fair criteria that was deformed in the act of "giving" following the dictates of a sick heart that did not think that this "giving" would be followed by an "asking" that deforms human dignity ... And graver still is the fact that this "giving," with its deforming "asking" has not only been applied to the material aspect of a few beans ... but also to influences, recommendations, distinctions, favors, let's say, of moral or at least intangible sort.

We should recall our previous reference to networks of compatriotism, shared lived experience, and collaboration, which clash with the dissolution of action that we find here. We still see a network of connections that are established through physical space, but here they are dependent on a system removed from the space and time of the suburbs, because it radiates from the city and sees them from above and far off in an almost divine fashion – divine in its moral affectation, infallibility, and even ineffability – and it imposes a structure that perceives the treatment and renovation of the suburbs as a mission. In doing so, the identity of the inhabitants of the suburbs is erased under an idea of coherence that strips them of their agency. However, what most stands out in this example is how Candel's voice becomes the cohesive element that binds them in protest to create not a community or structure but a collectivity. By collectivity here we understand cohesion, grouping, but not necessarily coherence and consonance (Delgado, *Elogi* 133). Candel becomes that "viajero interestructural" [interstructural traveller] about whom Delgado speaks in *El animal público* (117): his visualization of different structures disturbs that which is considered order and, in his opposition to critics of the slums, he reveals and recovers their residents' stolen agency.

From spatial experience a "we" emerges speaking about "us," giving way to a new human, geographical, and social cartography:

> És en aquest aspecte que jo crec que formen més societat al marge els immigrants, una gran majoria dels immigrants, els seus genuïns representants: en la seva misèria i en la seva injustícia més que no en la seva catalanitat o manera de catalanitat; en el fet de donar-los pa o certificats de bona conducta per fer-los callar i terure-se'ls del damunt, o de crear un món a part amb el seu pintorenquisme, el seu perniciós pintorenquisme, o de creure que són així i han d'ésser així. (*Els altres* 296–7)

> It is in this aspect that I believe that immigrants, a large majority of immigrants, their genuine representatives, better represent the idea of society from the margin than do those at the centre: in their misery and injustice more than their Catalanness or way of being Catalan; in the fact of giving them bread or certificates of good conduct to shut them up and get them off their backs, or creating a separate world with its picturesqueness, its pernicious picturesqueness, or believing that they are like this and have to be like this.

Let us appreciate, in the first place, how the immigrants make a claim to their own voice, as "genuine representatives," a representation based on their acknowledgment as "society," as a collectivity. Second, using the order that the city establishes through its language, organization, isolation, and paternalism, Candel re-elaborates the suburbs from a new perspective in which their "misery" and "injustice" form the basis for a rhetoric of denunciation that sets up a new network of relations. It is no longer, or not exclusively, about being Catalan; that is not what makes integration possible. Space is what enables integration: their treatment by structures that regulate space makes them part of the city, recovering a discourse of the basic rights of citizenship that evokes their humanity and presses for grassroots democratic action. In this way, starting with the vindication that he launches in *Donde* through his criticism of the structure that makes slum dwellers disappear and continues to develop in later works, Candel's writing establishes the foundation for an "escuela de ciudadanía" [school of citizenship] that opens the door to dissidence within the regime's structure. If, as Miquel Carminal claims (8), this grassroots citizenship serves to show the connection between neighbourhood associations and opposition to the dictatorship, since these groups become an alternative to Francoist city government, privileging a grassroots democratic structure that leftist parties and others opposed to the dictatorship oriented towards the struggle for democratic and national freedom in Catalonia, Candel takes it a step further. He lays claim to rights by criticizing precarious economic and living conditions and seeking redress in the form of material benefits like fair housing, by incorporating participation by the suburbs' underclass into the city's structure, and by insisting upon the dependency between city and suburb from different perspectives – albeit inserting them in the same economic system of capitalist exploitation. His dissent, however, although circumscribed by the context of dictatorship, establishes a dialectic opening that creates a mechanism for protest that will outlast the dictatorship, creating a place for the suburbs within urban structure, the bedrock of Francoist identity.

Put another way, Candel's search for a geographically based identity of the suburbs could be criticized for falling into the error of returning to the idea of an urban structure that supposes a moral and aesthetic order (see Harvey, "New Urbanism" 2–3). As Fraser informs us (*Henri* 148), thinking that the neighbourhood imposes a pattern of relationships is to admit that the planned city imposes a rational and inorganic structure over the city in practice. If dialectic thought attempts to mobilize an object, Fraser continues, to return it to a social dynamic that is not at all monolithic and is always negotiated through conflict, wrapping it up in the meaning of a spatial narrative means recreating a monolithic structure. However, Candel employs the language of urbanism precisely in order to create and mobilize a channel of dissent that cannot be closed. It is true that Candel elaborates his critique based on specific geography and develops an identity based on the material want that geography imposes on its inhabitants, however he also acknowledges social relations as inevitable and boundless and prioritizes them ahead of space:

> Per acabar, voldria insistir que si bé la difusió del llibre *Els altres catalans* es va estancar, com és normal en la vida dels llibres i de la majoria de les coses, l'esperit del seu enunciat continua ben viu, així com el leitmotiv que forma el cos del llibre, la seva ànima. És como si amb la publicació de l'any 1964 haguéssim "encetat" un tema, igual que es tasta un meló.

La diferencia és que el meló s'acaba, i el tema, no. El tema de la immigració, d'una immigració concreta i de la immigració en general, segueix sent, des d'aquell "encetat," des que el vam tastar, un tema candent, incandescent, imperible i intemporal. (*Els altres* 402)

To wrap up, I would like to insist that even though my book *The Other Catalans* ceased having an impact after a few years, as is normal in the life of books and most things, the spirit of its declaration is alive and well, as is the leitmotif that forms the book's body and soul. It's as if with its publication in 1964 we had "started" a topic, like how you try a melon. The difference is that the melon runs out, and the topic doesn't. The topic of immigration, whether concrete immigration or immigration in general, is still, since that "started," since we tasted it, a hot button issue; it's incandescent, timeless and undying.

The city, space, provides Candel with the groundwork to stress the link between form and content and to dissolve the stable morphologies, material as well as social, imposed on the city by Francoism's purported stability – or later conservative Catalanism "tan influent mes tard en la vida política catalana" [so influential later in Catalan political life], which set "la barrera entre catalanisme y no catalanisme ... deixant per a un segon terme la divisió entre depredadors i depredats, entre explotadors i explotats" (Riera 55) [the bar between Catalanism and non-Catalanism ... relegating to the background the division between predator and prey, exploiters and exploited]. Therefore, the dialectic, as in Lefebvre, is not chaotic in Candel but rather the gateway to an ongoing discussion that prevents the fossilization of the social landscape.[20] For this reason, his is not a politics of political parties. In point of fact, he does not belong to any party. Rather, he is trying to find a place from which to arbitrate the differences produced by structures that are, again, social or physical. The evolution of Candel's discourse, that is, the move from the notion of suburbs isolated from the city and dependent upon an imposed and foreign structure in order to survive (as we see in *Donde*) to the constitution of an identity with its own voice and agency inserted into a larger whole that exists beyond the boundaries of the suburbs and expands the relational network in which they participate (begun in *Donde* but more fully fleshed out in *Els altres*), establishes the connection between material and social domains, shrugging off the imposition of a single, all-consuming order. As his work matures, Candel homes in on the insertion of social and economic specificity in urban matters, such that they stop being a "framework" and become a practice that directly impacts the lives of those who live in the suburbs.[21]

Identity and Social Organization

The critique of strategies of absolute space and the conceptualization of a grassroots democratic structure in the collective gaze of the suburbs' inhabitants make us ask: what is Candel's place in the constitution of neighbourhood associations and later social movements? Both in his novels *Donde* and *Han matado*, as well as in *Els altres* and articles published in journals including *Destino*, *CAU*, and *Serra d'Or*, all of which chronologically predate the creation of social movements, we can already find traits that authors like Jordi Borja (*Movimientos* 196) will attribute to neighbourhood associations: highly effective organizations with continuity, strong social identification, organizational development, and institutional response. Candel's writing is essentially an "effective organization" that enables direct communication with the city and its governmental apparatuses, in his perception of the suburbs seeking and achieving results including acquiring immediate social assistance and configuring a protest-based identity that shifts the balance of power.[22] That is to say, articles like "La vida catalana" [Catalan life] are seeking out social assistance, always related to a question of identity as we can see in the title of this same article (which shows, moreover, the author's direct connection to neighbourhood associations and the process of evolution at work in his writing). But in addition, Candel initiates an epistemological turn with regards to identity and then later in the construction of the suburbs that allows him to lay claim to a collectivity, social presence, and grassroots democratic values that will give way, as Carme Molinero and Pere Ysàs explain vis-à-vis neighbourhood associations and social movements, to an alternative political culture rooted in solidarity and democratic participation ("Introduction" 22). Institutional response takes the form of censorship but also a change in the perception of the city by, for example, the professional urban planners and architects that collaborate with *CAU*.[23] The humanistic turn initiated with Candel – or the "human dimension" as the editor of *CAU* called it in the title of the first part of its special edition dedicated to the suburbs – is the next step in the urban turn, an evolution that is perceived thematically in this sort of publication that shows how different interested parties settled on an agreement of the importance of the social and cultural concerns being espoused by Candel since the publication of *Donde*.[24] In Candel's wake, the urban, which up until this point took the form of a movement that was critical but nevertheless operated within the confines of the city,[25] goes on to contemplate the urbanistic and, from there, the marginal, escaping the walls erected by nineteenth-century urbanistic form and simultaneously beginning to expand the city through new projects such as the many housing complexes that were popping up.

New structures imply new ways of making critiques, extolling the human and social dimensions overlooked by urbanism and architecture. Certain aspects of urban social movements, including direct action and protest against the material flaws and shortcomings in housing focused on people and distanced from formal political parties, can also be found in Candel's writings, although he does not engage in systematic mass protest tactics. The author does not, however, discount the fact that his books and articles set in motion a line of critical enquiry grounded in the characterization of a collectivity and the right of the inhabitants of the suburbs to be part of the city, taking advantage of the discursive turn of the dictatorship: "Rompía lanzas repetida y reiteradamente, como tantas veces de entonces en adelante haría, en pro de la gente pobre, humillada y ofendida que vive de espaldas a la ciudad porque es la ciudad quien les da las espaldas" (*Dios* 140) [Time and again, like I would go on to do so many times in the future, I stood up for the poor, humiliated, and victimized people that live with their backs to the city, because the city turns its back to them"]. Candel appears all the more exceptional in the context of the different housing organizations that emerged from the political machinations of the regime and the Church, such as the Obra Sindical del Hogar (OSH), which was severely criticized by Candel in *Dios* (214–24). Candel understood these organizations as an "instrumento de producción del urbanismo de tolerancia que se [había] propiciado durante 30 años" [production instrument of the tolerant urbanism promoted over a period of thirty years]. They prolonged the typical "urbanismo subintegrado, marginal" (Borja, "La promoción" 79) [underintegrated, marginal urbanism] characterized by a lack of awareness of the human component of the everyday lived experience of the slums' inhabitants and their particular needs; instead, these organizations prefered to uphold the status quo and the regime's worldview. In keeping with the politics of José Luis Arrese, the minister of housing, these organizations sought the construction of the greatest possible number of housing units, the real-world expression of a rhetoric of social justice and defusing of potential disagreements that could activate political opposition (Bordetas 51). However, Candel rediscovers this connection between neighbourhood, city, and dissent, making his discourse evolve over time into a political discourse in a dual sense: what starts out as a critique of state and local governments' zoning and their concomitant implementation of regulations that exclude, discriminate, and segregate ends up attacking the structures of the dictatorship through a class-based discourse that the state sought to suppress precisely through the application of urbanism. It is along these lines that we can see how Candel reuses the regime's discourses and practices to take them in another direction. Moreover, he opens the door to a social structure that will materialize in neighbourhood associations and the social movements that they will spawn.

The confluence of neighbourhood, city, and dissent allows Candel to broaden urbanism's handling of justice (*Els altres* 214), proposing the idea and practice of the right to the city based on integration and participation, which makes it a vital space in which to develop identity, culture, and social difference. Consequently, echoing Delgado's words ("Elogio y rescate"), in Candel we do not find a search for the suburbs' place within the Francoist worldview that claims to eliminate difference through the imposition of an allegedly neutral absolute space concealed under the fictitious social sensibility promoted by the aforementioned state and municipal organizations; nor do we find a desire for inclusion in the space of planners and administrators or in the bourgeois space of civic responsibility that purports to regulate the tone and tenor of social relations. Candel does not present us with a peaceful and predictable world free from conflict, nor does he confirm the existence of a space subjected to a utopia of territorialization and harmonious coexistence. Instead, in his creation of a genealogy for the suburbs, he shows us a space built on top of the violence of human relations unleashed by living in close quarters, understood as a paradoxical and heterogeneous accord that must be bolstered by the physical environment. Candel's is not a coherent city; it is a city of contradictions, even in the suburbs. Where the city tends to fade into the form of specific institutions (Lefebvre, *Writings* 142), Candel reclaims it for its citizens. And this is his principal form of dissent: in a society where citizens' voices are silenced by a dictatorial state, Candel restores the voice and agency that they are denied:

> [Les estructrues imposades pel règim] han destruït els llaços de solidaritat que, pel fet de pertànyer tots a una mateixa classe, els haurien d'unir … I ningú preconitza una acció col.lectiva ni operativista, per exemple, ni en vol saber res … Una vegada em va venir a veure una dona, a veure què podia fer, perquè l'havien treta de la seva barraca – tot i que era una barraca "numerada" – sense indemnització de cap mena i perdent els drets a pis, aquests drets tan problemàtics. Era un comiat per sanció. El delicte consistia a haver recollit una família que feia dies que no sabia on ficar-se … S'ha arribat en un extrem en què ni la teva misèria no et deixen compartir. Maten la caritat. (*Els altres* 214)

[The structures imposed by the regime] have destroyed bonds of solidarity that, by virtue of belonging to the same class, should unite people ... And no one praises a collective or operational action, for example, nor does one want to know anything about it ... One day a woman came to see me, to see what I could do, because they had removed her from her shanty – even though it was a "numbered" shanty – without any kind of compensation and losing her housing rights, which were problematic to begin with. She was evicted as a punishment. Her crime consisted of having taken in a family that for days had nowhere to go ... We have gone to such extremes that you can't even share your own misery. They have killed charity.

With its bureaucratic rationality, absolute space eliminates the possibility of identity claims based on class or even common humanity by manipulating basic needs. In true dystopian style, the regime creates an almost panoptical social system in which penalties take the form of stripping the city's inhabitants of basic rights. Consequently, the destruction of the city is brought about through depersonalization, the creation of anarchical sectors with nothing in common to bind them together except indifference and scepticism towards society and the city in which they live; it is the social version of the imposition of the straight line. However, through his person, and his critical and activist stance, Candel undertakes the consolidation of a grassroots suburban identity. He emphasizes the values of a culture fundamentally rooted in solidarity and pulls back the curtain over the regime's urban logic, searching instead for a type of urban planning other than crass economic development, preferably one based on reconstructing the urban fabric and putting residents first, with the goal of reigniting the mobility of social relations and making residents active agents in the process of urbanization. In this scenario, as Teresa Caldeira maintains (qtd. in Carrera 2), the suburbs, the metropolitan periphery, would not be a closed or isolated space, but would be spaces created and sustained through forever permutating processes of social and urban transformation that would make us rethink that whole system based on the peaceful coexistence of difference.

Now, Candel is the crucial piece of the puzzle needed to break down the walls that the regime put up physically and socially around the suburbs. He is the door that opens the threshold connecting both extremes and fills in the blanks that we see in his map of the housing complexes. In this regard, Candel himself is the margin and indeed a key figure in the genesis of urban social movements. He positions himself as the point of articulation where the diversity of urban experiences collides. In the discourse and practices of the city, the suburbs remain banished in a merciless separation of space, but he shows the right to connect, presupposing the other. As Georg Simmel explains, what is perceived as separate is connected in our conscience: "we have emphasized these two together against whatever lies between them" (5). What has been isolated previously from one another as the result of a supposedly pervious order is shown in Candel to be connected physically and symbolically. He creates a path that shapes the order of things and in which movement questions time and space: time by the construction of a chronology, offering an alternative to history; space by the construction of a spatial configuration that shows active resistance to absolute space. His voice, his writings, his walks symbolize that extension of the volitional sphere over space, as Simmel tells us when he talks about the door and the bridge. In this action we can also see the aesthetic value of Candel's work in the sense that by connecting and breaking with the dual city, his voice, his movement and, with them, the suburbs become visible. They give the eye "the same support for connecting the sides of the landscape as it does to the body for practical reality" (Simmel 6). The movement that connects city and suburb does not end, however, with Candel's wanderings; instead, in his creation of that connection and the visualization of a collectivity, he opens the door to new possibilities. That is, his narrative is not absorbed into a new material structure. It expands through time and space through the thousands of voices that he unleashes and alongside which he constructs the suburbs.

Candel's voice is the first to oppose the supposed naturalization of absolute space in its most basic form, material space, which is arranged into a particular unity according to a unique meaning. Candel shows us movement, connection, and, with it, malleability and change. As Simmel explains, "the [wall] is mute, but the door speaks" (7); Candel is that boundary with freedom, his narrative is "the possibility at any moment of stepping out of this limitation into freedom" (Simmel 10): he removes borders and creates new relationships not based on the "dead geometric form of a mere separating wall, but rather as a possibility of a permanent interchange" (Simmel 10). The plasticity resulting from the visibility Candel created using the materiality of the physical form of the suburbs expresses relationships that are invisible on different levels and stresses the importance of the body precisely because of how it can create or destroy social, economic, and cultural relationships.

Epistemological Turn

The critique that emerges from using a new narrative to break physical boundaries enables the (re)construction of the physical conditions and social memory of the suburbs, which in turn compels readers to reformulate their understanding of what the city is and the stereotypes they impose upon the margin. One consequence of this turn is that we witness what we could call an epistemological reformulation of urbanism. In 1964, as part of a eulogy of Bohigas' book *Del Pla Cerdà al Barraquisme* [From the Cerdà Plan to the slums], Josep Maria Castellet wrote a brief article in *Serra d'Or* entitled "De l'arquitectura al humanisme" [From architecture to humanism], where he highlights the concept of "urbanite":

> La Dolors, la portera, pocs dies abans del seu traspàs, ja greument malalta, contemplava la pluja darrera el vidres. De tant en tant, amb una convicció esgarrifadora, seguint amb el fil de la imaginació el curs de les aigües que les clavegueres del Passeig de Sant Joan engolien amb dificultat, exclamava amb veu lleugerament sinistra: "Déu meu! I pensar que vivim damunt de tota la porqueria que corre per sota la ciutat!" La seva, no era, certament, una visió urbanística pròpiament dita. Més aviat podríem dir que era una visió determinada per un estat emocional, sobre la base d'una realitat urbana, tan evident com parcial. Ara: és així, com el urbanites acostumem a veure les ciutats, la pròpia ciutat; no vull pas dir com a conjunt d'edificacions construïdes sobre la "porqueria" que canalitzen les clavegueres, sinó d'una manera mes o menys emotiva, subjectiva, feta de records, de la feina quotidiana, del nostre trànsit pels carrers, d'algunes reminiscències històriques, de les hores passades a casa, als habitatges familiars o dels amics, etc. En aquest país i en aquest temps, per altra banda, no ens és permès de participar activament i col·lectivament en la vida pública i, per tant, d'objectivar-la en una feina comuna. Com a ciutadans som únicament subjectes passius de processos municipals als quals no contribuïm, en definitiva, sinó econòmicament. Contribuents passius, doncs, relativament i, en alguns casos, adoloridament indiferents, res no ens ajuda a prendre consciencia objectiva d'aquests ésser viu que és – o que hauria d'ésser – la ciutat, la nostra ciutat. (26)

Dolors, the doorwoman, a few days before her transfer, already gravely ill, contemplated the rain through the window. From time to time, with a chilling conviction, following with her imagination the flow of the water that the sewers of Paseo de San Juan swallowed with difficulty, exclaimed in a slightly sinister voice, "My God! And to think that we live on top of all that crap that runs under the city!" Hers was not, of course, an urbanistic view per se. Rather, we could say that it was a view determined by an emotional state, based on an urban reality as evident as it was limited. Now, that's how it is, that's how we urbanites are accustomed to see cities, the city proper; I don't mean as a group of buildings erected over the "crap" that the sewers channel, but rather in a more or less emotional, subjective way, made up of memories, daily work, our transit through the streets, historical reminiscences, hours spent at home or at the homes of friends and family, etc. In this country and at this time, on the other hand, we are not allowed to actively and collectively participate in public life and, therefore orient it towards a common goal. As citizens we are only passive subjects in municipal processes which we can only contribute to, in short, economically. Passive contributors, well, relatively, and, in some cases, painfully indifferent, nothing helps us to become objectively aware of this living being that is – or should be – the city, our city.

Although he completely overlooks Candel's contribution, we can see the development of an awareness of the urban experience that unites material space with the lived daily reality of its inhabitants. The short-comings that Castellet mentions – the passivity of citizens in municipal processes, the lack of a public space for action, and, above all, the lack of awareness – are all elements criticized and reactivated in Candel's life and work. The 1965 themed issue of *CAU*, "Los suburbios," has the same reaction to these conditions as Candel, who penned the first text in this issue and who, having already begun to examine key aspects of the housing problem in *Donde la ciudad cambia su nombre* and *Han matado*, concluded that what was needed was a history of the slums, emphasiz-ing their human element and bestowing upon architecture a "geografía humana" [human geography] (Candel, "El amazacotamiento" 5). In a time where living conditions were predetermined by a "realidad mal-formada por las viciosas estructuras que hoy las determinan" (Bohigas, "El polígono" 29) [reality distorted by the vicious structures that be-get them], architects like David Mackay (17–21) and Oriol Bohigas ("El polígono" 29) start to emphasize, like Candel, the need to look from the inside – a criticism levelled by the slums' inhabitants themselves – and to research the physical and psychological needs of users.

  Similarly, architect Luis Nadal Oller explains that by building housing before urbanization took residents' needs into consideration, "el barrio nace sin vida" [the neighbourhood is stillborn], which causes its root-lessness (38), exactly how the map of the housing complexes illustrated in *Donde* showed. Human and material history should develop side by side, moving from the abstraction of urbanism to the concrete reality of the neighbourhood, and daily experiences and activities should be what gives meaning to the place, enriching the sense of belonging and the substrate of memory and identity in the neighbourhood. That said, what stands out in these articles is the authors' distance from the slums' residents, especially evident in Castellet's text, which effaces Candel entirely and ignores Bohigas' participation in the Special Plan for Montjuïc to be put into effect the following year. Moreover, when he speaks about "urbanites," Castellet is focused on residents of the city proper, not the suburbs.[26] And here we find what is Candel's most distinctive feature: what in Castellet is best described as complaint and dearth of action becomes pure action in Candel's work. No matter where he publishes, Candel cultivates language that is accessible to a heterogeneous audience; he neither includes nor excludes, but rather draws his readers into his project of creating another Barcelona, making language an essential part of the make-up of a suburban identity. The geography that he registers in his writing is the neighbourhood, the slums, where through the tales of their inhabitants/characters he develops a sense of everyday life that shapes the representational space which, as Lefebvre explained, cuts across and reformulates material and conceptual space. In other words, he reconstructs the signs used by the city to recognize itself, and he does it through the idea of neighbourhood and its relationship to place, not with the goal of stopping there, but of continuing to evolve within the open dialectic that is city. In this configuration, written language is essential, but so is urbanistic language, which links the idea of imagined community with Joan Ramon Resina's idea of contemplated community.[27]

Candel is aware of this connection: the construction of *Donde* takes the form of fragmented chronicles that break with the linearity of the city and construe a collective character whose life is told through multiple voices and stories, one of which is the urbanistic structure of the place. If one thing is made clear in Candel's novel, it is that there is no such thing as a single, stable memory: memories are continuously evolving, changing alongside residents, and they are made coherent precisely through their connection to space. This aspect of his work allows Candel to develop his own language, the language of the suburbs, such that "hem d'entendre per llenguatge la capacitat d'imposar la memòria pròpia, la pròpia consciència, no sols a través de les paraules, sinó també per mitjà dels edificis i plans d'urbanisme" (Vázquez Montalbán, *Barcelones* 124) [we have to understand language as the capacity to impose one's own memory and conscience, not just using words but also urbanism's buildings and plans]. It is not surprising, then, that *Donde* was criticized not just for its content, but also for its language, labelled as vulgar (see, for example, *Dios* 240 or Riera 60). However, that language, which like the space it represents was disassociated from bourgeois morality and the principles imposed by a social and cultural structure that did not apply to the suburbs,[28] is what creates uniqueness and difference, which in turn establish new parameters for the construction of identity. In this way, Candel reinscribes the meaning of this place, forcibly characterized from afar by the city, and through the rhythms of the human agency that fills it, his readers find space to be active, alive, and fluid. They, the inhabitants of the suburbs, are his protagonists, the ones who construct and produce space and identity, connected by a sense of belonging to a distinct although not necessarily static collectivity, as we have already observed.[29] Candel constructs a mobile space – mobile because it is a product of lived experience, sundered from the language imposed by/from the city[30] – and he redefines the place of the city, stressing the lived space of representation through his manipulation of the images and symbols that are imposed on it and which it is necessary to change in order to foster greater inclusivity.

Candel's importance as a margin is manifold: place and its materiality, which until this point only served to rigidly bind and restrict the slums' residents to a stereotype that expelled and excluded them from the city, becomes malleable and can be moulded by their actions; the margin, his narrative in this case, reinvents place, reconstructs the relationship between city and suburb, and establishes new power relations that can upend the predictability of what is considered real: "Aquests veïns m'han cridat perquè parli damunt el paper de llur situació. A la sortida del Metro de la Sagrera m'espera l'Hortet: ell ha fet de intermediari entre aquests veïns i un servidor, i ha estat amb ells en llurs reclamacions" ("La vida" 71) [These neighbours have called for me to write about their situation. At the Sagrera subway exit Hortet was waiting for me: he was the intermediary between these neighbours and me, and has helped them with their complaints]. As an interstice, an intermediate area to jump between place and space – or between two places – Candel serves as a common point to establish a dialogue. The following description details the route he had to take to arrive at the slums, and through his use of detail the author's movements trace the constitution of that space, making its characteristics visible, making them exist even:

> En un bar davant FENASA ens esperen uns veïns d'aquestes barraques. Traguegem i ens posem en marxa. Ens endinsem per un carrer a la dreta de l'Escola de Formació Professional Accelerada, edifici de línies modernes. El carrer pel qual passem fa com de magatzem a l'aire lliure … tot seguit, les barraques al.ludides. Són, si fa no fa, quaranta, arrenglerades com un tren, una darrera l'altra o una al costat de l'altra, com vulgueu, assentades damunt un mur de contenció de la RENFE. (71)

> In a bar in front of FENASA some neighbours from these slums are waiting for us. We have a drink and get on our way. We head in taking a street

to the right of the School of Advanced Professional Formation, a building with modern lines. The street we are going down is like an open-air
warehouse ... next up, the slums in question. There are more or less forty
shanties in a row like a train, one after another or each joined to the next,
whatever, all resting on top of a RENFE retaining wall.]

His description marks, first, the contrast between the city's buildings
and the material structure of the slums, but especially important is how
he shows their proximity and mutual dependency. Second, his description marks how the neighbours gather around him, which on one hand
shows his importance in organizing neighbourhood associations, and,
on the other, points out the fact of their existence, albeit on an informal
level:

> La unió fa la força, i aquests veïns estan units ... Aquesta bona gent, sen-
> zilla, humil i pobra gent no s'han adormit, i han procurat d'elevar queixes
> i denunciar llur situació. Han redactat instàncies ells, els capellans de la
> demarcació parroquial, d'altres, fins i tot personal tècnic, diguem-los així,
> com un metge ... [i] dos aparelladors del Col.legi Oficial de Catalunya i
> Balears. (72–3)

> There is strength in numbers, and these neighbours are united ... These
> good people, simple, humble, poor people have not been idle, and have
> managed to raise complaints and denounce their situation. They have
> drafted petitions, assisted by their parish priests, and others, including
> professionals, such as a doctor ... [and] two engineers from the Official
> College of Catalonia and Baleares.

Here we are witnessing the birth of the first neighbourhood associations, dependent at first on parochial demarcations but becoming ever
more independent and taking greater initiative. In this way, Candel
makes the space of the slums into a place, which is to say, as Doreen
Massey explains ("Conceptualization"), he shows how the experience
and actions of individuals humanize and fill space with content and
meaning by living in it on a daily basis, which makes it central to and
even the origin of the construction of an identity. The inhabitants of the
slums identify themselves as a group, belonging to a specific area, and
Candel sketches both – group and area – in his writing, fashioning both
the place and its inhabitants into a collective, rooted in a concrete place
that is part of the city. If, as Edward Relph explains, "ser humano es vi-
vir en un mundo lleno de lugares con significados: ser humano es tener
y conocer tu lugar" (1) [to be human is to live in a world full of places

with meanings: to be human is to have and know your place] and if "la gente es sus lugares y un lugar su gente" (34) [people are places, and a place, its people], then giving a form to that space, making it public and humanizing it, implies removing it from the realm of abstraction and stigmatization and revealing it through the daily life of its human users. The slums, as described to us by Candel, are an underground world propped up by the material structure that the city offers them – like the shanties "assentades damunt un mur de contenció de la RENFE" [resting on top of a RENFE retaining wall] – but they also prop up the physical, social, and economic structure of the city: "Nosaltres opinem que és denigrant que els barris més rics de la ciutat – puix que són els que allotgen la seva potent i poderosa indústria – siguin alhora els més pobres i miserables" (Els altres 222) [we are of the opinion that it is denigrating that the wealthiest neighbourhoods in the city – since they are the ones that house its potent and powerful industry – are the poorest and most miserable"], existing at the margin, ignored and invisible.

Candel strolls all over town and uses the experiences he has and the people he meets to create a representative public space in his writing; that is, he defines the social memory of this place, reconfigures its imaginary, revolts against its apparently homogeneous visual order, and uncovers its difference, singularity, and social and economic stratification for all to see. By applying the definition of public space claimed by Hannah Arendt in The Human Condition, we can see how Candel shows us a space defined by different participants through action and discourse; his writing opens a space of appearance "in the widest sense of the word, namely, the space where I appear to others as others appear to me, where men exist not merely like other living or inanimate things but make their appearance explicitly" (Arendt 198). Public space for Arendt is not the public space of the polis, in which, as Manuel Delgado explains (Elogi 130–3), both space and its user are subject to the demands of a political order. In Candel's case, yes, there are parameters for identity, but they are not linked to the monitoring and control imposed through the rhetorical and practical strategies of the dictatorship; rather, they exist in the "cruce de caminos e intersecciones con las que cada microgrupo y cada individuo levantan su propio mapa de la ciudad, que puede coincidir con los otros planos en sus puntos de referencia, pero no en su organización" (Delgado, Elogi 133) [crossroads and intersections where every micro group and every individual founds their own map of the city, which may coincide with other blueprints in their points of reference, but not in their organization]. His writing becomes public sphere, which becomes that space of appearance where – as we can also see in Benedict Anderson's idea of nation – "the presence of other who sees what we see and hears what we hear assures us of the reality of the world and ourselves" (Arendt 50), and, on the one hand, grants visibility and leaves traces of its existence, and on the other points out the active participation of diverse agents that create a territory and stand up for a plurality of interrelated communities.

In point of fact, this connection between writing, space, and identity is essential to understand both the protagonism of the margin and the relevance of these elements in the construction of a community. Lefebvre, Anderson, and Arendt stress the importance and protagonism of writing (or, more generally, art) in the production of social space. When Lefebvre speaks about "representational spaces," he acknowledges the importance of the everyday in the practice and production of space, but he also foregrounds artistic elements in order to stress the charge of possible meanings. Both Arendt and Anderson acknowledge the relevance, if not the exceptionalism, of telling stories in the depersonalization of private life that dwells in a "shadowy kind of existence" until "they are transformed, deprivatized and deindividualized, as it were, into a shape to fit them for public appearence," assuring us of "a reality of the world and ourselves" (Arendt 50). Clash and creation are the elements that shape a collectivity and produce a trialectics of spatial experience that invents, changes, and moulds identities. Candel allows the residents of these neighbourhoods to see themselves reflected through his chronicles, and as a result they identify with each other and then form an awareness of their collectivity,[31] which can be used as a basis to unite forces and, in the future, demand social and urbanistic improvements to their neighbourhoods, creating a civil society where they can cement their identities. These civil foundations are rooted in idiosyncrasy, spatial homogeneity, and residents' diverse origins, which Joan Costa and Adela Ros claim helps to create one's own identity and a particular dynamic based on residents' esteem for their neighbourhoods. Consequently, there is a direct connection between these new spaces and the configuration of their inhabitants, with an emphasis on the local element at play in the creation of a new cultural reality and the feeling of belonging to both neighbourhood and city.[32] Candel is not looking for a space for consensus; instead, he is pointing out and characterizing – following Arendt – a space for the construction and perseverance of the commons that does not suppress the heterogeneity of its constitutive components, participants, and agents, in fact doing quite the opposite: "Being seen and being heard by others derive their significance from the fact that everybody sees and hears from a different position" (Arendt 57), which implies a heterotopic relationship with the other. And this space for seeing and hearing opens the door to a democratic space that is just like the one defined by Lefebvre (*Le retour* 173), and which we have already seen in Amin and Thrift, a citizen-oriented democracy whose objective is to create a different social life, a direct democracy based not on action, but on the space and time being lived and experienced in that moment. Candel therefore focuses on everyday life and how it is manifested in and through the presence of multiple bodies, in the process establishing the parameters for a new city, which conform to Lefebvre's description of a city that

> complemented by the right to difference and the right to information, should modify, concretize and make more practical the rights to the citizen as an urban dweller and user of multiple services. It would affirm, on the one hand, the right of users to make known their ideas on the space and time of their activities in the urban area; it would also cover the right to the use of the center, a privileged space, instead of being dispersed and stuck into ghettos (for workers, immigrants, the "marginal" and even for the "privileged"). (*Writings* 34)

In this regard, Candel makes his reader think critically about the myths and rhetoric of the urbanism of this time, acknowledging the tensions between unity and difference as an integral part of the dialectic movement that underpins the city and understanding it, as we see in Lefebvre, as a total concept that must be reconstructed without suppressing or discriminating against any of its parts. These tensions, which lie at the heart of the search for a more fair and egalitarian urban structure, are what enables us to characterize Candel's narrative as democratic, since it allows for the expression of a popular identity in an era when political repression forbade just that sort of thing. To that end, Candel finds tools inside, not outside, that structure, and also in the articulation of the many voices that comprise the city's space, including the voices from the suburbs.[33] In this sense, years later, Vázquez Montalbán will say of the neighbourhood associations that "[l]a mirada del veïnat articulat vigila qualsevol intent especulatiu i el desarmament polític i legal es canvia per un democratisme de base que fiscalitza cada gest del poder sobre la ciutat" (*Barcelones* 299) [the view of the articulated neighbourhood polices any attempt at speculation, and the dismantling of political and legal rights is exchanged for a grassroots democracy that oversees every exercise of power over the city]. In Candel's work, we have the initiation of this field of vision and its articulation, in the author's own words and voice, of a new form of democracy that demands new materials: "no a la pedra, el vidre, la fusta, sinó sobretot als materials invisibles, aquells que no són substàncies sinó relacions, nusos, connexions, però també sobtades fragmentacions, vertígens" (Delgado, *Elogi* 163) [not stone, glass, or wood, but especially not the invisible materials, those which aren't substances but rather relationships, knots, connections but also sudden fragmentations, vertigos]. These fragmentations and vertigos point out an epistemological turn not just in how we understand urbanism, but also how this new approach to the material environment creates dissent, how it breaches urban and political modes of perception.

It is true that Candel makes a call for integration,[34] but not integration based on the ideal of universal equality; he wants integration predicated upon difference and the material space of the city, which is no longer an abstract entity but a collective creation in which citizens are those who should directly intervene in the governance of its form. His is an idea of citizenship that seeks acknowledgment of its diverse ways of living and appropriating urban space, unleashing new notions of belonging and solidarity. In this regard, Candel creates an unprecedented claim on the city and expands citizenship to a social base that the dictatorship was trying to break. And he does so by shaping and mobilizing a new source of citizenship that originates in a form of self-rule that is based on urban space and questions the official structure of the regime. That is to say, Candel conjures a social and political space that is based on the material space of the city and talks about the suburbs but also the whole city, challenging the idea of urban centrality, breaking free from the mythologies of official discourses, and revealing the corrupt practices of Francoism. Here is where we find his dissent, which sets in motion a cultural mobilization that will begin to undermine the foundations of the dictatorship.

Chapter Three

The Quiet Revolution of Photography: The Barcelona of Joan Colom

Although changes in the urban environment are an important factor in the development and evolution of photography that takes place in the 1950s and 1960s, Candel's work is what really charges this landscape with a new meaning rooted in urban mobilization, capturing a city that until that time did not exist. He put the suburbs on the map of history, but more importantly, he made them a part of Barcelona, which announced a radical change in how the city was perceived, and created an opening for a new social, political, and cultural field that put the "sistema en escac mat" (Vázquez Montalbán qtd. in Sinca 388) [system in checkmate] and unsettled municipal plans both urbanistically and politically. He criticized the urban disorder found not in the slums per se, but in the problems and solutions originating from and applied by the regime's governmental structure, the housing complexes, "vertaders monuments al mal gust, la barra i el menyspreu social a les classes populars" (Vázquez Montalbán, *Barcelones* 250) [true monuments to bad taste, the abuse and social scorn of popular classes]; in the process, he opened a previously unimaginable front to criticize Francoism. Candel's urbanistic voice is distinct from the many voices that professed the critical rationalism of the Grupo R [R Group] – which in spite of trying to drum up critical awareness and in spite of some of its members, notably Bohigas, being drawn to the role of social pressure in the reconstruction of the city (Vázquez Montalbán 254), nevertheless held a perspective far removed from daily life in the suburbs – and also from the speculative projects that were typical of the "estética oficial de mal gusto" (257) [official aesthetic of bad taste] carried out by Porcioles' city hall. In comparison, Candel was the only one who stood up as a representative and spokesperson for those who had been cast out of the city and were living in its shadows; he was the only one who dared to make noise about noise, the urban discord occasioned by/ from the suburbs, instead choosing to acknowledge and embrace it, not to hide or suppress it with the regime's crushing force or the idea of the suburbs as a mere discursive articulation. In the social and political domain, his stance and practice announce the creation of a public space for expression and presence that was non-existent at that time and suggests the development of a grassroots democratic system that prefigures and establishes a direct connection with the work that will later be undertaken by neighbourhood associations and the social movements of the 1970s.

Insofar as urbanism and architecture are concerned, this grassroots movement lays the foundation for intellectual activity devoted to a more social critique of the city, seen in figures such as Oriol Bohigas, Salvador Tarragó, or Jordi Borja (Moreno and Vázquez Montalbán 50).[1] In the cultural domain, Candel initiates a new form of critical urban journalism and gains disciples such as Josep M. Huertas Clavería, who will closely follow Candel's work not just in his critical articles, but also in the construction of the history of suburban neighbourhoods and the development of democracy through neighbourhood associations.[2] Moreover, Candel ushers in a new type of novelistic production that wades, metaphorically speaking, into the margins in order to criticize the capitalist geography of a Barcelona created for consumption. Juan Goytisolo, Juan Marsé, and Jaime Gil de Biedma are the most notable examples of this critique; however, the action in their novels and the Barcelona they capture are imbued with the staticity and rigidity imposed by the regime;[3] they do challenge and criticize, but theirs is a conquered Barcelona, one which accepts its suffering without the cries and pleas that we hear in Candel's writing, which was heavily censored.[4] Candel's influence is also exerted on photography, but not just thematically, opening the doors to a space that enables the young photographers of the Nova Avantguarda to expand upon their rebellion against form, but providing a way of being in the city, to immerse themselves in it. With Candel, as we will see with the photographer Joan Colom, we do not look from afar, through a window, like Juan Goytisolo's characters, whose use of different types of telescopes reminds us of the camera lens of, for example, Josep Brangulí or Gabriel Casas; nor is our experience like the stroll taken by the poetic voice in Gil de Biedma's "Barcelona ja no és bona," who hears the voices of immigrants from afar without seeing them, always keeping the other outside, in spite of his promises that they will one day triumph. The other in Candel and Colom is among us, it is us. Like the photograph that Xavier Miserachs took of Candel visiting the Sagrera slums in 1965, which appeared on the cover of *Serra d'Or* in May of that same year, [5] or like the doctor's visit to the Montjuïc slums in *Donde,* marginality makes Candel and, as we will see through his photography, Colom, an interstice, a bridge between different worlds.

As we can see in this photograph (figure 3.1), it feels as if Candel "drags" the camera lens, our eyes, to new places, offering new possibilities for understanding the city in terms of its movement, change, and difference. He makes us look in another direction. His body, his voice, becomes the point of entrance to a new space, expanding our viewing field. We experience, once again, a total immersion in that space, showing the urban decentring of the city through the discovery of a new pole of reference. From this new perspective, the city, the place of the city, is a complete illusion: absolute space claims the city as a utopia, but that is a reality that does not exist anywhere. Regardless, the search for and imposition of the terms of this illusion – transparency, light, circulation – are carried out through official discourses and urbanistic practices. Consequently, Candel is relevant not only because of his choice of subject matter, but for the way in which he approaches it. It is not a condemnation, a term that in this context inserts him in the regime's narrative (the prudish discourse of the bourgeoisie that denies and hides the presence of difference, like immigrants and prostitutes), or it is not only that, given that we cannot eliminate all of the possible readings that photography capacitates;[6] rather, it is a way to understand the city that diverges from the regime's parameters, instead shaping users into citizens. And Colom, knowingly or not, follows in Candel's footsteps.

Joan Colom teaches how to cross over to the other side, how to break with exoticism and find everyday lived experiences that are considered out of place. In that regard, Colom's approach to urban and urbanistic space is similar to his experience with photography. An accountant by trade, for him photography is a way to engage with day-to-day life in his free time, and the language that he uses is as clear and direct as the reality that envelops his existence. He took up photography quite late, at thirty-six years old, inspired to participate in different contests. In 1959, his work landed in the hands of the Agrupación Fotográfica Almeriense (AFAL) [Almerian Photographic Association], who included him in an exhibit of Spanish photography organized by the Spanish embassy in Paris, and in whose magazine he was published for the first time in 1960. Inspired as a photographer, the following year he had an exhibit in the Sala Aixelà in the Raval entitled "El carrer" [The street], a project that he started in 1958. Although he never abandoned the Agrupació Fotogràfica de Catalunya (AFC) [Photographic Association of Catalonia], which could be read as a kind of moderation when compared to the rebelliousness,[7] as we will see, of certain of his contemporaries, including prominent figures such as Oriol Maspons,[8] his work was always socially committed and granted no concessions in that regard. His photographic career met a precipitous end in 1964,

Figure 3.1 Xavier Miserachs, "Les barraques de la Riera Comtal" [The Riera Comtal shantytown] (Barcelona, 1965).
© Herederas de Xavier Miserachs. Photograph of Francisco Candel in the shantytown of the Riera Comtal. Published in *Serra d'Or*, May 1965.

in the wake of the scandal caused by the publication of *Izas, rabizas y colipoterras*, his collaboration with Camilo José Cela in the collection "Palabra e Imagen" [Word and Image].[9] From this moment on, his work was intermittent, and he did not resume his activity fully until 1990.[10]

In his work in the period under consideration in this chapter, as we will see in his performance of the Raval,[11] Colom uses the space of the city as it is meant to be used and from many different perspectives: as a man, as a voyeur, as an inhabitant of the neighbourhood – different ways to be in the same place.[12] He, as a margin, conveys the uses of the city, full of the contradictions that shape it. It is true that in this case dissent will not take the form of direct protest like Candel winds up formulating; nevertheless, we see a use of the city's urbanistic qualities and a conception of the urban experience that reveal an understanding of photography and city that transcends the regime's strict parameters. Colom gives us new coordinates from which to contemplate those parameters and propose new possibilities, breaking free from the imminence of Francoism's absolute space that attempts to control the social movement of the city's inhabitants. That is, following Pierre Bourdieu in his introduction to *Photography: A Middle-Brow Art*, here the practice of photography plays with ethos and those supposedly objective and common internalized regularities to which photography and city are subject; this play is predicated upon a breakdown of what simultaneously is and is not photographable, and of what is and is not socially acceptable. If, as John Tagg claims when speaking about portraits, their purpose is as much the description of an individual as their inscription in a social identity, then we could say the same thing about capturing urban space, the portrait of a city, whose purpose is as much to describe space as it is to insert the city in a determined social space. Just as happens with the urbanistic plans of the time, photography catalogues and defines the city, and it is in the movement of the Nova Avantguarda and Colom where we see a break with the Francoist cartography of Barcelona, although Colom takes matters a step further than his peers. If photographs are fragments that crop and frame the city and, by their fragmentary nature, acknowledge a border, a frame, as Susan Sontag tells us, then they give rise to questions about the consequences of the imposition of such a boundary on vision and the understanding of a landscape, since they restrict the visual field, a space that separates and emphasizes the meaning of whatever it frames (22–3). Photographs thus simultaneously bestow a new notion of information, establish relationships and new meanings, and question the official discourses that give shape to the city. In this regard, Colom creates dissent by playing with these two spaces, the photographic description of portraits and the configuration of urban space, revealing and challenging the canons de rigueur at this time through the establishment of new relationships in the city's place.

We would be remiss to suggest that the changes experienced in photography were exclusively due to Candel's influence, even if his influence was essential in a society that was progressively more visually oriented, especially in a moment in which the urban turn had come to determine the discourse and practices of Francoism. The union of photography and urban environment was already set up in the international practice of humanist photography which, following the Second World War, was based on constructing the image of a popular subject formalized in "la gente corriente" [everyday people] or "el hombre de la calle" [the man in the street], making the city the perfect environment for this new modernity to play out (Ribalta, *Paradigmas* 30–1). However, the connection of this type of photography to the transformation of urban landscape and the appearance of housing for the lower classes at the outskirts of the city makes Candel an inevitable inflection point since, despite being in the presence of a widespread phenomenon, he does bring to bear on artistic practice a specificity that did not previously exist.

In the move from Candel's literature to photography, we can see how dissent is not always expressed in the same way and does not depend on the written word, as we can deduce from studies on social and political change in the 1950s and 1960s.[13] Rather, in a context such as the urban turn, dissent metamorphizes together with practices that maintain some urban and urbanistic connection as they branch out through the substrate of the city's physical space and seek out the popular voice that democratizes expression. Urbanism is one of those forms of expression; photography, by way of its connection to urbanism, is another.

In the same way that urbanism was perceived, before Candel, as a tool without an ideological bent, as pure distribution of the urban environs, photography under the dictatorship was similarly limited: it was reined in by parameters that, while perhaps not neutral, were monumentalizing. Thus, photography was relieved of any relevant social discourse through photographic associations and *salonismo*, inheritors of nineteenth-century landscape painting in decline everywhere except Francoist Spain where it was held in great esteem.[14] In the aftermath of the Civil War, there was a dramatic about-face in the innovative production seen in the 1930s through photographers such as Pere Català i Pic, Josep Renau, and José Suárez. During the war, the work of photojournalists like Agustí Centelles was inspired by photographers of great international stature, such as Robert Capa and David Seymour (also known as "Chim"). After the war, however, the dictatorship took steps to impose strict limits on fields considered artistic, as Carlos Cánovas explains: "Front al 'morbo característic de la cultura humanista europea i liberal,' Giménez Caballero hi oposava 'un art universal, integrador, fecund, ecumènic i catolitzant'" (10) [Against the "characteristic titillation of liberal European humanist culture," Giménez Caballero opposed "a universal, integrating, fertile, ecumenical, and Catholicizing art"]. In this context, Cánovas goes on to explain, photography is a curious case. Because it was not considered art, it was enough to ignore it or allow it to operate within the confines of self-censorship: "clausurades les puntes de llança avantguardistes, desapareguts els seus mentors, es tractava simplement de no estimular, de cap manera, cap actitud innovadora i, menys encara, crítica" (10–11) [the avant-garde spearheads shut down, their mentors gone, it was simply a matter of not encouraging, in any way, any innovative and, even less, critical attitude], a state of affairs reinforced by a dearth of photographic supplies due to the ban on the importation of foreign materials.

Of course, we are not claiming that censorship somehow did not apply to photography, given that it operated like any other form of publication,[15] but because openings for expression became limited to what Fontcuberta called "agrupaciones apolíticas" [apolitical associations], groups that at no point questioned the legitimacy of the new regime and which esthetically implied a style characterized by an academicism that sought the creation of images with "patrones compositivos muy elementales y rudimentarios, de origen netamente pictórico" ("Barcelona" 78) [very elementary and rudimentary compositional patterns, of a clearly pictorial origin], the practice of photography was limited by its own form and channels for expression, which, due to the censorship of foreign influences, did not allow it to discern other possible paths. The break with this "hegemonía de salonismo y fotoperiodismo oficial" (78) [hegemony of *salonismo* and official photojournalism] came around the middle of the 1950s, with the emergence of what Josep María Casademont calls the "Nova Avantguarda" of photographers like Francesc Català Roca and others who appeared a few years later around the AFC, from which they broke off in search of new aesthetic criteria opposed to classicism, clustering around Casademont and the Sala Aixelà [Aixelà Salon] and giving birth to the Barcelona group: Xavier Miserachs, Ricard Terré, Ramon Masats, Oriol Maspons, Joan Colom, Leopoldo Pomés, Julio Ubiña, and Paco Ontañón.[16]

On the provincial level, several groups stand out as centres for disruption, including AFAL, among whose members we find some of those from the Barcelona group like Miserachs, Maspons, Terré, and Colom, and in Madrid, the group La Palangana. There was a tight connection between these groups, and, in spite of the geographical distance between them, they shared ideas and work. The principles behind their disruption were indirectly put forth in an article by Oriol Maspons entitled "Salonismo" and published in *Arte Fotográfico* in 1957.[17] This was the first open critique of its time to harshly attack traditional photography, revealing a new stance and links to contemporary European and American photography, although some of Maspons's ideas had been individually expressed by photographers such as Gabriel Cualladó and Paco Gómez. The opposition to traditional photography characterized this new photography by a discourse of renewal that declared itself to be incompatible with art, recovering the discursive tendency of the 1930s, according to which – Casademont explains – "es [deixa] de banda la pura creació plàstica per tal d'endinsar-se en una fotografia aplicada" (qtd. in Ribalta and Balsells, *El carrer* 15) [it leaves aside pure plastic creation in order to immerse itself in applied photography].[18] And this application came hand in hand with the urban epistemological change enacted by the intersection of new expressive parameters that, once again, were a response to the emphasis on cities. That is to say, the urban turn offers, especially in Barcelona, an emerging field of action in the new discursive practices and tendencies of the dictatorship that expands the expressive possibilities of photography.

Off the Map: Rupturing the Visual Rule

The reconfiguration of the urban constructions of the Nova Avantguarda's photography was preceded by a shift in the orientation of American and European photography.[19] Otto Steinert in Germany with *Subjektive Fotografie* (1951), Henri Cartier-Bresson in France with *The Decisive Moment* (1952), and Edward Steichen in the United States with the organization of the exhibit *The Family of Man* in the MoMA (1955) propose a new way of approaching photography through the movement of bodies in space.[20] Although each of these photographers or projects had their own personal style, they all coincide in their attempt to capture the intrahistorical moments of daily life. They distance themselves from artificiality in favour of spontaneity, taking snapshots in which bodies, both the photographer's and the subject's, challenge the limits of traditional framing and what is considered to be photographic objectivity, and they use fragmentation, arbitrary framing, and immediacy to flesh out an abstract relational space of perspective. The exchange between the general – physical and social spaces – and the particular – the body – enable the visualization of the dialectic exchange between the abstract concepts that shape spaces and the concrete analysis of daily life. "Subjective photography," wrote Steinert in his founding manifesto in 1951, "means humanised, individualised photography and implies the handling of a camera in order to win from the single object the views expressive of its character" (qtd. in Schmalriede 22), the principle by which he sought to distance himself from the increase of commercial, documentary, and journalistic photography occurring at that time. This type of photography concerned itself with visual criteria that authorized autobiographical elements to mix with formalism and pseudo-lyricism (Chevrier 120), or put another way, the recognition of the impact on any narration by the subject that writes it. As a result, the construction of the historical project is no longer in the hands of a privileged minority that claims to represent the majority; rather, it is in the hands of a plural subject whose presence brings with it a change in categories and language, giving way to the new avant-garde that Casademont will later describe. The photographer's creative endeavour will highlight this change in perspective – choice of camera and perspective, developing techniques – which reveals the possibility of creating new meanings, but also draws attention to exactly how those meanings are created.

William Klein (*New York*, 1956) and Robert Frank (*The Americans*, 1958) take these tendencies a step further by questioning their predecessors. Although like those who came before them they continue to echo the centrality of the photographer, who is the person that decides what is relevant and, therefore, indicative of the process of selection at work in the construction of any narration, in their photographs they attempt to capture life in its most trivial or insignificant manifestations, taking Cartier-Bresson's "decisive instant" a step beyond and capturing what Nicholas Dawidoff described in Robert Frank's work as "the emotional rhythms ... [that] portray underlying realities and misgivings" (Dawidoff). These rhythms make the body central to his photographs, and its movement comes to inform the shape of both urbanistic place and social space. Furthermore, keeping in mind this idea of rupture, the associations of photographers grouped under the label of the Nova Avantguarda accentuate not just their break from the preceding photographic movement, *salonismo*, but also their relationship to avant-garde movements of the 1920s and 1930s and the subsequent development of a critique that goes hand in hand with a direct connection to a history related to a cultural moment that precedes the dictatorship, which disrupts, once again, the linearity and narrativity of absolute space or the organicity of the discourse and practice of the regime through fragmentation of, first, the movements of the body and, then, the paradigmatic connections that disrupt the regime's temporally linear and supposedly fixed and unique structure.[21] This context elucidates the posture of dissent that we saw in the photographers that have been

mentioned already, in whose work formal and thematic innovation becomes manifest in the action of bodies that conjugate space and time in
the search for moments that – taking Cartier-Bresson's concept a step
further – lead to the development of what Lefebvre will call "a theory
of moments" that stress the formal, thematic, or social innovation that
occurs in those meaningful instants in which existing orthodoxies are
challenged, when the state of things has the potential to be annulled or
radically altered (qtd. in Elden x). This moment sets up a challenge to
pre-existing rhythms and enables dialectic confrontation between abstract or absolute space and relative space.

In spite of the importance that the photographers of the Nova Avantguarda had in the creation of a new visual language, spaces for the circulation of images, expansion of the social role of photographers, and
above all the formation of a future generation that will play an essential
role in the Transition,[22] these photographers were outside of the main-
stream. Their work will circulate in the form of books, exhibits, and
graphic journalism, but, in the words of Laura Terré, they will have "una
existencia discreta en los límites de su trabajo de encargo, y pocas veces
alcanzan un reconocimiento cultural más amplio en exposiciones o pub-
licaciones ajenas a los medios de prensa" (qtd. in Antich 3) [a discreet
existence at the fringes of their commissioned work, and rarely do they
achieve wider cultural recognition in exhibits or publications beyond
the press]. We could go so far as to say that, in many cases, the work of
these photographers has been acknowledged after the fact, beginning
in the 1980s, when on the one hand urban consciousness reclaims the
experience of the suburbs and slums, and on the other, we find a re-
newed interest in the photography of that earlier time.[23] Nevertheless,
these photographers, in their marginality and silence, initiated a line of
dissent that generated its challenge to the status quo through the constitution of a popular urban environment that reconfigured what was
considered part of the city. As was the case with urbanism, the diminish-
ment suffered by "official photography," the concept used by members
of AFAL to refer to photography that upheld the values imposed by the
regime through *salonismo* and contests, gave photography at large what
we could call a path towards freedom of expression, which would allow
for the development, albeit limited, of a practice of dissent in the 1950s,[24]
when the prominence of graphic journalism propelled photojournalism to its peak and introduced European and American influences into
Spain. As a result, certain books of photography were widely distributed
and had an outsized impact on the urban imaginary, "convirtiéndose
en la imagen popular dominante de Barcelona, al menos hasta práctica-
mente el periodo olímpico" (Ribalta, "La dictadura" 110) [becoming the

dominant popular image of Barcelona, at least until the Olympic period practically], creating an open channel for communication not limited to an elite audience.[25] The city as protagonist, changes in architecture, and the opening of the regime to the outside world bringing an influx of tourism and consumer culture, all encourage the creation of a new photographic language that, like we saw with Candel, gives rise to a popular and humanist urbanism in which a counter public sphere emerges where identities opposed to the regime can be developed. There, in this intersection, we find the freedom of expression that facilitates work like Joan Colom's. That said, the kind of dissent we find in the photographers of the Nova Avantguarda varies according to the work that each of them does and, in some cases, winds up blurring into a type of Costumbrism that, instead of generating resistance, becomes entangled with the practices and discourses of the regime.

The urban turn that we see in the discourse and practice of the dictatorship opens a new expressive front in photography in which we find a working-class approach to the city and the privileging of a space in use. In its handling of this subject matter, the work of the photographers of the Nova Avantguarda gives society "a certain sense of unease" (López Mondéjar, *Historia* 78) since it breaks free from the apologetic and indulgent spirit of the discourse of official photography. The local, that which exists on the street level, takes on a prominent role and shapes a new urban collectivity, in spite of the identity imposed by absolute space. Whereas according to absolute space what defines identity is monumentalism, symbolic appropriation, and the conquest of space through the imposition of physical codes that tightly control spaces of representation, the photographers of the Nova Avantguarda, as we see in this image by Ramón Masats (figure 3.2),[26] proudly proclaim vague terrain, purposefully cultivating a lack of definition and the ambiguity that enshrouds the indeterminate nature of uses registered by/in the streets. But in this example, Masats is not just trying to capture the essence of what it means to be urban, "la pura dispersión" [pure dispersion], "la máquina subsocial" [subsocial machinery], the almost impossible to control "conglomerado orgánico de instituciones momentáneas" [organic conglomerate of momentary institutions], as Manuel Delgado describes (*Memoria* 9); he wants to configure the city through a fragmentary materiality that defies the politicized urbanization of the state. He draws attention to the false coherence of place through a fragmented composition of the city, as Miserachs will also (figure 3.3).

Periphery appears as part of this city in chaos where urbanism defines places through the uses made of space.[27] Above all, what is emphasized are contrasts, the large infrastructures of the modern city set against the backdrop of the new housing complexes. *Barcelona: Blanc i negre* (1964) by

Figure 3.2 Ramón Masats, "Sense títol" [Untitled] (Barcelona, 1954).
© 2020 Artists Rights Society (ARS), New York / VEGAP, Madrid.

Xavier Miserachs is a prime example: fragmentation, contrast, and contradiction are the defining urban and urbanistic characteristics of Barcelona.
Miserachs constructs a cartography that, similar to the Situationist psycho-
geography, breaks away from absolute space's imposition of order. His
book is noise, movement, and excess, whose action strips away the dictatorship's homogenizing order. If, as Amos Rapaport explains, what urban planners seek is to "calm" urban disorder and reduce difference to
structuring images that embody values and simplify our view of the world

Figure 3.3 Xavier Miserachs, "Sense títol" [Untitled] (Barcelona, 1962).
© Herederas de Xavier Miserachs.

(qtd. in Delgado, *Memoria* 11), then Miserachs's photographic narration, through its use of collage, denounces the functionalist excesses of Francoist urbanism by eliminating the tranquility and silence of the straight line. At times this movement reaches us through photographic montage, directly through collage, as if multiple photographs were in the same shot, trying to capture the frenetic movement of day-to-day urban life, echoing the narrative style of William Klein in his book *New York*: "imágenes aparentemente mal hechas, llenas de grano, de contrastes pronunciados y con encuadres simuladamente erróneos" (Formiguera, "La segunda" 164) [obviously poorly constructed images, grainy, with pronounced contrasts and simulated erroneous framing].[28] At other times, the sensation of collage is offered directly by the environment itself, as in these photographs (figures 3.4 and 3.5), where the city itself imparts chaos without any kind of filter.

Here not only does Miserachs capture the transformation of the city, one of the major themes of his photography, but he also captures the roughness of space, offering a new perspective on the monumentalization of the city. Accordingly, his is a multiple discourse, in which architectural vestiges play a role in the evolution of the social realm, which could be interpreted as a political gesture in which the morphological and moral profile of the city is laid bare. That is to say, Miserachs keeps the references to the city's monuments that predated the dictatorship and

Figure 3.4 Xavier Miserachs, "Sense títol" [Untitled] (Barcelona, 1962).
© Herederas de Xavier Miserachs.

formulates a traditional identity that expands with time, uniting past and present, creating a new genealogy, a new narrative of the city's identity.

The construction of this multiple Barcelona has important precedents in the work of Francesc Català Roca,[29] Eugeni Forcano, and Leopoldo Pomés,[30] although they construe a more harmonious Barcelona, without Miserachs's noise and disorder. Català Roca was the first to show "el cambio, la arquitectura moderna en la ciudad, las periferias, la espalda de la ciudad, el terrain vague" (Ribalta, *Paradigmas* 34) [change, the modern architecture of the city, the peripheries, the city's backside, vague terrain], and already he portrays the reconstruction of a Barcelona of tales "unitari[as] por la intención y unitari[as] por el tiempo" (Mendoza and Pomés 23) [united in intention and time], which stresses the will to construct and, therefore, the will to break with existing discourses. Here we see the displacement of vision that we saw in Candel once again applied to the cartography of the city.

However, unlike Candel, these photographers kept their distance from the spaces they photographed, staying away from the lived realities of their inhabitants, which, as Ribalta tells us, promotes "esa representación del sujeto popular victimizado propia de los códigos de la fotografía humanista" (*Paradigmas* 35) [the representation of victimized popular subjects

Figure 3.5 Xavier Miserachs, "Barraques de Can Tunis" [Can Tunis
shantytown] (Montjuïc, Barcelona, 1962).
© Herederas de Xavier Miserachs.

typical of the codes of humanist photography]. Consequently, the dissent that we find in these examples lies in their divergence from official maps. In the metaphor of cartography, if the line of place produces a space, if walls and streets map out the boundaries between socially restricted zones and territories through a regime of visibility, then space and its social use also modify that line; that is, these images deconstruct and alter the limits of what is considered city and the content of absolute space, showing how urban space is not neutral and convincing us of the productive effects of opposition. However, we should approach this idea of dissent, and therefore possible opposition, carefully. In the case of these photographers, this dissent is plunged into a silence that muffles it and waters it down to a matter of perspective. In other words, the difference that is kept away from the space of the city by the dictatorship and urbanistic practices and reincorporated by these projects that make it visible is subjected to a question of morality and order that, instead of challenging the regime's structure, seems to uphold it in the guise of a type of Costumbrism based on capturing the everyday qualities of modern urban life, seeking to portray an identity that at that time comes from living in the city.

This attitude is a response to the climate of the day; that is to say, we are in the presence of a moment of rebellion against "la mediocridad, la sordidez y el hastío de un aparato de poder que no dejaba oportunidades de crecimiento personal ni moral" [the mediocrity, sordidness, and boredom of an apparatus of power that allowed no opportunities for personal or moral growth] among new generations, but which respected the political and social structure of Francoism (Gracia García and Ruiz Carnicer 209), in part responding to the self-censorship about which Casademont speaks. This situation is what leads both Fontcuberta ("De la posguerra") and Ribalta ("AFAL") to claim that we could polemicize the critical dimension of the photography produced by the members of the Nova Avantguarda, who in spite of their opposition to the idealized and monumentalist photography of that time and their connections to Italian neorealism (Fontcuberta, "De la posguerra" 417) did not oppose the discursive parameters imposed by the regime.[31] Although certain historiographical interpretations, such as Laura Terré's in her history of the AFAL group, claim that these young people "se ensañaron [contra la dictadura] desempolvando las tristes estampas de la España negra como una forma de contradecir la fachada del progreso y desarrollo que el régimen pretendía transmitir" (Fontcuberta, "De la posguerra" 417) [took their revenge against the regime dusting off the sad pictures of Spain's Black Legend as a way of contradicting the facade of progress and development that the regime intended to transmit], in reality, Fontcuberta explains, there could be no "verdadera denuncia" [true denunciation] for several reasons: because the censor's office would have nipped it in the bud; because there was no true critical impulse behind it; and because the diffusion of the media made it difficult to reach a widespread audience, because of which the regime showed a degree of tolerance ("De la posguerra" 417). Fontcuberta concludes by saying that, without a doubt we see a change in style, but as far as critical content is concerned, that could just be a matter of readings made after the fact ("De la posguerra" 418).

Insofar as the urban/Costumbrist characterization of their photography is concerned, Ribalta and Fontcuberta hit the nail on the head. The work produced by the photographers of this time related to the Nova Avantguarda, including Maspons, Miserachs, Marroyo, and even Leopoldo Pomés and Eugeni Forcano, to mention a representative and varied selection, is characterized to a degree by photographic Costumbrism that seems to distance itself from any and all criticism. Their monographs amount to a collection of picture cards that appear to characterize and define an era that, however harsh it was to live through, and in spite of the inclusion of the suburbs in a new cartographic configuration of the city, does not necessarily construct a consistent critique of the regime.

If we focus on the question of space, then the city presented to us by, for example, a photographer such as Francesc Català Roca, whose work inaugurates the era of the Nova Avantguarda, without a doubt captures "the urban"; that is, in projects like *Barcelona* (1954), through images that function independently from the text that accompanies them – emphasizing the border or limit that Sontag was talking about – he elaborates a cartography of the city that captures daily movement, in all its harshness and contradictions, but marked by structure. Although his work implies a break with the idealized image of the city promulgated by works such as Carles Soldevila's *Guía de Barcelona* (1951), which "presentaba una imagen edulcorada y pintoresca de la ciudad, previa a los códigos de la fotografía humanista" (Ribalta, *Paradigmas* 34) [presented a candy-coated and picturesque image of the city, prior to the codes of humanist photography], the Barcelona constructed here is based on a new form of daily life that respects the spaces of the modern metropolis and continues to map them in a narrative that presents the city as an aesthetic object, which will become the new tenor of how Spanish cities are represented.[32] As in all cities, we find contrasts in their modernity, but Català Roca's Barcelona is unabashedly bourgeois, ruled by the directives of place, which look upon the urban with a degree of exoticism. It is a superficial way of visually consuming the city, which makes it Costumbrist. Català Roca always remains at the gates.

Although his photographs often include the margins and map out a city produced by everyday, working-class living, there is nothing in

Figure 3.6 Francesc Català Roca, "Boy from the neighborhood of huts of
Sants" (Barcelona, 1953).
© Photographic Archive F. Català-Roca. Arxiu Històric del Col·legi d'Arquitectes de
Catalunya.

them that challenges the moral, social, and political parameters of the
regime. His photographs of the slums are precisely what they should
be, a paternalistic and exotic representation of the margin. In the photo
of the suburbs (figure 3.7), Català Roca does not break free from the
structure of the city. While it is true that he introduces the margin into
the network of urban connections, and from there the reconstruction
of cartography that we previously mentioned, there is nevertheless no
break from the discursive format of the regime, and his body remains far
from those he captures through his lens. Everyone, users and photographer, follow the established path, and even the title of the photograph,

Figure 3.7 Francesc Català Roca, "Outskirts of Barcelona" (Barcelona, c. 1956).
© Photographic Archive F. Català-Roca. Arxiu Històric del Col·legi d'Arquitectes de
Catalunya.

"Outskirts of Barcelona," marks and signifies Francoist topography, that
is, the fragmentation of the city rather than a questioning of an order
that separates and hierarchically divides. Ricard Terré's series on proces-
sions and other religious celebrations is another example.[33]

The violence of Terré's images in the most quintessential documentary style clashes, for example, with the Spain construed by José Ortiz-
Echagüe, an image adopted by the regime, but, again, it does not cross
any lines. Yes, the movement of bodies is the defining feature of these
photographs; however, these bodies are governed by a rhythm marked by
place, and the books that fashioned the popular image of Barcelona back
then also remain bound by these parameters, even a book as supposedly

Figure 3.8 Ricard Terré, "Semana Santa" [Holy Week] (Barcelona, 1957).
© Ricard Terré.

revolutionary as *Izas, rabizas y colipoterras*, which, in its transgression of the space of the Raval, only wound up responding to the morality of that time. That said, we cannot agree with the after-the-fact imposition of meaning that Fontcuberta referenced: the emphasis on the photographer's subjectivity in the changing climate of the 1950s and the ever more obvious appearance of an opposition to the regime – especially in cities where, as Jordi Gracia García and Miguel Ángel Ruiz explain (210), apolitical sectors of the population become more and more politicized, and where figures like Candel begin to appear – reinforce the possibility of a defiant attitude in the work of these photographers, however subtle and regardless of the fact that these photographs are largely perceived to be apolitical.[34]

Figure 3.9 Ricard Terré, "Semana Santa" [Holy Week] (Barcelona, 1957).
© Ricard Terré.

It is untenable to hold that these photographers were oblivious to the social, physical, and political changes happening in cities like Barcelona, since we can see how they developed new urban maps that left behind the monumentalization of the city and broke loose from functionalist order through detours and wandering, crossing over/through different zones, rejecting and altering prescribed uses. These photographic projects initiated a dialogical exchange, albeit within the parameters of Francoism, in which their works engaged with the limitations on the visibility and representation of the visual public surface of the city in which they reinscribed the practice of culture. Through the creation of a city built on the foundation of daily life as the undeniable marker of the presence of human activity and difference, they acclaim those strokes of history and memory directly and materially imposed on urban space, eschewing illusory images that, in absolute space's monumental city, can only signify absence and be bereft of meaning. Therefore, although dissent becomes diluted in the lived realities of day-to-day experience, this change of perspective ushers in a new way understanding the social, cultural, and political environment and will allow Joan Colom's work to dismantle discourse and social practice. Through this same environment that will go on to shape the country's new identity, Colom will utilize urban and urbanistic elements to change the way he understands and practices photography, much like his generational peers, but he will craft a previously non-existent public space that will defy and crack the regime's parameters. His photographs are urban projections, visualizations that uncover all of the relevant urban points in the construction of the city from multiple angles. Their reach will extend beyond the limits set down by the dictatorship, even while occasionally acting within them.[35]

Photographic Reconstruction in Joan Colom's Urban Practice

Photography shows how experience ceases to be dependent upon a stable point of view constructed according to the dictates of a ruling elite, and space is seized through movement and the independent identity of bodies, unstable and mobile identities. The question is no longer what is "real" space, but rather what new forms of the "real" are called into being by the movement of bodies that use space. Those who perceive – whether as users, writers, or photographers – become a through line created and guided by their own movement and interactions with others in the circulation and exchange with passersby that happens in urban (but in this case, not urbanistic) space. In the process, the monocular model of both urban planners and the dictatorship's city, whether fascist or capitalist, collapses and is replaced by an observer-based model predicated upon greater modernization and the deterritorialization of vision and space.

With this change, we are in the presence of a mobile and available producer who evokes an equally mobile and interchangeable space, in terms of signs and images. The embodiment of the visual field and space in discursive and practical movement erodes the foundations of a supposedly given and fixed reality. This articulation of the body and movement, which takes us back to Lefebvre's question of rhythm, connects vision and space to time, fracturing the alleged atemporality – or extra-temporality – of urbanism's or the dictatorship's rationalized plan of the city.[36] Time marks the discursivity of space and bodies and shows them to be constructed and malleable. The conjugation of body, space, and time reveals to us the image as it is seen. Moreover, by showing what is visible but not revealed by place's order, the invisible rhythm just under the surface, the conjugation of body, space, and time also accentuates the transgression taking place. It gives a shape to space that is not considered by the coordinates of place. This conjugation also reveals a condition of superposition and simultaneous presence that, even if it were to be identified or could be identified with place's order – because as de Certeau explains, place is the centre that organizes the world and provides what we could call the "scenario" for space to come to be – it cannot be understood on structure's terms, since the margin does not try to order or regulate difference. The margin holds those interstices and boundaries open, and subverts the geometric form and the discourses and practices it would seek to impose.[37]

Colom is an example of this will and desire for opening. The paradoxes and contrasts that we will see in his work will reconfigure vision, which will lead us to reconfigure our senses, the movement of bodies and, therefore, space. He decentres vision, shifting it using the crosshairs established by the urban map. In doing so, Colom breaks and dismantles habitual practices, stripping them down to find a new perception of otherness, which he reveals and accepts. In order to shake free from the Cartesian gaze, the margin follows movement, bodily movement, and with it finds the possibility of generating intimate physical and visual experiences that directly affect the composition of material and social space. And once again, we see the myth of two cities shattered, this time by dispersing the origin of vision among multiple focal points, multiplying the gaze, and doing away with the oversimplification of a bipartite structure. In the margin, the body's capacity for vision is discovered, focusing on lived time and challenging abstract order. Of course, the body, whether urban or human, is charged with meanings imposed by those who look and becomes a visual representation of the construction of the power relations that are central to social space, but precisely because of that, the margin is relevant, because it challenges and breaks the visual norm.

In two photographs (figures 3.10 and 3.11), that will serve as an introduction to the photographer's construction of urbanity, Joan Colom

Figure 3.10 Joan Colom, "Passeig Marítim" [Boardwalk] (Barcelona, 1964).
Museu Nacional d'Art de Catalunya, donated by the artist, 2012.
© Joan Colom, VEGAP, Barcelona, 2020. Photographic reproduction: Museu Nacional
d'Art de Catalunya, Barcelona.

simultaneously captures the impression of both the imposition of a my-
opic linearity and visual logic by official reforms and the break with
this structure.

These images of the Somorrostro, the shantytown situated on the
beach, were taken as part of an assignment for *El Correo Catalán*, whose
article, "La liberación de Barcelona continúa: El Paseo Marítimo, una
gran obra urbanística con proyección social" [Freedom in Barcelona
continues: The boardwalk, a great urbanistic project with social im-
pact], showed the evolution of construction in this part of Barcelona.
However, these photographs go beyond the intention of the news article. These images reveal the imposition of the bourgeois reticle that
constructs a fictitious duality between them and us, those on the inside
and those outside, between movement and stasis, between the formal
and the informal city. The Paseo Marítimo splits the city in two, imposing an architectural and urbanistic discourse that also reproduces the
discourse of the dictatorial regime. And here we are not exclusively referring to an ideological concern but also to the question of the control

Figure 3.11 Joan Colom, "Sense títol" [Untitled] (Barcelona, 1964). Museu
Nacional d'Art de Catalunya, donated by the artist, 2012.
© Joan Colom, VEGAP, Barcelona, 2020. Photographic reproduction: Museu Nacional
d'Art de Catalunya, Barcelona.

of space, fruit of the fascist desire to impose an absolute physical space
(Santiáñez 30).

As we mentioned earlier, the Plan Comarcal of 1953 established strict
zoning that implied a spatial and social stratification to the city, a stratification that had already been put into practice with the residences of
the Congreso Eucarístico (1952–62), thanks to an initiative by the church
with the backing of the state, delineating the new ideological orientation of the regime. Following an organization derived from the rational
style of modern architecture, the board established the geographical
and professional make-up of the inhabitants of the residences, even going so far as to require that they "hubieran prestado servicios de interés
de la fe, la patria o la familia" (Cambril Soriano 86) [had loaned their
services for faith, country, and family]. Behind the construction of these
residences lies a matter of urban social image, beautification, and ennobling of urban spaces, since it was because of the celebration of the
Congreso Eucarístico residences that the slums on Avinguda Diagonal
were razed.[38] As we saw in the idea of both absolute space and organic

democracy's space, the spatial configuration of Barcelona responds to an idea of community that institutes a political and social order of "divine" origin in which each individual has an immutable place and fulfils their assumed obligation (Morcillo 17), revealing the political discourse that undergirds the supposedly neutral form of urbanism.

Keeping this principle in mind, in the first photograph (figure 3.10), the camera establishes a frame and an angle that imitate aerial panoramas and the distance of the supposed neutrality of the straight line of urbanism. Consequently, the spectator takes up the separation between seeing and being seen, which imposes a process of division and urban fragmentation that establishes not contact but rather distance, and in doing so objectifies the margin. The predominance of a view from above is reinforced by the presence of the men who look from the top down, establishing a social frame that accompanies the inexorable advance of concrete. In this example, separation and the act of viewing from a distance announce an element of authority that emphasizes dissociation from what is photographed. This distance is all the more highlighted by the distance taken by the photographer: his demiurge's vision, above the physical margin and the people who are looking out over the edge, repeats the Cartesian gesture of the urbanist and, in this way, personifies and underscores the distance from the centre, of both city and knowledge, and the alleged neutrality of a foundational all-knowing and all-seeing gaze removed from the body and space that is, therefore, unique and unequivocal. The frame of the lens imitates the boundaries that the Paseo Marítimo establishes as it tries to impose order precisely through the presence of the straight line and visual distance. The suburbs are seen from afar, implementing a hierarchy and producing a notable contrast between the bodies that look and those that are located in the background; the former are active while the latter are passive.

As can be appreciated in the second photograph (figure 3.11), from the perspective of the people below, the formal city also remains at a distance, beyond reach and unattainable. The clash between the two cities seems unavoidable here, just like the relentless advance of the formal city represented by the threat of the Paseo Marítimo that is almost on top of them. However, the distance between the two cities and the change of perspective in the second photograph, in which the photographer has descended to the area of the shanties, disclose the complexity of the relationships that are conjugated in Colom's photographs and introduce movement that is contravened by urban place. On the one hand, in these photographs the urban dualism advocated by the official city acquires a physical shape, the architectural infrastructure that becomes a tool for control. Official language perpetuates urban segmentation through an oversimplification that ignores the complexity of the photograph, the confusion of the margin – the lack of a centre, multiple perspectives, gazes that can be seen and others that are announced only as shadows on the pavement. On the other hand, the mobility acquired by Colom through his role as photographer allows him to create a movement that fluctuates and breaks with the fixed patterns established by urban place, placing both cities in dialogue with each other and thus revealing their mutual dependence. The perspective of the second photo implies a turnabout in the origin of authority and the dissolution of the panoptification of the built environment. Borders, in this transformation, become mobile, unstable. The lens does not look straight on and its frame does not capture what is established by urban order but rather its possibilities: everything is in constant construction. Disciplined space, represented by the Paseo Marítimo, is utilized as a tool to lay down the rules for and govern the lives of those who inhabit Barcelona, both in its formal and informal manifestations. But in the actions of the photographed bodies, we see the recovery of dialectical movement that generates spatial practices not anticipated by the basic structure of the Paseo Marítimo.

In figure 3.12, the children from the shanties break the strict division of the straight line since their movement cannot be contained. No longer positioned above looking down on them, the camera is at their height as if it were one of them, another shadow among those cast on the ground around them, which, as Lefebvre explains, breaks with the material and architectural hierarchy and discovers an urban phenomenon that can only be known through the eternal movement of bodies (*Rhythmanalysis* 20). The fragmentation of the photographic frame contrasts with the clear division of the bourgeois reticle, which continues to be materially present in the background as the division between the Paseo Marítimo and the shanties, and which also, when compared with the photo with which we began this disquisition (figure 3.10), becomes a satire of the organized, rational, and utopian city of Ildefons Cerdà and later plans, such as the Plan Comarcal of 1953. Immigration, an essential protagonist driving urban topography in this period, reinforced a discourse of relations between "us" and "them," between the "legitimate" inhabitants of the city and immigrants, which in turn gave rise to a dual city in both practical and discursive terms. In this context, the margin, Colom himself, breaks with and reworks place's original expectations. The margin is characterized by an ephemeral action that circulates through places as if these were fluid, and leaves a trail that ends up modifying the places through which it has

Figure 3.12 Joan Colom, "Passeig Marítim" [Boardwalk] (Barcelona, 1964).
Museu Nacional d'Art de Catalunya, donated by the artist, 2012.
© Joan Colom, VEGAP, Barcelona, 2020. Photographic reproduction: Museu Nacional
d'Art de Catalunya, Barcelona.

passed. The margin, be it suburb or interstice, can be seen through activities despised by the city for the ways in which they call attention
to its wants and needs, and is comprised of different discourses and
practices that are free to move through place and space. This discursive and practical multiplicity may be linked to a physical space, be it
a periphery, a building, or a specific place in the city. But it focuses on
the rupture of that boundary through the movement of the photographer, as we see in the two first photographs (figures 3.10 and 3.11). It
is like a scar that opens up in the middle of the established order and
exposes dependencies that are meant to remain hidden. In the city's
entrails – in the marginal, peripheral neighbourhoods in this case – we
see its multiplicity and its potential. It is an otherness that destabilizes
what precedes it, but it is temporary, in constant movement, and makes
spatial and cognitive expansion continuous, without limits of any kind.

   In other words, we are dealing with the construction of an ordered
official image that, nevertheless, is broken down through the figure
of the photographer and the movement of the bodies captured in the

photographs. The stasis and distance of the first photograph enable us to see the imposition of the straight line, the triumph of concrete over the informal city, but by crossing to the other side, Colom changes this perspective and reveals the connection between the planned and unplanned city and their intimate dependency. The photographer's leap to the other side allows us to see the construction of a journey that refutes officialdom and which describes a path of mobile topography that goes beyond official parameters and established routes. In this visual interruption urban movement is perceived as a world of limitless possibilities. And it is here, in this visual interruption, where we see the margin: the photographer's action draws out the physical margin of the space marked by place and shows it in a new light. He makes the margin visually predominant and turns it into place. If, as Tuan notes (161–2), a part of space turns into place when it makes the eye pause, makes it distinguish the presence of something ignored or overlooked and gives it meaning and relevance, then the selection made by the camera illuminates a new area of urban experience and becomes the centre of a new cartography that creates its own space, one that is not imposed but lived in the movement of bodies. It is not only a matter, then, of showing the clash between the two cities, but of seeing how the action of the photographer disarrays that duality and visualizes dissent against the status quo. Thus, the margin allows us to dismantle both the definitive viewpoint of urbanism, and the photography of Joan Colom, which outlines the contours of this social and urban fissure that questions the predominance of a sole image of the city. Here, a visual awareness of the city persists, but instead of showing the static city of maps and official plans, Colom exposes a Barcelona that is contingent, in constant motion, a combination of individual "Barcelonas" conjugated to represent what was, what is, and what the city may someday become.

Colom's photographs reveal precisely the notion of urban margin through the fragmentation that he captures: because photography is always fragmentary – as we saw in the words of Susan Sontag (22) – because it is the act of cropping in itself, it intrinsically contradicts the notion of totality and is therefore the perfect vehicle to question the social, political, and material status quo. From his surroundings, Colom makes a "picture," inheriting Martin Heidegger's concept of "the structured image that is the creature of man's producing which represents and sets before" (Jay 134), which makes the city manifest itself as an image, as a construction, "putting the world in a frame" as Martin Jay will tell us when describing Heidegger's work (104). In this way, Colom highlights urban fragmentation and, consequently, breaks away from the conceptualization of the city as a fictitious totality through the action of photographing it, which he uses to disrupt and deconstruct the apparent coherence of Francoist absolute space, already in the very perspective of the subject.

By challenging the dominant visual protocols of that time through a new urban cartography, going a step further than his peers, he also challenges those who hold the power of the gaze by questioning not only who can look but also what can be looked at by questioning what is visible and what is invisible in the space of the city. Thus, he exposes and subverts the social order of the dictatorship's Barcelona, making a more open city. That is to say, the contrast between staticity and movement personified in the body impels us to recognize and dismantle the duality built into the material city. He shows us a point of contact where the lack of a sharp definition of the limit makes us question the structures of knowledge that demarcate our surroundings. It is there, in that point of contact, where Colom's margin surfaces. Following de Certeau (93), it is the hollow that enables the creation of uncontrollable and illegible movements that erode given structures; it is the mobility that signals a different spatial possibility and escapes the imaginary totalities produced by the eyes. It is the dialectic that engages in a controversial appropriation of urban space based on the incongruence of the relationship between space and place, a product of the law-breaking of everyday users of space. And it is in this appropriation that we see the birth of dissent and, simultaneously, a new configuration of public space.

Public Space

The conquest of public space through the actions of neighbourhood associations and social movements initiated the decline of the regime towards the end of the 1960s, a period known as late Francoism.[39] Opposition to the regime was no longer exclusively connected to workers or political parties; opposition had been growing on different social levels that, as we have seen, were rooted in the practices and uses of urbanism. As an expression of that growth and expansion, the street became a public space, that is, a space where visibility, presenting oneself before the other, takes on a democratic and civic connotation, "entendiendo la democracia no como forma de gobierno, sino más bien como modo de vida y como asociación ética" (Delgado, El espacio 21) [understanding democracy not as a form of government, but more like a way of life and ethical association]. Although up until this point social protest had been contained by gradual measures that punished participation in protests with jail terms, sanctions, and fines (Mateos 10), the repression of opposition and political dissidence was more selective after 1962, when Francoism's objectives were discursively reoriented towards a language of reconciliation, a consequence of the opening of the country to the outside world.[40] Nevertheless, already in the 1950s we begin to see a space for public appearance and representation take shape where, in the wake of the autarchy's strict control, the social structure of Francoism begins to be challenged. Of course, by opposition here we are not referring to large scale protests like the ones that took place in 1951 with the streetcar strike, or the student strikes and the Huelga Nacional Pacífica [Peaceful National Strike] convened by the Communist Party in 1956; rather, we are referring to dissidence on a smaller, more immediate social scale that began to erode structure from the very base of society. Candel is already a harbinger of this change, as we saw in the role he played in the creation of a grassroots democracy and the creation of a public space for expression, which configured and moulded a collectivity based on urban and urbanistic space. Now, with Colom, we see that same collectivity taking shape in a public space directly related to life in the street.

Under the dictatorship, the concept of public space was non-existent, and space in the street was conceived above all as the fulfilment of an ideological value in which empty and circulatory spaces were "filled" with appropriate uses and meanings that were imposed by official structures; above all, however, the street was a territory of exception, which is to say, it was characterized principally by its capacity to "expulsar o negar el acceso a cualquier ser humano que no sea capaz de mostrar los modales de clase media a cuyo usufructo está destinado" (Delgado, *El espacio* 10) [expel or deny access to any human being that was incapable of displaying the middleclass customs for whose usufruct it was destined]. In this space, the regime sought to persuade or dissuade any dissidence, any capacity for challenging or resisting, and any appropriation of the street deemed inappropriate, by violent means if necessary, but first and foremost by disqualifying or disabling under the abstract principles of good neighbourly conduct (27–8). The space of the street, then, is meaningful: it is a political category that organizes and configures politically (28), ratifying absolute space. For this reason, control of the street and the imposition of social order during the autarchy was linked to a question of political repression and opposition to the regime.

However, once the law of 2 March 1943, which conflated activities related to public order with the crime of military insurrection – a law that in spite of the regime's discursive shift remained in effect until 1960 – and the Law on Banditry and Terrorism of 18 April 1947, which made all opposition to the regime a political crime, were no longer enforced, control of the population and social order became a matter of "seguridad en tanto que estabilidad social" (Ortiz Heras 22) [security as social stability]. This change is indicative of a turn in the nature of opposition to the regime. The Law on Banditry and Terrorism was replaced by the Law of Vagrants and Criminals of 1954, which decoupled social control from political opposition, but was sufficiently vague to be applicable to both in many different ways.[41] Now the powers that be turned their attention to ruffians, habitual vagrants, prostitutes, drunks, and homosexuals, which created a Francoist system of control based a priori on national Catholic customs and morality. In this context, it makes sense that the emergence of social unrest takes shape precisely in those spaces that, like the Raval or the suburban shantytowns, are characterized by elements that are deemed "illegal" but which configure a space of collectivity directly related to the material environment. If, as Jordi Gracia García claims, the resistance to brutality has to start by "reaprender la lengua, aprender a rechazar el utillaje verbal de la propaganda franquista y repudiar la retórica idealizante del fascismo falangista" (15) [relearning the language, learning to reject the verbal tools of Francoist propaganda and repudiate the idealizing rhetoric of the Phalangist fascism], then rejection in the form of the reappropriation of public space using elements considered out of order must be understood as a breach of morality and the social uses it imposes: it is a matter of relearning the language of space by putting it to use.

Accordingly, Colom's dissent is silent, echoing Gracia's "silent resistence" since we are not in the presence of a "loud" or "explosive" change or resistance – although that does not make his dissent any less important, since it lays the foundations for the noisy resistance that will come later; it is dissent "in a soft voice" inserted into the citizenry's daily life as lived at that time, "lacking decorum." Although as we see in the photographs shown above Colom moves within established parameters, given that the images were commissioned and appeared in an official regime-sanctioned publication – which would be an example of the conflict that Ribalta and Fontcuberta talked about – Colom questions officially imposed structures, be they material or social, and configures a collectivity predicated upon space, breaking clichés and stereotypes. But the epistemological turn produced by his photography could already be seen in an exhibit prior to the publication of these images, "La calle" (Sala Aixelà, 1961), where we can see the importance of photography not just as a way of capturing reality, but also as a challenge to the parameters of what was considered socially acceptable at that time. Because, as Jerry L. Thompson asks, "shouldn't photography – which began as a hyperdetailed record of our shared visible world – provide a close, critical examination of that world, the kind of jarring irritant able to rouse viewers out of a complacent, forgetful slumber, and into a wakeful regard of what is?" (4). Colom creates a narrative in which, using a vague reference to "the street" – not the Raval, Barrio Chino, or District V – he reveals a world beyond the thrall of Francoist parameters where a democratic space of life can be founded. His Barcelona, his street, is disarray, dislocation, showing new possible arrangements.

Through this dislocation Colom shows how two regimes of visibility – one legal, the other social – face off. In each there are rules and codes that determine what can be seen and what cannot, granting or withdrawing visibility. If, as Jacques Rancière observes, the political is represented in "the partition of the perceptible," which regulates, divides, or distributes the visibility of power (in our case through urbanistic form), and if "politics is first of all a way of framing, among sensory data, a specific sphere of experience … a partition of the sensible, of the visible and the sayable, which allows (or does not allow) some specific data to appear" (10), then Colom's reference to a Barcelona described by "the street" disrupts the system of borders and spaces created by Francoist urbanism and applies the nature of public space in the Raval to the whole city. Colom transgresses and appropriates space in a creative act that, as de Certeau explains (93–101), reorganizes the dominant bourgeois image that we find even in the works of Català Roca or Pomés. Through the emphasis on fragmentation that we see in his photography, Colom's street appears at the intersection of these power-generated regimes, disputing the rationalization and partition of the visible within the legal regime through the visible and public intervention of the social regime. That is, whereas the city visible from place is constituted by the imposition of a Cartesian order that fragments urban experience according to a set of moral and social parameters that restrict social practice, Colom reconstructs it by reinstituting the fragmentation of the urban chaos of the street. It is the vindication of visibility against the ubiquitous control of a normative experience that makes the city a zone of guarded visibility, the uncontrollable everyday nature of the street and daily life. Public space acquires new parameters of visibility that directly affect the grip of power: if being visible means being acknowledged, then simply existing – crafting streets defined by the collective coexistence of difference – can reformulate what constitutes identity and offer new possibilities for being that do not conform to power-imposed identities, which implies the creation of a new symbolic space and a new urban space that modify the city. If the space of the dictatorship restricts and controls visibility, Colom establishes a new parameter of visibility and creates a public space in which precisely what is emphasized is the quality of being visible, legitimizing forms and uses that are excluded and forbidden by official practices and establishing a counterpractice that exemplifies de Certeau's and Lefebvre's analyses of the appropriation of visual public space in the city.

Capturing the Street

In this reconstruction of public space, the Raval is essential; it is where Colom recovers a notion of the public by conjuring the space of unreason that is unleashed in the heart of the city and threatens the very foundations of place. Where unreason is eliminated by the Cartesian logic of urbanism, Colom legitimizes it with a public sphere that vaporizes the claimed bourgeois "reason." If the state wishes to guarantee social order by promising to take care of the needs of the private sector (again, we return to Arrese's quote, "a country of property owners, not proletarians"), the concept of public consequently becomes a question of social benefits. This representation of the public domain takes on a new significance in the hands of Candel, and now Colom, in whose photography we find the formation of a civic space for coexistence that breaks from the public space of the regime's Barcelona. Colom creates a mirror image of public space, where we see the contrast between what is chosen to be seen and what is chosen to be hidden, an inversion of values that begins to manifest itself formally in the photography of the Nova Avantguarda. Here is where dissent comes from. The public domain, in Francoist urbanism, is fragmented into marginalized groups, many of which have neither access to nor voice and representation in the public spaces of the city. Through the street, Colom recovers the continuity of urban topography, breaking with the collage of incongruent urban reforms that speculative urbanism seems to seek and which, later, will take the form of a supposedly revitalizing gentrification; instead, he tries to find the totality of the metropolis, not in nineteenth-century harmony and order, but by constructing a city that breaks with the image imposed by Francoism's sterilized and apportioned abstract space. He manages to achieve this feat through his exploration of daily life in the street, where he finds an open and fair society that lies beyond the grid, both materially and socially, and he reconceptualizes the public part of urban planning.

The idea of the street as a creative force unites the photographers of the Nova Avantguarda, but Colom's work takes this a step further, linking the street to the idea and practice of citizenship. So, if urbanism drives urban form in both a real and abstract sense, as we see in Francoism's absolute space, Colom subverts this form with the movement generated by users' uncontrolled bodies, which disregard the legality that presides over movement in the city's place.

This manner of taking photographs is intimately linked to the place where Colom centres his work. The Raval, as its name indicates, has been considered a margin since its beginnings. It has maintained the provocative character that distinguished the extramural population of its origins – workers, travellers, prostitutes, thieves, etc. – and gave rise to the literary and journalistic discourse of the end of the nineteenth century and beginning of the twentieth (McDonogh, "Geography" 174), further evinced by its infamous denomination as the Barrio Chino.[42] The margin here is the disposal site that Michel de Certeau talked about, where poverty, filth, and violence are seen manifested physically in spaces and bodies. We can see traces of what we have been defining here as margin in Colom's explanation about what attracted him to this neighbourhood in the first place: its diversity, its richness, and what he called "la qualitat humana dels personatges" (Ribalta, "Entrevista" 36) [the human quality of its characters]. As a photographer, he straddles the margin, cancels out dualities, and gives shape to the faceless masses.

In this context, the heterotopic and marginal characterization of the Raval serves as the point of departure for Colom's photography; however, we are talking about no longer understanding the Raval as it was defined by the official city – as an area of poverty and violence exoticized by the journalistic discourse – but rather, by understanding it from within so as to uncover all of the complexity and movement in the never-ending parade of bodies that give it life. Echoing Jane Jacobs' urban conceptions, Colom sought spaces that represented street life and chose a place where taboos do not appear to exist and where the boundaries between public and private disappear. A place where it would be possible to discern spaces; a place where there was no fear of being exposed, no fear of seeing or being seen, although Colom did hide his camera because of the implicit transgression of carrying the Raval's secrets beyond its strict borders but also to be able to capture the nature of the space. In this regard, the Raval resembled what would years later correspond to the public space of democracy, a space in which to explore discourses apart from those claimed by the law. Therein we understand public space not as a juridical concept, but rather as a margin, which is to say, as a space of relations in which the urban order imposed by the materiality of the city is substituted by the disorder of the movement of its passers-by. In this space, it is possible to contemplate new urban relationships that enable what Jordi Borja calls a "dialéctica de movilidades-centralidades" [dialectic of mobilities-centralities], which is "una cuestión clave del urbanismo moderno" ("Ciudadanía") [a key

Figure 3.13 Joan Colom, "Sense títol" [Untitled] (Barcelona, c. 1958–1961).
Museu Nacional d'Art de Catalunya, donated by the artist, 2012.
© Joan Colom, VEGAP, Barcelona, 2020. Photographic reproduction: Museu Nacional
d'Art de Catalunya, Barcelona.

Figure 3.14 Joan Colom, "Dona i nen" [Woman and little boy] (Barcelona, c. 1958–1961). Museu Nacional d'Art de Catalunya, donated by the artist, 2012.

Figure 3.15 Joan Colom, "Sense títol" [Untitled] (Barcelona, c. 1958–1961).
Museu Nacional d'Art de Catalunya, donated by the artist, 2012.
© Joan Colom, VEGAP, Barcelona, 2020. Photographic reproduction: Museu Nacional
d'Art de Catalunya, Barcelona.

concern of modern urbanism], a space not free from conflict between
individuals and collectivities, but one in which the visualization of
the other is possible. Here we find the possibility of the coexistence of
heterogeneity in society and a venue where differences are overcome
without having to be altogether forgotten or disavowed. Colom's work
highlights public space as a way of life, not a form of governance, coming back to the idea of democracy based on citizenship that seeks to
create a different social life.

   In this regard, Colom indirectly keeps with later theories put forth by
Chris Ealham, who describes the Raval as a space of collectivity whose
opposition to order is rooted not in immorality, but rather a rejection
of the morality and cultural politics of urban elites ("Imagined" 390).
Colom's work, however, was inserted and continues to be inserted today
in the conservative ideology of the regime through works like *Izas, rabizas y colipoterras* or the articles published in *AFAL*, which either branded

his work as denunciation, exalting precisely those aspects, such as prostitution, that constrained the neighbourhood to what Ealham calls "the myth of the slum" ("Imagined" 390), as is the case with *AFAL*, or took advantage of its exoticism, as Camilo José Cela did in *Izas*. Colom himself, even then, disagreed with that characterization, as well as the selection of images chosen by *AFAL*, which focused on photographs of prostitutes in search of precisely the reading that the author denounced (Terré 207):

> Tal vez la crítica que, en general, ha sido muy halagadora, tal vez inmerecidamente, ha ahondado a mi pesar demasiado profundamente, en el aspecto social de la misma, cosa de la que nunca durante su realización me preocupé ni advertí. Incluso había quien escribía desde el boletín de la RSF [Real Sociedad Fotográfica] de Madrid algo así – escribo sin consultar los originales – como "motivo de intervención por parte de la Autoridad Eclesiástica" o algo parecido. (Colom 8)

> Maybe criticism, which has been generally flattering, perhaps undeservedly so, has gone too deeply, much to my dismay, into social aspects of my work, something I never paid attention to or was aware of when I was doing it. There was even someone who was writing for the bulletin of the RSF [Royal Photographic Society] of Madrid something like that – I am writing without consulting the original – with "motive of intervening on the part of Ecclesiastical Authorities" or something like that.

Colom is silenced in his discrepancy in a "Nota de la dirección" [editor's note] that follows the above text in his autobiography:

> Si bien estamos de acuerdo con Colom en cuanto dice en los tres últimos párrafos de su autobiografía, no lo estamos tanto cuando parece quejarse de que las críticas de su Exposición se haya magnificado un tanto el aspecto social de la parcela humana que él retrató. Aun admitiendo que sea total y absolutamente sincero al decir que ese aspecto ni lo advirtió siquiera cabría que por modestia quisiera eludir esa intención sólo pone esto de manifiesto que la propia fuerza del tema le turbó de tal forma, que no comprendió la denuncia que estaba realizando al encuadrar con parcialidad seres y actos que fuera de su propio ambiente son rechazados por la sociedad. (9)[43]

> While we agree with Colom about what he says in the last three paragraphs of his autobiography, we agree to a lesser extent when he appears to complain that the critiques of his Exposition magnified the social aspect of the human landscape that he portrayed. Even admitting that he was totally and absolutely sincere when he said that he never even noticed that

aspect, it is possible that out of modesty he wanted to avoid that intention, which shows that the very force of that subject bothered him to such a degree that he didn't understand the denunciation that he was making by framing a biased image of people and actions that outside of his own environment were rejected by society.

The rationale for including this discrepancy is twofold: first, for how it shows the rejection of not just the possibility of a new spatial and social configuration of the city, but also a reading of the social domain that is not a denunciation; and second, for how it modifies Colom's work. That is to say, Colom insists on the importance of creating a narration, seeking "continuidad temática" [thematic continuity] (Colom 8); however, AFAL's insistence on the denunciation leads them to even modify the order and presentation of his photographs, just like Cela does in Izas, a work in which denunciation is replaced by exoticism, imposing a bourgeois discourse and making the space of the Raval – and, by extension, the public space created by Colom – become regulated and controlled by the gaze of absolute space.[44] If what Colom is seeking is the construction of a narration, then separating images into those that can be read as a denunciation and those that cannot means modifying his narration and reorienting it in a completely different direction that reveals the parameters within which the regime operated and which were inserted into the Raval, drawing attention to the discourse of sterilization that Francoist urbanism sought to apply there. It also implies the rejection of a different reality that forms a dialectic opposition in the chaos of the relationships that make up the neighbourhood and also the urban construction of place.[45]

Consequently, Colom's work shows not only the deviation of the margin, of his photography and himself as a photographer, but also the fictionalization of urban place in how the street breaks with the legality of place. On the one hand, his marginal photography provides a subversive, questioning filter over the image of the city, largely due to how he took his photos. The work on the Raval was carried out over three years (1958–61),[46] during which time he visited the neighbourhood with his camera hidden at waist-height and took photos without looking through the viewfinder. The photographer thus becomes an invisible witness who attempts to capture the everyday activities and transactions of the neighbourhood, seizing fragments of this forbidden space and attempting to find specificity in the shapeless mass of this suburb. On the other hand, Colom's naivete, how he captures life in that space without social considerations, shows the search for a democratic space of coexistence that contrasts with the social control we see exercised outside of the neighbourhood. The coexistence of prostitutes,

families, homosexuals, of difference in general, going about daily life
without judgment, constructs a space for expression that directly opposes
the space of morality that we saw expressed, for example, in the articles
of *AFAL*. The boundaries established by his fragmentation reveal the
arbitrary nature of both the images and the orders that are constructed
through them. Susan Sontag explains, "Anything can be separated, can
be made discontinuous, from anything else: all that is necessary is to
frame the subject differently" (22). Photography thus reinforces a nom-
inalist conception of reality by emphasizing a vision of the world that
negates continuity and interconnection between diverse photographs
and the order that they create in the world to which they refer (22). The
contingency of photographs confirms the arbitrariness of discourses and
the practices that derive from them. This is not to say that photographs
do not provide any information, since as Roland Barthes states, "[pho-
tography] points a finger at certain vis-à-vis" (*Camera* 5), which is to say
that any practice reveals a positioning before the world. In this fashion,
Colom evidently constructs a frame through his photography and in doing so reveals the discursive limits and determinants that can be found
in any cultural practice. Through photography, the urban place ceases to
be unique and static, and instead becomes open to multiplicity as this art
form emphasizes the existence of innumerable frames and, in the process, shows that every practice reveals a positioning before the world.

In this sense, a poetic image of the city's marginality that is more
attuned to the exoticism of life in the large modern city takes precedence over critical testimony, which is not to say that, a posteriori,
political or ideological consequences cannot be derived from these images, whether or not that is the explicit intention of the author. Here a
bipartite image of the city is re-established: aspects overshadowed by
the bourgeois social order, such as sex and poverty, are recovered in
spaces that only the camera can disclose through furtive excursions to
the margin, giving to the urban form new meanings that reshape the
understanding of the neighbourhood.

In figure 3.16, for example, we can see how the masculine gaze defines
not only the body of the woman but also, in a repetition of the gesture of the
official city, the urban space that we have before our eyes. The man's body
serves materially as a frame for the photograph and for the female
body: the darkness of his suit makes him practically invisible, resulting
in the spectator's eyes being drawn to the woman's body; while the male
figure is thus to a degree overlooked, it is simultaneously accentuated
by the objectification of the female body that it enables. It is true that the
camera's focus encourages this reading, but the composition of the photograph reveals much more: the street and its materiality, which allow for

the presence of pedestrians and sketch out a daily routine that changes our interpretation. Our blindness, which makes us ignore the street and direct our gaze towards the overtly sexualized female body, implies our insertion into a discourse that we accept dogmatically.[47] However, by composing the photo with a wider scope, Colom shows us other possibilities that transgress the reading imposed by the formal city, the one that transforms the Raval into the Barrio Chino. And here the idea of narration that Colom defends in his "Autobiografía" is important, since these images cannot be understood in isolation; they require a linearity that gives them meaning when taken as a whole and reconstructs the idea of public space that we see in his work.[48] The selection of objects and of people chosen by Colom, his framing, and the order of the images as a whole creates a rhetoric that cannot be ignored, which is what Cela does in *Izas* and what the commentators on Colom's exhibit do in *AFAL*. Discarding the form of Colom's images in favour of a purely social reading is to eliminate the constructed element that is present in any narration and jam his work into the absolute space of the dictatorship where the Raval, or the street, can only be read in one way, through one unique lens.

Nevertheless, the coexistence of these opposing perspectives is what provides the complexity that characterizes the city as an urban space. And in his clandestine stroll through the neighbourhood and in his anonymity as a passer-by, the figure of the photographer is the force that transgresses the heterotopic rationality of the Raval. Sontag relates these hidden incursions to the image of the flâneur, since photography, as she describes it, becomes an extension of the middle-class gaze of this wandering figure:

> The photographer is an armed vision of the solitary walker reconnoitering, stalking, cruising the urban inferno, the voyeuristic stroller who discovers the city as a landscape of voluptuous extremes. Adept of the joys of watching, connoisseur of empathy, the flâneur finds the world "picturesque" ... The flâneur is not attracted to the city's official realities but to its dark seamy corners, its neglected populations – an unofficial reality behind the façade of bourgeois life that the photographer "apprehends," as a detective apprehends a criminal. (55)

While is possible to think of Colom as presenting himself as a bourgeois dilettante who sees at a distance, and who makes aesthetic and, later, social observations from that distance, he does not belong to the bourgeoisie nor does he seek to expose any supposed "exoticism." The way in which he pierces the margin reveals an entirely different agenda: similar to the bourgeois authors who went to the margin because it was

Figure 3.16 Joan Colom, "De la sèrie Districte 5è" [From the series 5th District] (Barcelona, c. 1960). Museu Nacional d'Art de Catalunya, stored collection of the Government of Catalonia. Col·lecció Nacional de Fotografia, 1999.
© Joan Colom, VEGAP, Barcelona, 2020. Photographic reproduction: Museu Nacional d'Art de Catalunya, Barcelona.

there they could enter a space where what was forbidden by official discourse could be expressed, where they could expose themselves, Colom goes to the margin in search of a space for expression and public relationships that was otherwise non-existent at the time. Through this positioning, the Raval acquires a complexity that goes beyond its mere consideration as a heterotopic, "exotic" place: the margin puts the intimacy of urban place on display. This is what makes Colom not a flâneur but a "stranger," to borrow Georg Simmel's concept; he is both inside and outside, committed and indifferent. Unlike the flâneur, the stranger's actions are not linked to habit or precedent, which grants him a certain degree of objectivity since he is not connected to the actions that he registers (Simmel, "The Stranger" 405). Colom is a marginal element, a cultural hybrid on the verge of fusing, in this case, with two different types of group life. For this reason, the margin is part and parcel of urban place, not alien to it; the figure of the stranger recovers this unity through the celebration of the heterogeneity and anonymity that new urban dispositions attempted to eliminate, and by making the opposites movement/motionlessness converge in one point and become essential characteristics of the place.

In this way, Colom discloses two processes to be kept in mind at all times: first, that the construction of his own space takes shape through his meanderings, which create a unique itinerary that will later be captured in the spaces of the unknown passers-by; and, second, that he probes the construction of the margin based upon the established parameters of the formal city. In the intersection of these two processes, Colom's photography makes clear the physical margin, and that he himself is a margin. That is to say, his presence, like we saw with Candel, is interstitial. It is a point from which the city's movement can be perceived, where it is possible to glimpse the construction of constructions. His photography uncovers those points of contact and in the process becomes the frontier where it is possible to behold the multiple city.

This flight from official parameters has caused Colom to be described as a street photographer rather than as documentary photographer. The distinction between one and the other is by no means totalizing or clear, but from their contrast there emerges a type of photography that classifies and clarifies what Colom does, what we have been calling margin. According to Clive Scott, the language of street photography is not amplified, as can be the case with documentary photography, which moves to another rhythm. Documentary photography fixes vision, freezes the image, and subjects viewers to a series of demands through the gaze that stares back at them (57–8). Street photography, on the other hand, is characterized by the fast, jerky style that results from its ambulatory nature, making for sometimes aimless composition and a peculiar perspective from which the straight line is replaced by oblique angles.[49] Quickness of gesture and of view is reminiscent of the tactile vision of Impressionism, but also of the lines of force of the urban experience of Expressionism and Futurism, all of which implies lines that are materially and thematically blurry and shift between various urban professions and archetypes while simultaneously promising multiformity and registering both the happenstance and the precariousness of life (64). Colom accentuates a "blind field," using Scott's understanding of the term (60), meaning that he does not impose a social or historic context in order to show what can be known but rather shows what can only be known as an imaginary space. Colom does not explain; he invites deduction and speculation. The disappearance of point of reference is achieved through a plunging, peripheral, and asymmetrical vision that disperses the foreground, which, in principle, should draw in the spectator, and his photography gives a physical, almost material form to the fragmentation and selection that emphasizes the disconnection from and resistance to the official regulations of the city of order.[50] And here we also find a disconnect from Colom's predecessors, breaking the distance that we see in Català Roca, for example, in how Colom fuses his body to his surroundings, not just by using the space but also by touching the bodies in his movement. Colom does not document, he uses the space.

By using space, we see a reconfiguration of the urban space. In Colom's photos we can observe streets that show no apparent relation to the others that surround them (for example, figure 3.17). They appear to go nowhere; they are instances that promise a past and a future because they are in motion, they come and go, but with no specific origin or destination. These instances reveal the nature of the city, including its composition and necessity of spaces, and the discontinuous chronology that confronts the ordered and fictional chronology of urban place. They break with any official discourses' imposition of time and their selective criteria for deciding what is and is not relevant in urban place. All of this can be seen here through the unusual angles and the precariousness of the images, which suspend the clarity and order prized by official discourse.

Colom approaches the urban space's margin from outside, without prejudice, and allows himself to be absorbed by its confusion and disorder. Aimlessly adrift, the artist can introduce chaos into what is ordered and has a purpose. He can map itineraries that do not correspond to the spaces and places marked out by the official city. And in doing so, his street photos reveal not just the boundaries of the margin, but also the margins of the official discourse staked out by governmental organizations. We can perceive Colom's drifting in the way he left framing and composition to fate, decisions that in turn allowed his photographs to emphasize the contingency that they captured.

In figure 3.18 we can see out-of-focus pedestrians, which emphasizes the instantaneousness of the image. We can clearly see the speed, movement, and spontaneity of how the photograph registers this meeting point. Here, Colom captures the dynamism of the street, the never-ending movement of its users, and the multitude of social relations that are concentrated in the space framed by the camera lens. This is everyday life, the experience of others, but it is also his own since he is necessarily present as well, as a sort of witness photographing the clandestineness of relationships that cannot be seen not because they do not exist, but because they exist under the veil of habit.

In this photograph, bodies inhabit space rather than the material environment. They function as a point of entry to the construction of the margin. Structural clarity disappears and instead the labyrinthine, confusion and uncontrolled connections are highlighted. All of this is daily living in the public space of the street. Furthermore, Colom uses this photo to examine sexuality: the woman's body in the foreground and the mischievous smiles of the children that are looking at her expose often infringed notions of morality and prurience. This photo shows the darker side of the margin that subverts the narrative linearity of the formal city.[51] In urbanistic terms, we can take all of this to mean that Colom establishes a new relationship with the architectural environment of the city. The photographer captures the city not by photographing its buildings, but by registering the heightened social interactions that the urban environment favours. These interactions are conspicuously absent from new Rationalist construction, which is distanced from the city centre and can be read as projects that do not support the human scale of urban relations.[52] From there we can appreciate Colom's interest in the margin, because it is the space in which it is possible to find this type of urbanity. Or in other words, he seeks out the social cohesion that has disappeared from the formal city due to the dictatorship's tight grip on the one hand, and new architectural and urban forms of life in the suburbs on the other.

The fact that Colom's Barcelona is exclusively marginal gives rise to a new order that prioritizes vanishing points and offers a different place from which to look. Thus, Colom photographs a city in which the interplay of social, economic, and cultural discourses highlights those selfsame elements of its relentless effervescence: commerce and immigration, two key aspects that lie beneath and prop up the bourgeois city. He does this not by adding individuals to the masses that inhabit the formal city, as happens with rational architecture, but by giving shape

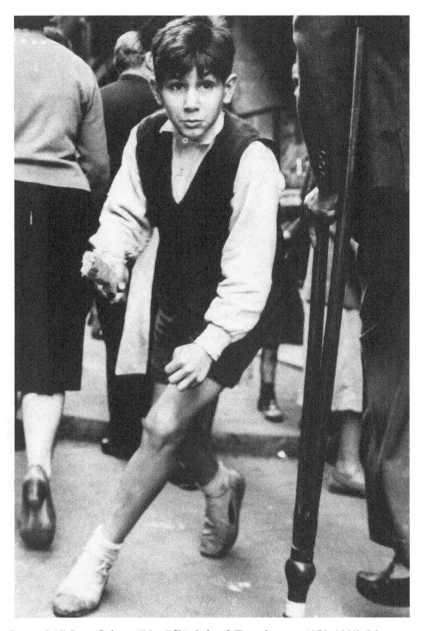

Figure 3.17 Joan Colom, "Nen" [Little boy] (Barcelona, c. 1958–1961). Museu
Nacional d'Art de Catalunya, donated by the artist, 2012.
© Joan Colom, VEGAP, Barcelona, 2020. Photographic reproduction: Museu Nacional
d'Art de Catalunya, Barcelona.

Figure 3.18 Joan Colom, "Sense títol" [Untitled] (Barcelona, c. 1958–1961). Museu Nacional d'Art de Catalunya, donated by the artist, 2012. © Joan Colom, VEGAP, Barcelona, 2020. Photographic reproduction: Museu Nacional d'Art de Catalunya, Barcelona.

to a society characterized by interpersonal relationships. Here, he confirms that the margins are the gateway to change, announcing the city of the democracy in which pedestrians like Colom resignify the vocabulary and syntax of urban planners and engineers.

Nevertheless, even faced with a completely marginal and changing city in perpetual motion, the bourgeois city continues to be present as the invisible framework that structures the whole. This framework of place contextualizes Colom's photographs and explains why they can sometimes be shocking or surprising. Colom wades into the Raval from the parameters of the official city that sees it as a forbidden place. This in turn further contributes to the negative reputation attributed to it by the formal city. However, once there, Colom sees what is hidden behind the ruin of the margin and the Raval's plastered walls and condemns that posture as artificial, as only one discourse among many, and he puts it into dialogue with the Raval's movement.

The artfulness of the street comes marked by the formal presence of boundaries and distances. Because the images are shot from below, Colom's presence along the edge of the margin in the photographs of the Raval can be seen formally through the slanting composition that betrays the hidden position of the camera, as seen in figure 3.19. This posturing provides distance through the liminal space that the photographer occupies, but it is not the only distance present in this photo. There is appreciable distance between the liminality of the threshold occupied by the woman in the shot, the depth of the street, the shaky image of a supposedly forbidden neighbourhood, and the reference to a sexualized female body, all of which occupy the same space and create an image that distances itself from established order. This is a space with a confluence of different gazes: the photographer's, the woman's, those of the people in the background, and the gallery spectator who looks at the photograph. It creates an open and infinite dialogue that always penetrates much deeper than the solitary narrative line. Indeed, all of these gazes are part of the urban geography of the margin, part of the architecture that Colom shows: a narrow street without asphalt where cars do not pass and where pedestrians block part of the road; buildings on top of each other and clothes hanging from balconies. This is, yet again, a human-scaled city.

This dialogical opening is reinforced by the instability that arises in these photos as a consequence of its subjects being captured in motion and therefore often out of focus. Blurring captures the temporality of the margin and the innate border-like qualities of these photos. Space is as unstable as the photographs themselves, in the sense that it is impossible to situate the photographer or the place being photographed. There are no wide-angle photos, no monuments or famous buildings to

Figure 3.19 Joan Colom, "Sense títol" [Untitled] (Barcelona, c. 1958–1961). Museu Nacional d'Art de Catalunya, donated by the artist, 2012.

contextualize the action. Streets are indistinguishable from one another. They all look alike: they are narrow, dark, and surrounded by buildings that are impossible to identify. What does stand out is everyday life. Like Jane Jacobs, Colom sees the city going about its business; he captures the quotidian nature of its space. He accentuates the unmappable labyrinth and the confusion of the street. In opposition to the structural clarity of the Modern Movement, he opts for the permanence of the values of the photographed space instead of its ex novo configuration.

Sontag proposed an idea of anonymity that emphasizes that something must be discovered, revealed, because it is imperceptible or because it is in perpetual motion and the everyday gaze is incapable of capturing it (120). This characteristic imperceptibility and movement are present in Colom's work. The space occupied by the photographer is unseen; what is seen is the space of the anonymous citizen in everyday transit as a passer-by. This subject is part of daily life on the street, one voice more among the throngs that inhabit the city. Colom recovers street users' voices and moulds the city according to their point of view. In the end, what he emphasizes most is a city in use, where public life governs all public places. And public life is, above all else, spontaneous reflection and direct experience.

If what modern architecture intended to do was eliminate the street because it considered it a place of crime and sickness, an opinion that lies at the heart of all of the reforms carried out in the Raval and the suburbs, in these photos we see the exact opposite: a pre-industrial city and the architectural context for public life revealed. This contrast does not result in exclusion; it creates an intermediary space characterized by its complexity and the possibility of coexistence between the different parts that make up urban space. In Colom's photography, closed spaces continue to exist, albeit as the possibility for the indefinable, creating a space for difference and coexistence.

Urban Projections

In all of Colom's photographs discussed here, we find a change of register that shows the margin as a space for interaction and encounter. The street is a space of flow and exchange in which, once again, movement, social interaction, difference, and the heterogeneity of the margin are the rule of the day. This new register underscores the spatiality of urban place, and we should keep in mind that Colom sought to represent street life, the essence of the city. If the Raval is remade into "Chinatown" by artistic and social discourses, if it is made into a place whose order is characterized by the discourses of sin and the forbidden, then upon entering this neighbourhood and walking its streets like one of its inhabitants, Colom cancels out that immobility as he discovers the intersections of mobile elements that construct new itineraries and spaces that reject the homogenizing discourses of the city of order. Indeed, his organizing principle is the dynamism reflected in the movement that he captures in his photos. In the end, the margin according to Colom is the disorder that nullifies the geometrization of the grid and the straight line.

As we mentioned before, an important element in these photographs is the gaze. Here, the photographer is not the only one who looks. In fact, we could say that in a way he does not look, since he snaps the photos without focusing or using the viewfinder. There is no game of reciprocal gazes; what we have is more complex than that. People are always looking at other people: men looking at women, men looking at the photographer – not the camera. Looking does not establish a centre; quite the contrary, it rejects conventional notions of composition and framing, and therefore the possibility of a unique, dominant order. Both subject and spectator are doing the same as Colom: recognizing otherness and, through it, the paradox that gives life to urban space. These photographs centre on the otherness of the bodies that they see, just like all of the different gazes that they register. The presence of bodies, the ultimate place of movement, takes on a special meaning in these photos of the Raval. That Colom finds the margin in action and the movement of bodies underscores the multiple discursive crossings built into the diversity of their actions. Once again, we confront the pre-eminence of space over place, because space is by default built into bodies and the temporality and mobility of their actions, which makes their personal itineraries the epitome of the Raval.

In the context of Colom's work, architecture and the order established through the discourse of urban place are subordinate to use, the unforeseen, provocation, and the unexpected, that is to say, subordinated to this idea of public places organized by the mobility that sweeps through them. In sum, there is no fixed and stable linearity. Borders and boundaries, which depend on the gazes and movements of pedestrians, are continually being adjusted, creating a city characterized by the interaction of the multitude. This perspective marks urban place not by what it finds but rather by its constructedness and processes of selection, both of which are indicated by the photographer's perspective as well. And that is why Colom homes in on the bodies that fill his spaces. He perceives in their movements and activities the fragmentary quality of daily life and the immediacy that fractures what is supposedly fixed and stable. By focusing on bodies – by including the body among what he captures and also inserting into that space the body of the spectator who looks through the format of an exhibit – his visuality is not just optical; it is multisensorial, as we saw in Candel. As Michael E. Gardiner explains, to conceive of the world geometrically relies exclusively on sight, which alienates and reifies, which negates the qualities and potentialities of the human body (348). But in Colom – and here we return to Lefebvre once again – we do not find a spectacularization of the body, whether urban or human, but rather a body in use, which emphasizes experience as its defining quality. From there we can extrapolate the body's contradictory nature, the manifold reality of space, and its unlimited production.

And that is dissent: just like we saw with the suburbs, Colom does not reproduce cultural, political, or social values, nor does he reproduce the physical form of the city that the regime sought to impose – which is what the declarations of denouncement imposed on his work ironically wound up doing; rather, he emphasizes the dialectic nature of coexistence in the street, precisely that which the housing complexes were intended to eradicate, as he renews the contact between bodies. Against repressive urbanism, Colom's street shapes a space for movement and agency and the right to claim space for one's own use. Instead of inserting physical margins into the regular, calm surface of the street, as urbanistic plans aimed to do, the margin – Colom's city – disrupts the supposedly coherent urban image that at the time was created by neutralizing anything considered formally or socially chaotic and making it disappear; he legitimizes chaos, offers it as another possibility, as another order in its difference, and thus he is able to counteract the discursive and practical campaign waged against the city's physical margins. And thus, his urban configuration gets inserted into the material city as an argument over visibility, over how social and political structure consists of being visible, and therefore limited. Sure, the "bourgeois reticle" remains, but now it presents just one of many navigable routes, as the layering of temporality and movement over the city's immanent spatiality blurs the once-fixed grid; the city ceases to be a well-ordered tableau and functions with a new dynamic. And so, marginal spaces dissolve into individual itineraries that seem impossible to capture and which give shape to a city full of infinite possibilities, a city made of urban projections. Colom's photography allows us to see the city from the margin, from the wings, as it breaks free from the canons of proportion offered by official structure, inserting his spectator into the performative activity of Barcelona's space, in a game of encounters and clashes that provide the most basic consensus of a democratic society.

Chapter Four

A ~~Female~~ City: Colita and the Conceptualization of Barcelona

Until now, the perspectives that we have placed in opposition to each other in the construction of the city – official discourses and practices and their marginal counterparts – all share one common trait: their gaze is always masculine. Urban space is developed through the language of the patriarchy, and if it is not neutral in terms of class, neither is it in terms of gender. It is always masculine. Consequently, when dealing with the body that moves and acts in these spaces, these perspectives presume a male form. Of course, this approach does not mean to imply that the female body is absent; however, because the act of looking is carried out from a male perspective, it affects the representational strategies simultaneously employed by female spectators, who accept and identify with the position of a male spectator. That is to say, the uses of space made by the male body establish codes and assumptions that become internalized in the language of the city, relegating the female body to a "sight" rather than a "gaze." But, what happens when the "gaze" is shifted to a female body? This restructuring of the gaze's ascendency brings us yet again to the epistemological turn that we have traced in the ways that the city is constructed: it is not simply a matter of urban construction, but rather of what is allowed. It is a matter of the reciprocity between space and body, of how they mutually act upon each other. The city is reconstructed and reconstructs, taking a step closer to dissent, utilizing urban space to defy conventional representations and shape a new female body that is essentially characterized by its agency. That is, the act of granting visibility that we have pointed out up until now configures identities and alters the conventions established by the power of the gaze, complicating the observer/spectator position and challenging the constitution of gender through urban space.[1]

The act of looking is central to the formation of power, as Luce Iriga-ray explains, and it directly affects the construction of bodies, whether urban or human:

> L'investissement du regard n'est pas privilégié chez les femmes comme chez les hommes. L'œil, plus que les autres sens, objective et maîtrise. Il met à distance, il maintient la distance. Et, dans notre culture, la préva-lence du regard sur l'odorat, le goût, le toucher, l'ouïe, a entraîné un ap-pauvrissement des relations corporelles. A partir du moment où le regard domine, le corps perd de sa chair. (50)

> Investment in the look is not as privileged in women as in men. More than other senses, the eye objectifies and masters. It sets at a distance, and main-tains a distance. In our culture the predominance of the look over smell, taste, touch, and hearing has brought about an impoverishment of bodily relations. The moment the look dominates, the body loses its materiality.

Privilege, materiality, and spatiality become essential elements in the configuration of the city. As we saw with the idea of fragmentation in pho-tography and, by extension, in urban place/space, the gaze characterizes. It constructs and deconstructs, gives and takes away. It is pure selection. But, when it comes to questions of gender, in a world ruled by the male way of seeing, it is selection from a distance; it ignores the needs of the body because it does not come to know the body through proximity. By virtue of this distance, our reality is separated from that which the eyes register, and that separation in turn leads us to contemplate the body from out-side, as Elaine Scarry reminds us, as parts, shapes, and mechanisms more than in terms of capabilities, needs, or as a source of life (285). Through its being seen, the body loses materiality and becomes a discourse that can be manipulated without regard for the consequences upon whatever sur-rounds it, be it a social or an urban space. In this context, the female body is objectified and stripped of its agency. However, this cartography acquires new directives once the female body and eye are given precedence: if it is through the body that we see and experience urban space and the social space that it in turn produces, as we have seen in Candel and Colom, then it stands to reason that a new conjugation of these constitutive elements – body, gaze, city – will enable the development and construction of a car-tography that breaks away from the hegemonic forces that restrain them.[2]

The underlying basis of this analysis, which we have also seen in pre-vious chapters, is the contrast between stability and mobility. On the one hand, place has the ability to apprehend lasting meaning, as explained by Teresa del Valle in *Andamios para una nueva ciudad* [Scaffolds for a new city], which applies more convincingly if we keep in mind the construction of abstract space on the part of the dictatorship; on the other hand, however, this very same place allows for a dynamic in which movement – whether material or physical, for example, a change in the interpretation of history or the construction of some determined type of space – leaves that discourse behind in the place where it came from, voids it of meaning and updates it, constructing a narrative in which the past becomes a shadow that precedes the present (Del Valle 102).[3] In this way, contingency and continuity reshape movement, but in both cases the experience of everyday life is what gives it meaning; lived-in space is the key.[4]

This quotidian quality is what street photography attempts to capture, where the photographer, as a sort of flâneur, captures movement through the performance of the everyday walk, in the process rewriting the urban text and searching for new readings in that materiality that appears to be permanent. When it comes to women photographers, as Marsha Meskimmon explains (20–3), the interaction between bodies and city becomes discontinuous and flexible. They outline the parameters of the masculine city, but bend the structure to find and show how identities are mobile, fluid, and unfixed, given that they are constantly changed by the different ways they see and move through the city.

And here, photography grants us the necessary distance to perceive the contingency/construction of meanings in the quotidian, given that a photo – as we have already mentioned – like space, does not narrate anything on its own except when it establishes a link between its viewer and subject matter. Once this link is established, however, both are inserted into a narrative, in a story that moulds and constructs. This back and forth suggests predestination towards change, in spite of both the city and space being based on notions of inevitability and durability that have become part of the same culture that created them.

If capturing the everyday is what enables dissent, in this chapter I posit that the nature of the everyday shifts in an unexpected way: it is not the rupture of the suburbs or the visibility of the Raval, but the quotidian that lays behind the female eyes. Martha Rosler puts it this way: "Henri Lefebvre, quoting Hegel, notes that 'the familiar is not necessarily the known.' It was feminism that underlined for me that it is life on the ground, in its quotidian, thoroughly familiar details, that makes up life as lived and understood but that bears a deeper scrutiny" (*Decoys* ix). As Ribalta had it, the photographs taken by the Nova Avantguarda constituted the image of a popular Barcelona that would remain until the Olympic Games of 1992. The popular quotidian, the familiar, comes out from their work. In other words, these photographs become the quotidian; the spectator absorbs them as a common memory of what the past was and which defines us as social entities. We assume their accuracy in capturing the past, as if they covered the totality of experience. However, if we apply some of that deeper scrutiny that Rosler was talking about, we notice that all these images are constructed by men, but because of "the commonsensical notions that things are as they are," as Rosler will say (*Decoys* ix), then this masculine view becomes the supposedly neutral city, and, as happens with the photographic genealogies that shape the popular narration of Barcelona, that space is already known as it must be, which is to say, naturally masculine.[5]

In this context, we cannot see this patriarchal perspective unless we introduce a disruption. Candel disrupts the formal city by talking from the suburbs and extending the topographical limits of the city. Colom disrupts the idea of visibility in public space by immersing himself in the Raval and creating a new concept of public being/space. And, now, Colita (born Isabel Steva i Hernández in Barcelona in 1940) gives us through her camera – using once again Rosler's words (ix) – the disclosure of the decoy's otherness that unsettles certainty and disrupts expectations. The margin, in this case, uncovers another fictionalization of the city: it is not only the opposition of two cities, but also the construction of a city where women cannot see or be seen. Of course, as we see in the work of Forcano, Català Roca, Pomés, and Miserachs, women are in the streets, but as they should be, as if the street becomes the interior space that defines their self.[6] In the context that we are examining, the city determines the movements of its users, which is why we see dissent in Colom and in Candel, because they rupture the uses determined by the place. But this never happens with women: they are where they are supposed to be, and Colita takes this opportunity to rewrite their identity in relation to the place they occupy in the city, making the masculine gaze visible and breaking away from it.

Thus, the idea of visibility reappears here with more strength than we have seen in Colom or Candel. On the one hand, due to the lack of it. If "collective transformation requires communication" (Rosler x), it is very important to consider the fact that most of the photography developed by women during the dictatorship had no visibility or, if it did, was in the circuit of contests and the ties of *salonismo* – with the exception of a few photographers, among them, Colita – which made them supposedly irrelevant in many ways: in the impact of the construction of the city, in the importance in the rupture of a masculine society, and in the construction of a photographic genealogy,[7] a history from which they are still absent.[8] On the other hand, due to the relevance of visibility as a tool of control: as we have seen, the gaze is not a neutral phenomenon, but an active cultural element in power relations used to create the illusion of appropriation through abstraction. Keeping this in mind, when we look at the images of the photographers of the Nova Avantguarda, women's bodies seem to solicit the gaze; they are always eroticized, which reinforces the power relations that constrain the female body. Hence, we have, first, a lack of public presence and, second, an excess of public exposure, which is confirmed by the success of a book like *Izas*. In this context, dissent is then about making noise through the gaze, in relearning structures, about letting women see and letting them be seen; it becomes a matter of politics of gender, which, in the context of the dictatorship, is a question silenced under a structure that suppresses the presence and voice of women. How can we talk about dissent if there is no possibility of seeing it? It is a matter of, as Maria Aurèlia Capmany will say years later in Colita's *Antifémina* (10), "visibilizar el reverso de la imagen de la fémina al uso" [visibilizing the opposite of the image of women being used], which is what Colita will do.

The presence of the street and women's presence on it, then, is of the utmost importance in this case, not a presence characterized by the objectified body but as a subject of agency whose body and, furthermore, the body in the street, becomes a place for social identity and an expression of self-determination that reveal the public and the political in the personal. By taking their personal space and making it somehow public, women photographers call attention to the deficiencies of urban space, question limits, and redefine the role of women. So, photography in this case helps us to appreciate the distance that, through perspective, emphasizes how the gaze organizes the space that it registers, but also how, being conscious of its creative and organizational power, it at times tries to offset that lack of physical closeness through a critical reading that emphasizes precisely its own shortcomings. Photographs are therefore constructed but also construct discourses and are not therein related only with the act of taking photos per se but also with institutional practices, social contexts, and discourses of transmission and circulation. Indeed, these relationships are what give power to the act of seeing and create the possibility of developing a new narrative through the eye that emphasizes the gendered construction of spaces through the perspective of the photographer, noting the existence of stereotypes, the renegotiation of predominant narratives that reshape space, be they visual or textual, and redefining the role of gender in public space.

Another concept to keep in mind here is that of perspective, for how it amplifies the coexistence of scopic regimes and questions the representational strategies imposed upon the female body by emphasizing the limits of narrativity, while simultaneously eliminating the idea of a naturalistic discourse. If urbanistic discourse and practice insist on a voiding of perspective that naturalizes the space of women in their isolation and distance from the public domain, what the work of these photographers does is precisely emphasize perspective, which effectively amounts to the limitation of vision. Through the collaboration between photographer and spectator, in which the former creates and the latter decodifies, photography is made out to be a construction of visual narratives, and so reading images, "visual records of time past," is a way to construct versions of history (Davidov 3). From this point of view and following the theoretical stance of Hayden White, interpretation implies assigning categories of meaning to the images and ordering them in a sequence of visual and verbal language in such a way that, from these pieces, a narration or discourse begins to take shape; this narrative or discursive whole can then take as its central focus countless different features (chronology, a linear mode of perception based on different criteria such as gender, class, etc.) and in being open to such approaches create narrative patterns that are potentially as varied as the readers of the images (Davidov 3). In this fashion, both the photo catalogue as well as the exhibition become narrations that include but also exclude and, therefore, marginalize and open discursive spaces in different parts of culture: the viewer of the photograph conjugates various spaces characterized by sequence, including one that we could call syntagmatic, where the photograph is read in the order created by the exposition and the catalogue, and another that we could call paradigmatic, where the photographs are read in the order created by the experience and knowledge of the viewer, and thus can vary widely according to differing viewpoints. This same phenomenon occurs with the space that surrounds us and with which the image is (re)constructed. We seek out those parts that we recognize and assign them meaning within our own discourse, which is how the city or the photograph also takes shape:

> This city can be known only by an activity of an ethnographic kind: you must orient yourself in it not by book, by address, but by walking, by sight, by habit, by experience; here every discovery is intense and fragile, it can be repeated or recovered only by memory of the trace it has left you: to visit a place for the first time is thereby to begin to write it: the address not being written, it must establish its own writing. (Barthes, *Empire* 33–6)

We can draw from this distinction a double reading that will be useful for the analysis of the city portrayed by the photographers we are going to analyse. First, we have what could be considered stable: the narrations we have seen until now can and do create canon and therefore can be considered as representative and constitutive of a supposedly unique reality – that popular memory that Ribalta was talking about.[9] Then we have movement: the image and the multiplicity of readings that can emerge from it enable the existence of a new way of looking that branches off from the canon and heeds different aspects and in doing so gives new form to the photograph, its context, and, by extension, what we describe as "reality."[10] Here movement, the unexpected, memory, and the posterior visualization of these routes that have created a new reading of social and urban context show us just how uncontrollable these urban, social, and cultural discourses are. This operation recognizes the canon (whether spatial, social or cultural), is aware of the malleability of its boundaries, and critiques and deconstructs it. As a consequence of this expansion beyond the canon, a decentralization of place results and together with it the possibility of (re)construction through ambiguity, movement, difference, and conflict, all of which point out the possibilities for interstices opened by the everyday that can alter the permanent – or, at least, longer-lasting – discourses imposed by the physical presence of streets and buildings, or the action of social structures or a canon. Physical permanence imposes an urban map just as it establishes a social reading; the attention paid to these uncontrollable movements and discontinuities creates a new sequence of spaces and readings and, consequently, the refutation of a singular, canonical reading. In this sense, photography, as a visualization of urban wandering and the *real* rendered image, can allow us to uncover new discourses and possibilities in urban places while simultaneously encouraging a spatial memory that lays out a way of narrating built upon the traces left behind by the city's wanderers. These new readings offer the possibility of reintroducing the female body and its gaze as a force with the capacity to create through a multiple urban and photographic subjectivity both urban space as well as the photographic canon. The remnants collected by photographers such as Milagros Caturla (1920–2008), Carme Garcia (1915–2015), and Colita become essential pieces of this new urban narrative as they unleash a destabilization of conventional meaning in urban discourse.[11]

The immersion of the body, and the camera, in the rhythms of the space that we saw in Colom are substituted here, first, by a distance that amplifies the staticity of female space, and second, by the creation of a body of dissent shaped precisely by bestowing it movement. It is this contradictory development that bends the city and shapes it in a game of presences and absences. In other words, the work of these female photographers does not negate the space assigned to women but, by asserting the presence and agency of women in the city, these works violate the dominant formal canons that typically subdue them. And, by this, they are the beginning of a long trip towards the end.

Contexts

Even though the neutrality of urbanism is produced in part because bodies are removed from its equation, because it ignores the everyday quality of those who inhabit structure so that it can objectify the representation of what is tangible, which in turn facilitates its characterization as absolute space, its constitution depends on the close relationship between body and urbanistic form. From the nineteenth-century organicism of Cerdà to the organic democracy that Aurora G. Morcillo talked about, the intersection of body, gender, and sexuality established itself as an essential directive in the construction of the city, which was accentuated during Francoism with the establishment of the female body as an essential directive of the nation. In this context, it makes sense that the presence and agency of the female body became the point of intersection that allows us to visualize the dialectic complexity of both urbanism and female body, and, from there, dissent.

It is well known that during Francoism women became second-class citizens. They saw the revocation of rights that, during the Republic, made their participation and intervention in politics, culture, and society possible (Di Febo, *Resistencia* 128), and this loss entailed limitations on their physical, cultural, professional, and individual movement as they became subject to men, who obliterated them as independent social beings and stripped them of basic rights, depriving them of their participation in society as full-fledged citizens. As Irene Abad Buil indicates (245), women having their rights taken away and being made socially subordinate necessarily makes dissidence in their case a question of gender, and also makes opposition to Francoism just as social as it is political. It is not until the mid 1960s that women began to take part in political protest, specifically, in calls for amnesty,[12] which led to the dawn of the first women's groups that would lead to the formation of the Movimiento Democrático de Mujeres (MDM) [Democratic Women's Movement] in 1964, which would act as an alternative to the female associations arranged by the Sección Femenina and the Church through legal associations such as the Asociaciones de Amas de Casa [Housewives Association] (Di Febo *Resistencia* 154–9).[13] The objective of these organizations that arose from protest was to embed women in the development of social and political movements and to raise awareness about general social and political topics, as well as female-specific ones (159). The basis for the development of the MDM partly depended on, as was the case with Candel and the neighbourhood associations, concerns related to the urban environment, that is, the problems vexing the inhabitants of the periphery. Again, it is the urban turn, the shift in urban structure and the discourse of the construction of the nation and, therefore, identity, that encourages the development of a line of grassroots protests that, in this case, will give rise to a feminist protest movement that will gain momentum and really become consolidated in the 1970s.

In this context, the work of photographers like Colita and, a little later, Pilar Aymerich (1943) establishes itself as important for how both document this movement and make it – and women more generally – visible as constitutive elements of society with their own agency and identity.[14] This popular movement was accompanied by a surge in intellectual and legal movements that consolidated the presence and rights of women in Spanish society.[15] In spite of this discursive and practical turn in Spanish society, Anna Caballé claims that politics was designed and implemented – and still is today– without the inclusion of women (270). Be that as it may, we can see the creation of a channel for public expression that allows women to come out of their seclusion and move about "in the street," in the process redefining their position in society and the characterization of urban space. That said, parallel and even prior to this more narrowly focused political mobilization, we find the development of a movement of dissidence predicated upon reconfiguring everyday structures, breaking the "códigos de silencio" [codes of silence] alluded to by the historian Giuliana Di Febo ("La lucha" 257).[16] This first step is necessary to lay the foundation upon which to cement later public protest, expanding the scope of women's presence and action. That is to say, the works of these women, but especially Colita's, raise an awareness of gender that pushes back against the limits socially and culturally imposed on them, and they fight for the acceptance of women in social discourses and practices and their right to make contributions to them. Dissent, then, lies in the constitution of a discourse and practice related to the rights of women in a moment when everything is subjected to discourse and political practice, and this dissent begins to challenge and erode the social structure of the regime. In other words, in a moment in which everything is framed by the anti-Francoist struggle, Colita sets out to develop a discourse of female identity that challenges the dictatorship's patriarchal structure.

Of course, this does not mean that one discourse or another is eliminated, but rather that a practice of dissent is simultaneously created
and begins to question the Francoist structure using a popular, everyday discourse that is not necessarily related to a direct and mainly political opposition, although social discourse is undoubtedly political, too.

The consecration of the female body through its establishment as a
political body by virtue of its relationship with national Catholicism
makes its presence in and absence from images from this time, whether
written or photographic, essential for what it reveals about identity.
That is to say, if, as Morcillo explains, bodies become indispensable
members of the mystical political body, their (re)construction, whether
in the social or cultural domain, implies a (re)construction of identity
and Francoist structure, which consequently calls for the presence of the
body to be strictly regulated and censored. Therefore, on the one hand
this approach justifies the reading of Colom's work as denouncement
and the success of *Izas*, a book where, apart from the curiosity aroused
by the exoticism of the theme of prostitution in relation to the space of
the Raval, the female body is, and is confirmed to be, a commodity to
be bought and sold. On the other hand, however, the presence of the
body emphasizes, as we saw in Colom's exhibit, the importance of new
dissident discourses that use the female body to deconstruct the social,
political, and cultural structure of the regime. This dissidence comes to
be associated with the opening of the country, beginning in 1953 with
the Madrid Pacts with the United States, which fostered the development of a counter-discourse in commercials, cinema, and television
through the creation of a female image opposed to the regime's view of
modernity and gender roles (Morcillo 21). In this context, life in the city
opens the door to a new type of visibility that will give way to the dissident photography that we see in photographers like Colita. The loss
of social power contrasts, therefore, with an increase in visibility in the
urban environment that, as we have already seen, continues to restrict
the female body to an interior space. In the street this translates into an
interiorization of public space, in this case understood not as we saw in
Colom or Candel but as the creation of spaces for appearance that are
restricted by an environment that continues to define women through
the exercise of certain gender-specific roles – wife, mother, or prostitute.

In spite of the reconstruction of public space as a space not just for
appearance but also the expression of the difference that both enable,
women are always subject to the structure imposed by this social and
cultural environment where they have no voice. In Candel's case, for
example, women disappear completely.[17] As Genís Sinca already indicates in his biography of Candel (210), female characters are scarce or

insufficiently developed, and Candel's wife, Maruja, is a phantasmago-
rical figure that moves through the background of his stories serving
whiskey and opening doors. Her role is as limited here as it is in the
broader society: "senzillament 'en les novel.les de barri, les dones són
les que donen suport al marit'" [simply put, "in the neighbourhood
novels, women support their husbands"] (Candel qtd. in Sinca 213),[18]
which is contradictory if we heed the testimonies of this time, which
explain how women were the ones who initiated and breathed life to
the neighbourhood associations, since they were the ones most directly
involved in day-to-day life in the neighbourhood.[19] However, just as
happens in the cultural space of the regime, the female body is mutilated, stripped of voice and action. In Colom, as we have already seen
and as we will see in greater detail, in spite of this search for public
space, a space of appearance, the female body continues to be subject to
the male gaze, just the same as with his generational peers. It is because
of this emphasis on the male gaze that the urban environment becomes
so important: if women are restricted to interior spaces, then their presence in public space and how it is captured shows a restructuring of
place, how it affects bodies and how it enables the creation of dissent
within an emerging countercultural feminism. If movement of the body
is what enables the creation of a multisensory spatial experience that
grants new meaning to place – a new epistemology of knowledge that
subverts the position of mastery assumed to be male – in this case the
body in space will (re)construct a social space in which women take on
presence and agency.

Out of Sight

If we observe photographs without regard to the gender of the person
who took them, we can ask ourselves whether it is relevant if the author
is male or female.[20] Eric Homberger, in his article "Transcending the
Agendas," asks if photography has a gender, concluding that it does
not given that, disciplinarily speaking, male and female photographers
share a language and a medium, which implies no separation between
them. However, this utopic approach cannot be considered when there
is a social and cultural context that represses the role of women; in such
a context, the eye behind the camera does indeed modify the content
of the images: the way in which the female body is perceived and portrayed, and how this perception and portrayal configure urban space is
undeniably influenced by the gaze. As Lefebvre will note when talking
about "The Right to the City," it is not a matter of eliminating differences, but of leaving the opportunity for rhythms to coexist, having

access to centrality and participating politically in decision-making. Hence the relevance of the body – and the relevance of the body that takes the photograph – because it counteracts the dominance of the visual, which in this context accompanies an abstract, violent, and masculine space.

These limitations or differences in context come to light if we set in juxtaposition the work of Joan Colom and Milagros Caturla, one of his peers.[21] Neither was a professional photographer, at least not at first, yet both attained recognition for an activity that started as a pastime. As we have mentioned in the previous chapter, Colom's photography became known through expositions in different centres and art galleries at the time, and the interest in his work was rekindled during the 1980s when expositions and publications rediscovered his work. The path followed by Milagros Caturla's photographs, on the other hand, was marked from the beginning because Caturla was a woman, which limited her work's exhibition almost to the point of disappearance.[22] Her work became known through a photography contest for women organized by the Sección Femenina, the women's branch of the Falange, in 1961. The photographs were displayed in the Salón de la Virreina, and Caturla won fourth place with her photo "Fervor." The AFC was charged with organizing the exhibit and its subsequent publication in the association's review (March, 1962), which includes Caturla's photograph. The AFC was divided into the "male group" and the "female group," with the former being in charge of editing and publishing the magazine that, as explained by Caturla herself in an interview, excluded the activities of the female group and, in turn, caused their work to be disseminated in far fewer professional circles with less exposure overall. Caturla continued to show her work in contests and exhibits,[23] although her name disappeared from subsequent genealogies of photography, despite the quality of her photographs and the fact that she rubbed shoulders with prominent photographers such as Eugeni Forcano.[24] As Carmelo Vega notes, in spite of advances for female photographers in Catalonia thanks to their participation in the heart of the AFC, this was a very private group, which imposed an important limitation on their influence and exposure (722).[25]

Joan Colom, despite his dissent when it comes to the configuration of space, maintains a masculine gaze that limits the female body. As we have seen, and returning to the idea of movement, we can see how Colom's photographs emphasize the idea of physical and discursive movement and through them question the nature of what the Raval was at that time, a place marked by crime and prostitution. However, the masculine gaze – both the photographer's and the one that characterized the Raval as Barrio Chino[26] – endures and colours the search for change even in his later work, which perpetuates the same place occupied by the female body in the 1960s even though the neighbourhood finds itself in a very different social and historical moment. We are not talking about a monolithic representation of the neighbourhood, but rather an example of the presence of the male gaze that objectifies women and dismisses them to domestic and family spaces.

In Colom's photographs, the female body is mutilated, like its place in urban space: she is denied her whole being, the ability to speak, and the subjectivity that her body should grant her. It is not just a question of how a woman is transformed into a woman of the street, but rather that her body is manipulated and fetishized, fluctuating between lack and excess. This mutilation allows us to perceive boundaries, which is to say that the photographer is conscious of the creative power harnessed through photographic techniques, here through framing and composition. The mutilated female body creates a visual axis that organizes the discursive space, but it does not transform this space, even though it occupies it. Here she has no agency; she is just another object that is part of the Raval's surroundings, like its buildings or streets, as is perhaps even more evident in a photograph that we have seen as an example of a confluence of gazes.

Let us observe one of Colom's photographs once again (figure 3.19). In this example, we can appreciate how the female body is the organizing axis of the image, as confirmed by the focus on her and the blurry background that takes up most of the image. Nevertheless, it is striking how the woman's body is absorbed by the architecture of the neighbourhood in the same way she is absorbed by the act of looking performed by the masculine gaze, not just the photographer's but also any and all who might pass by. She is under continuous observation as a spatial representation of the Raval in its most exotic context. Although Colom is attempting to reread the Raval not as heterotopic but rather as an example of interstitial public space in which the street is the essence of the Mediterranean polis inasmuch as it is the source of a unifying power that defines a supposedly real but nevertheless unregulated neighbourhood, the female body, in how it is construed, reveals the very discourse and practices that act upon and socially restrict it. The spontaneity of the photograph and the resulting emphasis on the idea of realism transmitted through Colom's technique, which seeks to capture a natural, uncreated space, reinforces the limited space of women that is characterized by a taken-for-granted and unavoidable daily life. Be that as it may, the framing of the female body in any given spatial configuration here is not the product of chance, however much it may appear so due to the way in which Colom took the photos: the use of a specific camera; that it was hidden; the use of black and white; the graininess of the images; the alleged lack of focus, even though corrected when developed (as can be seen in the contact sheets that are conserved in the gallery Colectania). These are all defining characteristics of street photography: the idea of wandering aimlessly through the streets, without formal structure or a theme so that photography is not defined by the photographer but rather by the surroundings, so that what is captured is considered more real. All the same, this search for liberty is carried out within a matrix of power relationships that (re) organize urban and social spaces.

These characteristics can be appreciated in other photographers of that same time and also the years that followed, like Francesc Català Roca or Xavier Miserachs, in whose photographs the women are largely a mute group, subject to the relations of power transmitted through space. In this sense, space is performative: the types of encounters implemented and captured construct the gaze's narration and structure, limit, and map space according to a determined tradition, one that is in this case masculine. We can see in their photographs a repetition of patterns that also exists in literature. Sandra Gilbert and Susan Gubar explain, in *The Madwoman in the Attic*, how the portrayal of women in literature responds to their position in a capitalist patriarchy, where men hold all *"authority"* and control all words. Literature and, by extension, art rationalize socio-sexual patterns that they see around them, creating a "biologización de lo social" [biologification of the social], to use Bourdieu's words (*La dominación* 14), in which a social construct is naturalized. If we apply this idea to Colom's photography, and then later to Caturla's, we see how both underscore the idea of a complex urban matrix characterized by a tangled labyrinth that is not exclusively physical and through which the power relations that act upon society become manifest, and therein we find an immaterial base upon which bodies are organized and mapped.[27] Nevertheless, perceiving urban space as a group of relations, even if these are power relations, does not mean the imposition of a fixed hierarchy, but rather quite the contrary: these are mobile and modifiable relationships since they are, as Pollock tells us ("Missing Women" 203–4), not realities but images and therefore malleable, changing spaces.

Keeping in mind this urban matrix of power relations, Milagros Caturla's work seems to be very conscious of how context contours the feminine. In her photographs where women are the protagonists, the ways in which the female body is given space to act draw attention to social practices that limit and confine, which can in turn lead us to designate her work as photographic *salonismo*.[28] Their movement in a supposedly exterior, public space is clearly demarcated, to the point of being claustrophobic. This limitation comes from the framing of the female body within a religious practice that determines where she can be in public places. In one of the photographs we can see a line of young girls walking down the street dressed for their first communion. At the head of the line is a female figure that appears to be a nun who is flanked by two other women dressed in black or with veils, whose purpose is to reinforce both the integrity of the single-file line as well as the social norms to which the girls are subject. The everyday, almost Costumbrist tone of the image, the use of black and white that emphasizes the presence of the line, *chiaroscuro*, and the dialogue between urban place and the human figure, and the image in motion all remind us once again of the techniques that we saw with Colom: the search for spontaneity and reality that comes out of capturing the momentary. In this case, however, the female body is not objectified by photography but rather its socialization within the parameters of a discourse derived from practices that engage the body. By offering a whole female body bounded by walls, the framing produces a perspective best characterized by proximity, trust, and acknowledgment, through which a feminine discourse that seeks out and individualizes the body is cultivated. Colom's limitation is breached here by Caturla's gaze, which peers into the photograph in order to explore and reveal its inner spaces. She also mutilates the body, but through its urbanity. This physical limitation is much clearer if we compare these photos with others that have masculine subjects, where we can appreciate a wider variety of themes that spread their physical presence throughout urban space.

Caturla's physical mutilation of the female body is very different than what we saw with Colom. In one of her photographs, she presents a close-up of a woman's feet. We can see her feet and ankles resting on the asphalt, up to what appears to be the bottom edge of a coat. The woman in the image has removed one of her high-heeled shoes and is resting her semi-nude stocking-covered foot on the other, still covered by its shoe probably so that the other one does not touch the ground. Her feet and the parts of her legs that can be seen are right in the centre of the image and allow us to catch a glimpse of the asphalt, but nothing more. The axis and centre of the image grant complete prominence to the woman's feet and emphasize her everyday femininity but also a tiresome modesty that demands she take a rest. Her body is the source of perception; it is simultaneously the point of departure for the construction of discourses that she uses to define herself from within, but it can also be used by others to define who she is. There can be a tremendous difference between these perceptions, which is evident through our contrast here of Caturla's work with Colom's. Caturla does not attempt to map an ideal body, like we see in the way advertising eroticizes the female form or how Colom packages it for consumption. We see the body in its intended use, in its reality, with the social restrictions that inscribe it. The woman in the photograph is not subordinated to her surroundings or the masculine gaze; rather, she seeks out her own femininity in her body and through her body. Unlike the previous images, her femininity is detached from her environment, just like she detaches her pain-inducing heel. The female body here produces knowledge and devises new ways to approach discourses that shape reality, while at the same time questioning the posture of the prior cognizant subject by making its personal and social profiles visible. The reprioritization produced by Caturla's fresh perspective does not remake the organization of the space occupied by the woman's body; rather, she confirms it, but by showing it from the other side, the woman's side, she establishes the base for the type of dissent that we will see later in Colita's work. The body unmasks the authority and powers that regulate the day-to-day life of women.[29] In both cases, Colom and Caturla, the boundaries between the public and the private converge upon the most intimate of our interfaces with the world, the body, which is also decidedly public and the means – and perhaps even more appropriately, the spectacle – through which experience is visualized. Along these lines, the way we read urban geography infiltrates and informs the way we read the bodies that permeate it.

The language of photography therefore becomes a system that repeats and (re)constructs, but also allows for the modification of established structures. Caturla inserts herself into feminine spaces that she knows and reveals them in all of their familiarity, as we can see in the photographs in the school for girls.[30] The photographer has no need to hide her camera like Colom did, because she belongs to/in this space and can pass unnoticed and blend in with what she captures. Otherness for her is not an external representation. However, these spaces are not exterior; they are interior, respecting the heterotopia of schools for girls, an institution that, like religion, gives structure to the urban matrix and the places occupied by bodies therein. Here urban space is identified with the male spectator. As happens with her city photos, here Caturla respects the limits in force, repeats the language of social discourse that limits the body, and in doing so, makes it visible and insists on the presence – and necessity – of other voices.

Seen from the Window

The movement that we see in the photographers of the Nova Avant-guarda, who use the street to pull the curtain back on everyday life in the city, takes a completely different form in the hands of their female counterparts. There is a physical, spatial restriction that forces them to rethink the concept of everyday life. The movement of their bodies is subject to restriction, and that restriction is precisely what becomes dissent. Therefore, it is not so much a matter of how bodies move in the urban spaces that make up the city, but rather of how this restriction marks and moulds the framing of their photography. It is true that in some ways this dissent does not carry the same force as Candel's or Colom's; it is more nuanced, in part because their voice is female and does not carry the same force of projection as that of their male colleagues. Indeed, it is not until Colita that we see that same force of disconformity again. That said, in both Caturla's and Carme Garcia's work,[31] to mention photographers whose work focuses on Barcelona and especially urban space, we begin to see the configuration of female figures that have agency and identity even within the limitations imposed by the regime's structure. John Berger writes that "all stories are discontinuous and are based on a tacit agreement about what is not said, about what connects the discontinuities" (285). Well then, this is a tale full of discontinuities that tells the story of the body from the other side, filling in the gaps that seem to remain in the story of place. This new perspective permits the creation of a new urban space comprised of simultaneous temporalities that affect the constitution of place because they break with its linearity.

This change implies, moreover, an epistemological shift in documentary photography: if what up until this time defines a "realist" approach to the environment is going out into the street, as we see in the photographers of the Nova Avantguarda, then in the work of these female photographers, we see a new configuration of that idea that, voluntarily or involuntarily, challenges both the parameters for considering what is urban and the photographic principles that guide the production of photography at this time. This new allegation of public space – as a limited space, with limited freedoms – becomes the basis for the photography of these women and paints a picture of a city beset by social and cultural restrictions. If, as Alan Sekula explains ("Desmantelar" 151), art is contingent because its meaning varies according to the conditions under which it is read, the same thing that happens in the creation of art also happens in the construction of the city: we have completely different spaces when the lived experience of space is totally different. That is to say, the harmony of Català Roca's or Forcano's city vanishes in a city hemmed in by walls that block memory, because they erase presence and heighten the perception of people as objects under control. In other words, the work of Caturla and Garcia tackles the question of social order by being buried under it; they invent a new concept of city and everyday life using the limited number of possibilities available to them, and precisely in that imposed limitation is where we find the beginnings of urban, social, and cultural dissent.

Keeping within the AFC, we find a professional colleague of Caturla, Carme Garcia,[32] whose work is remarkable for how it establishes a space for photographic and urban creation by leveraging the interstitial position that she occupies due to the limits imposed on her body. Where Caturla manoeuvres within the material confines that the city imposes on her movement, Garcia exploits the liminal zones of contact in those physical borders in order to "subvertir los cánones visuales" (Segura Soriano, "Carme" 6) [subvert visual canons] and urban structure. By looking out from her terrace or window, Garcia seizes the urbanist's distant view in order to show not its neutrality but the complexity of its narration, its limitations and intersections. Lefebvre notes that "to capture a rhythm one needs to have been captured by it ... Therefore, in order to hold this fleeting object, which is not exactly an object, one must be at the same time both inside and out," because it is from that point of contact that noise becomes distinguishable, flows disjoin, and rhythms interact with each other (*Writings* 219–20). By being both inside and outside of the window at the same time, Garcia's body allows her to capture the limits imposed upon her and simultaneously subvert them, interrupting the fictitious harmony of absolute space. And this interruption applies to both urban space and the female body.

In figure 4.1, Garcia's gaze is filtered through the negative in her hand and the window, and both limits are propped up by her body, which in spite of everything, including her own agency, continues to respond to a male gaze, as demonstrated by the propriety of her seated position, how she is looking from inside, respecting the lines as drawn, as if she were under a masculine gaze. However, she interrupts that normativity precisely through the act of looking from that posture, just as much because of her body as because of the environment, which broadens the conceptualization of what we see: simultaneous worlds, a conjunction of temporalities that (de)territorialize the city, that decentre the gaze. Her body's confinement, behind a window, is neutralized by the agency of her gaze: the metaphor of window as gaze created by the action of looking through the negative shows that what is on the other side is more than just what is on the other side of the window panes.

Figure 4.1 Carme Garcia, "Autorretrat" [Self-portrait] (Barcelona, 1959).
© Arxiu Fotogràfic de Barcelona.

It is what we can perceive through the act of looking; it is what we decide to include and what we leave out, and it reveals fragmentations.
Looking through the negative is a rejection of imposed boundaries and
a movement through margins that subverts spaces, contexts, and relationships. This action of looking reveals the presence of an interstice, of
a margin. It reveals, moreover, the epistemological turn that makes us
question the image's realism – how many filters do we have before our
eyes? – and the positioning of the body, since what is inside is not necessarily isolated from the outside. There is a mutual influence that pulls at
both of them. In this sense, Garcia's city is polyrhythmic, that is, made
up of multiple rhythms in the form of times, spaces, bodies, memories,
and identities that coexist in the view from the indoors looking out or

from rooftop terraces, which become a sort of living space contiguous to the street, "each part, each organ or function having its own in a perpetual interaction which constitute an ensemble or a whole" (Lefebvre, *Writings* 230). In this way, she offers a new configuration, a series of porous boundaries that create a new system of relationships that destabilize urban structure, and the rupture of what is considered to be civic politically charges her action even within its everyday nature.

Unlike Caturla's work, which never left the premises of the AFC or the Sección Femenina (with all of the consequences that such a restriction on the circulation of her images could entail), Garcia's work was extensively exhibited in solo shows starting in 1966, even though she never became a professional photographer in spite of the many offers she received to work in advertising.[33] She relentlessly shot photos and actively participated in the AFC, but her work remained separate from the art world outside the AFC. As Rosler says, this world "es fundamentalmente una trama de relaciones, éste incluye también todas las transacciones, personales y sociales, entre los grupos participantes" (*Imágenes públicas* 139) [is fundamentally a set of relationships that includes all of the personal and social transactions between group participants], which means that her individualistic character and outsider status as a woman kept Garcia out of the most important circles in photography, in spite of the fact that her work sought modern, innovative forms that rejected the traditional forms of pictorialism, as Nash and Colita tells us (106), and was thus very much in line with other members of the Nova Avantguarda.

In spite of this limited profile, Segura Soriano assures us that Garcia makes three essential contributions to the history of photography: (1) she blurs the limits between inside and outside, making the relationship between both spheres visible and politicizing the photographer's positioning through the relationship between body and gender politics; (2) her representation of the female body becomes a public manifesto, demanding a change in both representation and the way her photos are viewed; and (3) she visualizes a peripherical Barcelona, in as much a physical as a social sense ("Carme" 8). More importantly, however, in all of these contributions we see a breakdown of hierarchies in which the inside perspective becomes the more dominant, accentuating the human scale of her work. In this breakdown, Garcia formulates her dissent: she superimposes those ignored rhythms, gazes, and bodies over the structure of absolute space, stressing their everyday human components and thus the importance of the body that we track in the construction of the city, in this case, in order to break up imposed structures. She removes stereotypes that deny city and women their

Figure 4.2 Carme Garcia, "Felisa" (Barcelona, 1960).
© Arxiu Fotogràfic de Barcelona.

individuality, finding her own identity in both bodies by doing so. The connection between space, body, and identity is therefore all the more relevant for how, together, they show the ways that they mutually construct and influence each other.

The limitation of Garcia's perspective by material structure offers us a mutilated body, in this case the urban body, interrupting absolute space's narrative and the discontinuity it forces on the female body. That is to say, similar to her indoor photos, the urban environment is also a fragmented reality due to the limits imposed on the body. Garcia's city is framed in an experience that is straightforward in the image, captured precisely in distance that no longer purports neutrality, but offers proof of the fictionality of urban narration. These scenes or fragments that offer a new architecture/structure highlight an in-between, a new rhythm in which everyday life is an undeniable sign of human action, countering the illusory images of an absolute space that only indicates absence. The intra-history of the suburbs put forth by Candel takes on a new meaning here: against monumental architecture that zones and controls the social realm through the symbolic, a new perspective is inserted that completely eliminates the scopic and gnostic drive of which

Figure 4.3 Carme Garcia, "Carrer d'en Carbassa" [Carbassa Street] (Barcelona, 1960).
© Arxiu Fotogràfic de Barcelona.

de Certeau spoke. The city is now a landscape of roofs and rooftop terraces that do not offer panoramic views united under one single viewpoint, as we would expect from a position elevated over the city; here
we find fragments that do not allow us to see very far at all. The city is
almost unrecognizable, which reveals to us a new idea of the "real": an
image, as Pollock would say, that unmasks the artifice of the narration
of place and makes us question the idea of the "popular image of the
city" that Ribalta talked about, since this "familiar" Barcelona, familiar
in the sense of a family album, subverts the role that memory plays in
the construction of place. The idea of a "popular Barcelona," or whatever the idea of Barcelona is at that time, is an imposture, a memory

built by what others tell us. In *Novelas como álbumes*, Antonio Ansón, following John Berger, claims that

> las fotografías no cuentan nada, excepto cuando tienden el vínculo de la experiencia entre aquel que las posee y las personas o cosas fotografia-, das. Entonces sí que cuentan, importan y narran una historia tan personal como perecedera, a merced de la memoria que desata sus imágenes. (18)

> photographs do not tell any stories, except when they make the link between the experience of those who possess them and the people or things photographed. Then, yes, they tell stories, they matter, and they narrate a personal and perishable history, at the mercy of the memory that unleashes their images.

Their characterization as family albums emphasizes this idea, because photography unites with an idea of oral history that configures the history of the city. But it is here, at this point, where the discourse of place is subverted against the grandiloquence of official narration, the "oral" discourse and practice of those who live in the city, who lie beneath the surface of monumental Barcelona. At this point, it is a matter of representation and self-representation in which visual rhythm is precisely fragmentary; it is detached, individual moments, inside and outside, uncovering an identity that breaks and is broken, a multiple identity that is hard to capture with the linear narration of place.

It is also the creation of a new network of interaction with almost exclusive female participation that, although it respects the spaces allocated to women, spaces that transform the exterior into the interior – markets, spaces of almost exclusively female expression – it develops a new space for agency and collectivity that through its gaze redefines the formal boundaries imposed on women. This collectivity arises by creating photos of one equal to another, not looking down, upon those with little prestige or power, as Sekula defines them ("Desmantelar" 158), but rather with a horizontal gaze that connects those who coinhabit the city. Garcia breaks through the inside/outside divide by recreating herself in the fictionality of that dichotomy, creating a space for her voice in which the perspective from which images are taken emphasizes the act of looking, especially if we compare her photographs to Colom's or Miserachs's. In other words, although Garcia also goes out into the street, she always keeps her distance, marking the distance of bodies, hers included, but it is precisely this distance that marks the difference between them, perceived in how they move about the city with different rhythms – rhythms born of structure. Gender difference,

Figure 4.4 Carme Garcia, "Pis del nen, barri del sud-oest del Besòs" [My son's apartment, southwest of the Besòs] (Barcelona, c. 1970).
© Arxiu Fotogràfic de Barcelona.

then, is written into the urban landscape and, as a consequence, the optical is limited by the topographical.

Now, this interior/exterior in-between, this mobility/paralysis, offers the possibility of constructing a city whose hierarchies, especially the centre/periphery one, are challenged and redefined. As the title of the first photograph that we see in this sequence indicates (figure 4.4), the city expands through its everyday life, which produces a democratization of space. There is neither margin nor centre, only a space for daily life that expands how the city is experienced. The representation of place is local, personal, ignoring the social, cultural, and political patterns that applied to the body at this time. Here, the city fragmented into living spaces ignores the monumentalization and politicization of the spaces of daily actions. At the same time, we see a historicization of the city in terms of the onset of chaotic modernization fueled by rapid industrialization and commercialization, both processes that, in spite of being produced from within the power of place, eliminate the centrality and authority of a singular point of view by forming a new narrative, a city with multiple levels that clash with and contradict each other in

Figure 4.5 Carme Garcia, "La Zona Franca des de Montjuïc" [Zona Franca from Montjuïc] (Barcelona, c. 1970).
© Arxiu Fotogràfic de Barcelona.

the industrial and residential margins, both of which are put on the same level. In this way, the mobile perspective of pedestrians moving through the streets is replaced by the panoramic perspective of a static observer that reveals the place-based palimpsestic layers of scopic positions that coexist and oppose each other, among which are included the relationships between public and private spheres that Garcia captured with the interplay of near and distant gazes. And this approach applies to the female body that, in her photography, sheds its objectification.

If we compare figure 4.6 to "Felisa" (figure 4.2), we can observe how the identity of these women is blurred by the street. The things that bestow them with individuality and strength indoors seems to disappear

Figure 4.6 Carme Garcia, "La Rambla" (Barcelona, 1960).
© Arxiu Fotogràfic de Barcelona.

once their bodies move through public space. The bodies that walk down the Rambla do not look around; they become indistinguishable from each other. Their streetwalking is not a flâneur's, because there is no agency: they do not look around because they cannot, which contrasts with Garcia's action as photographer, who becomes, as Leet says about the flâneur, "a disembodied eye observing but remaining unnoticed or invisible" (280). She is an invisible flâneur, echoing the concept developed by Elizabeth Wilson in her article of the same name but carrying it a step further, since she controls the gaze and, therefore, the bodies. This makes her gesture a political act if we consider the importance of the gaze in a society ever more defined as a society of spectacle with women at its centre. However, here we have public circulation in which the sidewalk allows the female body to be present without sexualizing it, as happened in Colom's images. The bird's-eye view of the image makes way for a new architecture of gender that also configures the female body. The male gaze, relentlessly present in the photography of Forcano, Miserachs, and Colom, disappears, even from the point of view of those seated at the tables and whose feet are the only part of them that we glimpse; their presence is cropped out, eliminated on purpose, which gives total autonomy to the female body and eliminates the voyeuristic superiority of male visual control. The objectification of women is challenged by mutilation, in this case of male bodies, still there but nullified, which highlights the underlying masculinity of urban space, which is also assumed in invisibility, in the implicit masculinity of the figure of the flâneur, given that she still limits her movements to an indoor perspective. True, the body is still restricted by structure, but it is, I repeat, not subjected to the male gaze, an effect that Garcia achieves by eliminating the idea of detachment and acknowledging her own sense of identity in the place of the city. In these examples, the camera does not naturalize, or at least, not in the same way that Miserachs or Colom sought to do in their photography: as Sekula notes, the theory of photographic realism depends on a viewpoint that "no está implicada en el mundo que tiene delante, está sometida a una idealización mecánica" ("Desmantelar" 157) [is not implicated in the world that lays before it; it is subjected to a mechanical idealization]. However, here the camera and the eye are completely implicated in the surrounding reality, giving rise to a dialectic relationship that blurs the limit between observer and object. The limits imposed on bodies here challenge the notion of a distance that can capture experience without acting upon it. That is to say, Garcia captures the street with that idea of distance and happenstance that seeks to capture an intact reality, but by doing it from above, from the window, she reveals precisely the encounter between female body and city, not just physical limitations imposed upon women, but also how the gaze disrupts and categorizes.

For that reason, we can affirm that Garcia seeks the (re)construction of the public sphere by opening interior spaces to the outside world. Dissent is expressed through the presence and consideration of, and insistence upon, female space as part of urban space. That is, Garcia creates a city and collectivity based on internal rhythms that are hidden away or ignored; she establishes a dialectic relationship between them, emphasizing contact, friction, and the city as a structure made up of discourses and practices. Although it could characterize her work as a folkloric or Costumbrist endeavour that draws from a whole tradition of female discursivity centred on the interiority of private spaces, this emphasis on interiority accentuates the weight of structure, and, although her criteria for femininity continue to be imbued with the regime's discourse and practice, she unmasks the authority that regulates and restricts the female body on a day-to-day basis, just as Caturla did, while at the same time seizing authority by taking control of the gaze, both her own and men's, and reapplying it to urban and urbanistic space.

Bodily Ruptures

From the restrictions placed upon Caturla and Garcia, we can assume that the flâneur's attitude, movement but not necessarily gaze, continues to be male dominated, since it is men who, Wilson observes (93), occupy the public sphere and whose figure is conflated with being an artist, whether photographer or writer, a fact readily apparent in both literary and photographic genealogies. And it is in this context that Colita emerges, seizing movement in the city in her search for a female identity that reconstructs the meaning of the female body and its urban surroundings. Colita heads outside, breaks free from imposed restrictions, and rewrites a new territory that defies the regime's obsolete structures. Her rupture is even more dramatic if we consider that her work is contemporaneous to Caturla's and Garcia's, which intensifies the relevance and dissent of her gesture, the violence with which she intrudes into the urban panorama of the city, attacking those canons and structures where, as she herself claims, "el ser mujer es un serio hándicap" (*Colita* 10) [being a woman is a serious handicap]. That is, in her work outside of the photographic salons under the sphere of influence of the Falange's Sección Femenina and the AFC, under the tutelage of photographers such as Miserachs and Maspons, who would wind up being her colleagues – a term applied here to denote their shared professional footing – Colita breaks with the educational and social structures imposed by the regime's social and educational systems. Her work proclaims the visibility of a female body extracted from closed interior spaces and inserted into the public domain, casting aside the self-sacrificing femininity that we find traces of in Caturla and Garcia.

The interplay of photographic language and the relationship between photographers and images continues to be essential in Colita's work. One of the most important and famous photographers in Spain, she established her journalistic career in association with the Catalonian Gauche Divine (alongside photographers such as Oriol Maspons, Julio Ubiña, and Xavier Miserachs, who guided her in her professionalization as a photographer) and the Film School of Barcelona. Her work covers themes drawn from the social, cultural, and physical reality of Barcelona in the last four decades of the twentieth century: the city and its neighbourhoods, especially the Raval and Somorrostro; portraits of personalities from the worlds of literature, film, and music; flamenco and gypsies; performance and transvestism; and her work in daily journalism and reports published in magazines including *Interviú*, *Destino*, and *Triunfo*, where she reflected on political change, protests, electoral acts, and social issues like psychiatric centres.[34] This professionalization helps Colita develop a detailed consciousness of the photographic medium and thus separates her from the circles in which Caturla and Garcia carried out their work.[35] This statement, however, is not intended to characterize the work of Caturla or of Garcia as second rate photographic productions, or brand them with the label of "hobby" or amateurism in a derogatory sense: let us not forget that artistic and cultural production does not have to be professionalized to be of value, but it does if it is to have visibility.[36] Returning to Colita, although she herself has claimed that "sus objetivos, más que llevar a cabo una reflexión teórica sobre el medio para transformar sus estructuras, eran los de hacer una fotografía profesional que sirviera para ilustrar los artículos o la revista para la que trabajaba como freelance" (qtd. in Rosón Villena 59) [her objectives, more than reflecting theoretically on the medium in order to transform its structures, were to cultivate a practice of professional photography that would serve to illustrate the articles or magazines that employed her freelance], in her work we find a dialogue with the forms being developed at that time, which can also be read as a personalization of her photographic language, undoubtedly connected to a context of change.

In Colita's work we can see a true questioning of the photographic perspective in regards to the female body. Her photos that take women

Figure 4.7 Colita, "Jorge Herralde y sus secretarias" [Jorge Herralde and his secretaries] (Barcelona, 1970).
© Colita.

as their protagonists show a beauty and strength that transcends social parameters. They are conscious of the place of women in society but seek to counteract it with irony and a sense of protagonism that grants agency to the body. By irony we understand, as Donna J. Haraway defines it in "A Cyborg Manifesto," a figure that emphasizes the coexistence of contradictions "that do not resolve into larger wholes, even dialectally, about the tension holding incompatible things together because both or all are necessary and true" (5). In order to understand how dissent functions in our urban context and in terms of gender, it is first necessary to accept the coexistence of uncomfortable contradictions, which shows how dissent tries to destabilize the security of those spaces that we believe immutable, that is, the security provided by the walls and inner recesses that make us feel protected and sheltered.

Through irony, Colita plays with the objectification of women and in doing so emphasizes and critiques oppressive masculine discourse, as seen in figure 4.7. It is true that the context of this photograph is not urban, but it can be useful to demonstrate how Colita's photographic language works and how she is very aware in her work of the discourse and practices of oppression that govern the female body. In the first place, by adopting the women's perspective – limited to ground level just like the camera lens – she becomes the affirmation of resistance by imitating the gaze and logic of the masculine way of looking: she is still a body subject to the male gaze, bound by a socio-patriarchal structure that reins her in. The discomfort of this gaze highlights the containment of a subjugated and objectified space. What is more, here space is represented through conventions that take up the techniques of street photography and yet break with its pictorial references, capturing space according to the experience of those who live it. Objects and subjects are represented according to subjective hierarchies that the producer considers important. The image thus becomes a space of experience that is susceptible to different subjective, ideological, and historical inflections. And so, Colita's photography evokes how she perceives the spaces and places of women in the spaces and places of men; however, her images do not just show women subjugated to male will, but also a genuinely female perspective on physical and social space. This approach considers spaces represented and spaces of representation, and, more importantly, the social spaces from which representation is made and the reciprocal postures that are derived from there.

We can see, however, how this photo can be understood inside a discourse of oppression, where Colita, instead of criticizing the construction of masculine space, is embracing it. In other words, while it could be affirmed that Colita's critique or irony here does not necessarily arise from her prior intentions or the fact that she is a woman – since neither can be known directly through the image – they nevertheless become visible in how she composes and develops the language of photography in the photograph. Colita uses the language available to her and emphasizes, marks, and delimits it in the composition of the image, making it visible and showing its consequences on the female body. Joking and irony are essential parts of the image and the source of its inescapable critique. Furthermore, it is in images such as this one that we see the importance of gaze, because of how it restructures and reconstructs the perception of spaces and the place occupied by the body in them. Although some critics like Rosón Villena assert that Colita does not directly develop a theoretical schema of the gaze, understood as an active cultural element in power relations, not as a neutral phenomenon (60), in spite of the fact that it is one of the principle themes in the feminist critique of visual and artistic culture, photographs like this one make us doubt that claim, since here we can see a clear questioning of the gaze and the paternalistic and authoritarian discourses and patterns working on the female body, anticipating future debates.

Within these contradictions, Colita is very aware of the importance of the body, especially the female body, as a carrier of a politically charged meaning that will go on to represent the political and social tension of the Transition. That is, her photography is ahead of its time as it offers us an early look at the panorama of contradictions between feminism and the cultural production of the "destape" that will become evident later on and will dominate certain areas during the Transition,[37] creating a discourse of dissent based on the presence of the body not through its objectification but through its heightened visibility and the allegory of rebellion that will oppose different social and cultural fronts as references for the body of the nation. However, in this context, Colita performs a feminist – or queer – reading, as Rosón Villena claims (67), that contravenes the uses of the female body that will be made in film and some journalistic productions of the time. In this case, the body is not exploited by gaze and male desire; rather, a woman directs the gaze and its erotic impulse towards another woman, which shows self-determination, agency, and rule breaking, "desorientando las lógicas 'straight' que construyen la experiencia" (67) [disorienting the "straight" logic that constructs experience] and challenging the unique models that constituted the regime's binary male/female logic. And among the many possible "straight" readings we should include bodies as sexuality under control, "mecanismo necesario para que las mujeres continúen con su estatus de reproductoras biológicas y simbólicas de la nación" (Garbayo Maeztu 12) [a necessary mechanism so that women would continue to be classified by their status as the biological and symbolic reproducers of the nation]. The doubts that can arise from a feminist reading of this image highlight precisely the contradictions produced by irony and, above all, by deviating from the straight line. Colita upends the order of things, as can be seen in the positioning of the camera, the eye as the producer of a discourse of power that cannot be ignored and must be read precisely through that contradiction, in that dialectic of powers. Furthermore, it is the spectator's responsibility to learn to question, to abandon practices that constrain the body, and to grasp the eroticism here that challenges and filters power through the model herself, making her "un arma de contestación cultural y social" (Rosón Villena 69) [a weapon of social and cultural opposition]. We should use this same approach to Colita's more urban photography: how she shifts the gaze and perspective and in doing so challenges the preceding images.

This awareness of spaces of enunciation extends to urban place and reveals the urban matrix within which the female body has to create its own place of existence, as is expressly disclosed in figure 4.8. The space

Figure 4.8 Colita, "Putas del Barrio Chino" [Chinatown whores] (Barcelona, 1969).
© Colita.

of the Raval maintains the same conventions that we saw in Colom: the women are observed bodies and women of the street, as seen through the framing of their bodies by the men's gaze. However, there is an important change in perspective here; while it is true that the men, like the buildings, frame a specific reading of the female body, here they meld with the walls. This image echoes the language of the preceding photos: the bodies are shot from behind, in full movement in black and white, recalling the supposed spontaneity of the camera's snap.[38] The women's bodies, on the other hand, occupy the whole street as the centre and axis of the image, not to be objectified like the masculine gaze would see them, but to be given strength. The proximity of the camera to their bodies emphasizes this strength and breaks with the privileged gaze as it acquires and gives materiality to their bodies. In the way they walk and how they cling to and support each other, we can perceive an agency that fractures the street's structure; what we witness is not submission but rather protest. The framing, how their bodies spill over the physical boundaries of the photograph, move them beyond established limits in this act of protest. The reading of the physical place remains unchanged, but the use these women make of it calls into question and critiques established parameters of accessibility and respectability. Here we see the violence of everyday acts that was spoken of by Barthes and de Certeau: the image deconstructs from within established parameters and from within a photographic and urban language that is recognizable to viewers; its structures are made subversive through a clear and direct language that does not employ euphemisms.[39] The body is being heard.

Figure 4.9 is especially relevant if we observe how it blends the male figure into the background, makes it a part of place and, therefore, irrelevant. It is part of the story being told, but it is not the body being defined. The distance of the male body, those blurry figures subsumed by the space of the Raval, become a commentary on power, influence, and the construction of history. Gaze rules here and makes the male figure secondary although present; it is part of the palimpsest that constructs the history of the Raval, but if the body's noise is what the previous photograph (figure 4.8) allowed us to hear, here it is inaudible. The presence/absence binary vanishes: they are present and absent just like the female body, like the photographer's body, both spheres convoluted in a space of conflict. Space is essential in this configuration, since it continues to be defined within the parameters of what is considered to be the Barrio Chino, but Colita uses that characterization to undermine the foundations of the male gaze since here it is a female gaze that encroaches upon the neighbourhood's streets, breaking the structure of what is "morally acceptable" in order to show us an active gaze that acts just like the male one, but with a specificity that, by virtue of being female, becomes dissent, since her action is the same as a male photographer's.[40]

It is interesting to note how Colita uses buildings and signs to configure an environment that defines bodies, a quality absent in the figure 4.8 where the bodies are female, highlighting who writes the narration and how she changes these hierarchies, using irony to transform the structures that define and characterize bodies. In these photographs, we continue to see a direct dialectic relationship with the discourses and practices of the neighbourhood that precede her work. Like Joan Colom, Colita immerses herself in the streets of the Raval as just another pedestrian without offering us a guidebook of the streets or places, making the Raval just another neighbourhood with streets just like anywhere else, in the process making it a pure space in which we are all spectators and actors. The coexistence of an underground world in which women's bodies continue to be exploited once more points at the idea of selection and discursive narration that we have been considering

Figure 4.9 Colita, "Marineros en el Barrio Chino" [Sailors in Chinatown]
(Barcelona, 1969).
© Colita.

since the beginning of this analysis. However, Colita makes those bodies appear in other ways, questioning the way in which those bodies, of women both in the Raval and in the margin, are authorized to appear, misaligning, as Garbayo Maeztu writes, Francoism's community and corporeal ideology through bodies that "amenazan" [threaten] to transform us into others (20). Nevertheless, Colita's Raval is always a space where life happens, and to that end she emphasizes the figures of those who inhabit it on a day-to-day basis, without necessarily focusing on the neighbourhood's more exotic aspects, but rather blending her view with them, in the process toying with the monopoly of the male gaze and defying the discursive linear structure that shapes the neighbourhood and, by extension, the city in the narrative of place.

The Raval is always a contradictory space, defined by the different levels of life that compose it. The day-to-day realities of those who reside in the neighbourhood coexist with the activities of those who are only visiting. In figure 4.10, the topology of the street chokes the gaze; light and shadow coexist in the image, as simultaneous temporalities that are revealed in the palimpsest of signs and clothes hung out to dry. We can assert, then, that Colita shows us an open space, a border space, a margin, in which movement, dialogue, and change give protagonism to the idea of contingency and ephemeral encounter that enable a challenge to and reconstruction of the basic structures of urban place, and the Raval seems to be at the centre of it, precisely for the freedom that somehow it portrays.

That said, this focus expands beyond the conception of the neighbourhood as public space and the questioning of its organization according to a narrative that stretches out along its history. It is true that the objective of these images is to search for a new identity without renouncing completely the old one, but what stands out above all in Colita's work is a new characterization and positioning of the city and the female body. Both bodies are immersed in a new context that contradicts their alleged neutrality.

Monumentality, as we can see in figure 4.12, is undermined by the quotidian, the same way that the discourses imposed over female bodies are questioned when considered under the perspective of a female gaze. Colita offers us a response to that which is prized by the city. Urban space is understood here under a new ontology that breaks away from monumentalizing conceptions of space and time. The present overtakes the importance of the past through a "hereness" and "nowness" represented in the hanging clothes, highlighting the mutability of that which is considered eternal and representative of the city. In a similar fashion, characteristically female interior space is brought outside

Figure 4.10 Colita, "Sereno" [Night watchman] (Barcelona, 1969).
© Colita.

Figure 4.11 Colita, "Vieja y colegiales en el Barrio Chino" [Old woman and school children in Chinatown] (Barcelona, 1962).
© Colita.

Figure 4.12 Colita, "Ropa tendida en La Pedrera" [Clothing hung on the terraces of La Pedrera] (Barcelona, 1970).
© Colita.

Figure 4.13 Colita, "Madre e hija tendiendo ropa" [Mother and daughter hanging laundry] (Barcelona, 1964).
© Colita.

to the building's exterior and takes priority in urban (re)construction. The clothes become an indicative accent, a trace of what is hidden and not given to be seen in the city, revealing the relative blindness of an urbanism that denies certain presences. In this way, as we also saw in previous photographs, Colita writes over the structures that precede her, and she (re)conceives those spaces through a markedly female experience. Consequently, her corporeality, simultaneously present and absent, challenges the formulation of the city, particularly its basic principles of representation that are inherent and socially inscribed in masculine parameters.

The female body is embodied on several occasions in a pleasant image that eliminates and avoids overt references to its sexuality, but without dismissing its gender. In these photographs (for example, figure 4.13), Colita re-examines the inside/outside dynamic that we saw in Caturla and Garcia, always pointing towards a new urban geography that breaks with monumentalism and the conception of space as the product of a discursivity and practice removed from daily life.

On the other hand, the fact that these spaces are much more heterogeneous than those offered by Caturla or Garcia indicates a change of perspective in the female lens, an evolution that responds to a new type of gaze, a gaze that is changing the way we perceive social context in spite of the ways that the latter continues to impose limitations. Just as in the other examples, the camera lens moves at the height of passersby and neither discriminates nor shows the intention of framing; it captures actions in motion, centred on urban dynamism as it seeks out the elusive instant.

From this dialogue with a space that relegates women to the background, we can surmise a different knowledge of place: in Colita's photographs we see two distinct discursive spaces that operate on different levels at the same time. Thus, the temporalities that we saw in Garcia assume a more direct form here: now it is a matter of a direct action in public space, highlighting perspective and the creation of social bodies that constrain the terrain of the other, naturalizing what is considered deviant, contingent, temporal. All of these examples confirm how the spaces that make up the urban matrix, to return to Lefebvre's term, configure life, mobility, and the activities of women, and, in many cases, they express feminine stereotypes that become lived realities, as del Valle explains in relation to the creation of an urban feminine space (28). They are examples of how photography and space differentiate and organize hierarchies, building a generic space that is configured by the sexed construction of culture (32). All of these relationships – between male and female photographers and between/with space – reveal the structural axes of social life: time, space, and gender. In other words, space, be it physical or photographic, traps moments that configure and determine its usage, and in this context, the space from which one looks is neither abstract nor exclusively personal, but rather ideologically and historically construed, determining the point of departure of its producer and the position of consumption of its viewer.

What we should highlight in this case, then, is not the quasi-utopian perception of public space in the Raval, but rather how it is a place for encounters and, therefore, conflict, movement, and interruption as defined by Jane Jacobs. If in this context we have in mind how the performativity of public space in the Raval has been monopolized by a masculine gaze, the work of these female photographers goes on to identify this part of the city as an affirmation of women's space. The kinds of encounters captured and the ways in which the gaze's narration is constructed here structure, limit, and map space from a new perspective. This return to the Raval as a zone of resistance, with a nod to its anarchist past, is significant because it lays bare the urban, social, and gendered structures

Figure 4.14 Colita, "Paseo de la Barceloneta y barrio del Somorrostro"
[Promenade in Barceloneta and the Somorrostro neighbourhood] (Barcelona,
1964).
© Colita.

that identify this place. It becomes a synecdoche for those other conflicts
that shape social relations and structure urban spaces, whether they are
tourism, gentrification, or immigration. Here the intimate relationship
between public space, access, and the construction of identity – all essential elements in the construction of urban space – are made manifest.

The focus on the physical body and the construction of a social body
through the female form jointly recodify the social and economic relationships that constitute the city and shape its community through
the proximity of said bodies. All of the body's materiality, which is lost
through the gaze, comes rushing back in its proximity and centrality. If
the body facilitates a rereading of place, as de Certeau and Lefebvre explained, then modifying the body, its representation, and its construction by looking can also affect and reconstruct place. And this goes also
for the material space of the place.

Compared with Colom's photographs of the Somorrostro, where the
boardwalk is characterized by the presence of bodies that observe the
slums, in figure 4.14 Colita emphasizes isolation, the distance between

the structure of the city and the margin. The supposed modernity of structure does not break with the supposed disorder of the slums; rather, it underscores it and promptly overlooks it. In this case, we do not perceive the movement of structure towards the slums, but rather how it has sought to close off its access, leaving the residents of the So- morrostro in what seems like a perpetual "out of place." The thematic focus of the photograph reminds us of Colom or Ignasi Marroyo,[41] but so does the position of the camera: above the railing, like Colom's body was once perched, but cropping the view with structure itself, which does not allow us to see any further. The straight line, highlighted pre- cisely by the lens, characterizes the slums by their disorder, establishing an architectural linguistic hierarchy that Colita will dismantle in her photos of the shanties, whether in the Somorrostro or Montjuïc, where what stands out above all is proximity and day-to-day lived experience, and the photographer's admiration for gypsy life. The physical oppres- sion of structure, the containment of what is considered problematic, reveals the presence of a central discourse that attempts to structure the city's social movement. In this case, by marking precisely the straight line and its failure, just as she does with the female body, the photogra- pher disrupts that alleged harmony, challenging it through its own ineffectiveness. In this way, the political reality of a centralized state that consolidates a series of urbanistic, social, and cultural discourses is laid bare and defied precisely by the limitations that it imposes. Colita shows us a border space in which movement, dialogue and change give protagonism to the idea of contingency and ephemeral encounter that enable a challenge to and reconstruction of the basic structures of ur- ban place. Even in this photograph of the Somorrostro, the contingency appears in the selection of the moment in which Colita took the pho- tograph: although the photo was taken the same year as Colom's, the differences between them show the coexistence of multiple temporali- ties that we also saw in the Raval, and the impossibility of defining any space according to a single structure. It is the failure of the neutral gaze of urbanism and the gap that allows the expression of dissent.

Contesting the Gaze

And so, here there is a change in the perception of the city and its na- ture, which we observe through an opening of perspective and the amplitude of themes that emphasize the diversity of the city inhabit- ant that constitutes citizenship. In this way, movement continues to be present, but it is no longer unidirectional, which makes the spectator question the stable patterns that give shape to the captured space. If, as

I said at the outset of this book, both gaze and place create hierarchies, then the fact that the power to control social and symbolic space passes into the hands – or eyes – of the female gaze that voids and neutralizes as it searches for openings, implies that we recognize the categorization of this power and, in our new reading of it, modify and invert it. This shift does not eliminate masculine identity, but rather seeks to eliminate the masculine limit as an enclosure and make it instead an opening. The dialogue with the photographic memory and construction of, for example, the Raval and the understanding of what the suburbs are, thus becomes a reflection on social memory as it accesses the comprehension of mechanisms of power through the construction of the past and the present. Their images present themselves as the culmination, but not the end, of an evolution in which the male gaze begins to lose its monopoly on representation. In this new vision, feminine and public space is perceived as a collective that does not necessarily singularize or limit.

If in urban spaces we find monumental indications such as street and square names that mark a process of formal historical recognition, the spaces selected by these photographs as they ignore these indications and certain places and emphasize others imply the creation of an alternative and subversive space that gives voice to those marginalized groups. They construct a parallel narrative that undermines the structure of institutional place and emphasize the dynamic of change. The choice of the Raval, for example, establishes a politics of enactment aimed at introducing an egalitarian social memory in which women are the objective but not in a sexualized way, and they draw attention because they are included as an essential part of a much larger, more heterogeneous group that reshapes the social fabric and the places that make it up. Photography here opens a space for subversion that fosters the inversion of ordinary time and space and breaks with specifically gendered conditions as could only be allowed by the presence of female spectators and producers. It alters the logic of the masculine gaze and, although it maintains the language and distance that we saw with, for example, Colom – or maybe precisely because of that – it becomes a commentary on the containment of women, which in turn allows us to read these photographs as an affirmation of resistance that helps us see and understand how place is marked by gender in the societies in which we live. Photography, intimately tied to the idea of image described by Pollock, thus becomes not a place of memory, but a landscape that helps to (re)configure the cultural and political reality of a territory.

And so, we come full circle back to where we started: it is true that as a consequence of the privileging of the gaze the body loses materiality.

However, through the examples that we have seen in this chapter, we can affirm that through photography the gaze can also grant materiality to the body in the simple fact of making it visible, recapturing Arendt's concept of appearance. This new materiality, this reappearance of the female body, (re)constructs new corporal relationships and, consequently, new spatial ones that give a new shape to the place of the city. The objectification in the examples that we have seen gives way to a new selection and a new discursivity, which imply the resignification of the physical bodies of women and of urban place. Accordingly, the female eye mounts a new cartography by moving beyond cultural and ideological dictates that were believed immutable, and in doing so mitigates the footprint left by what was once considered original or "real." The gaze of the female eye uncovers the imbalance between the image and lived experience and results in a new female socio-spatial map that can account for her place in this world.

Dissent is then a multipronged tool that not only redefines the space of women but the politics of representation in general. The visual properties of photography establish a close connection with the visual definition of what urban space and the city is at this moment, but also, by the change of perspective, reveal the relevance of the photographer's eye and, by extension, the eye of the urban planner and the politician. The female perspective shows the constraints of structure and how the city absorbs and imposes said constraints on the bodies that inhabit it, but also how the body appropriates the fissures of both physical and enunciated place, and defies the forms used to represent it. This revelation is what allows dissent: again, it is the material structure that allows a supposedly neutral gaze where the camera introduces a disruption through the everyday life with which the official place seems to harmonize. The claim of transparency and neutrality attached to photography becomes then an opposing claim that emphasizes the difficult language of the photograph – its framing, montage, and juxtapositions – and that of the structures of the city.

Bodies, be it those of women or of the urban structure, become a way to question the discourse and practice of the regime by observing and questioning the normative space, by revealing the uses of space and its defective materializations. Hence, we can affirm, as Garbayo Maeztu notes (following Pollock), that the consideration of this work is not a matter of introducing the names of women in the history of photography or of the construction of the city, but to intervene in the construction of the place considering the positioning of women (27). The presence of a feminine body that lives, questions, and moves in an urban, social, and cultural environment is not only a question of gender but also an issue of identity of the self and how it relates to its surroundings and those who inhabit those surroundings. The presence of a body, a physical body or a body of work, involves a visualization of matters of representation that normalize the corporal parameters imposed over the female and the urban body. Women must be present in order to redefine the status quo, and their presence must be not only physical but also active, participating in creation, leading to "a seizure of a metaphorical site as much as an occupation of a particular spatial location" (Meskimmon 3). The body, the female and the urban, becomes then a quote, as Garbayo Maeztu characterizes it (33), which, on the one hand, implies the creation of a collectivity, as a meeting point, returning to the creation of a democratic space that we saw earlier, and the materialization of discourses that construct a physical presence through a not-considered-before practice, and thus also a resistance, because, on the other hand, it is also the "quote" of the structure imposed on the body, conferring a political presence that can change the constitution of the public sphere, as Arendt will have it (*Human* 222). The body is then a visualization of a rhythm ignored by the structure of the city, making it present in front of and as the other, questioning the significance of representation to issues of gender identity and cultural politics. But in our context here, we need the urban body/female body connection to grant visibility, in the same way that through its presence that body modifies urban space; they are mutually dependent, since urban bodies are and become public bodies that, paraphrasing Meskimmon once more, are the organizing metaphor for all forms of social discourse.

The Elusive Landscape

Through our analysis of their artistic endeavours, we have seen how Candel, Colom, and Colita used their work to create a space for visibility, presence, and acknowledgment, and how that space reconstituted the materiality of the urban landscape. The multisensorial element brought to the forefront by the presence and action of bodies – supplanting the dictatorship's reified and disembodied way of seeing, which denigrates the other senses and, consequently, other experiences and ways of being in the world – reformulates the city and simultaneously gives us a new code to read urban space. Their urban/urbanistic interventions show us a multiform city that, as Lefebvre, de Certeau, and Jacobs will later posit, is founded upon an empirical knowledge of space, based on the specificity of their experiences that in turn provide the source for dissent that will enable the creation of a participatory democracy. And here is where the exceptionalism of their work is laid bare: they are not just representations; they are performances that directly act upon material and social space, fracturing the structures, discourses, and practices of a regime that seeks to keep its tight grip on absolute space.

Consequently, Barcelona is materially remade through the daily experience of those who live there and make use of the city, although they are ignored by the discourses and practices of power. The work of these artists creates a new urban demarcation that allows us to see the city from different perspectives, with new patterns of mobility and communication, in the process levelling a critique against the imposition of boundaries and segregation, showing the city to be a dialectical space rooted in the multitudinous physical experiences of its many diverse inhabitants. These artists (re)formulate a public space founded upon the tension between presence and absence: they uncover the presence of rhythms, but above all the noise made by those who do not fit neatly into the constitutive harmonies of what is deemed acceptable, desirable, or productive. The presence of these people, their voices raised in dissent, directly acts upon the physical and social materiality of Barcelona. The city, then, is formulated through these new, multi-layered perspectives, coterminous in time and space, that are interwoven in the public space that the work of these artists represents.

Urban space provides the means to transgress the oppressive structure of the regime. That is, through the work of these artists, we find the creation of a set of identities predicated upon material presence of/in the city and the active engagement of subjectivities. Echoing the words of Amin and Thrift (131–5), Candel, Colom, and Colita formulate a notion of citizenship that depends on presence and grievance in order to be acknowledged, and this act of presence produces empowerment and civic engagement. In this fashion, their work, founded on heterogeneity and multi-sensoriality, speaks to us about literature and photography not as representations, but as material objects and social agents. They are spaces for establishing contact, building networks that are not necessarily political – in the strict sense of the word – but rather guided by the actions of citizens, the residents of Barcelona, and their neighbourhood associations that erode the absolute space of the dictatorship. Their work reflects possible changes, changes yet to come, and the hope for social and, later, political change. As Vázquez Montalbán tells us about Candel, "la seva vida i obra representen, imagina-t'ho, la reconstrucció de la Barcelona democrática" ("Barcelona" 384) [his life and works represent, if you can believe it, the reconstruction of democratic Barcelona], an affirmation applicable to all three authors.

Be that as it may, we should also read their work in relation to the present. We should not allow ourselves to be seduced by possible utopian connotations of this characterization. On the one hand, yes, there is rupture, (re)construction of the city, the creation of transgressive discourses and practices that challenge the social, cultural, and political order of the day and announce democracy. These authors initiate what will become an intangible social network that will extend beyond a purely social domain, showing us how social movements have always been connected to urbanistic concerns, as David Harvey affirms (*Ciudades* 8). In this regard, Candel, Colom, and Colita are the smoke that indicates the fire of soon-to-come social movements, becoming what Vázquez Montalbán calls "creadors de saber, de consciència crítica" ("La lluïta" 9) [creators of knowledge and critical conscience]. They are, in other words, the first signs of social movements that "al llarg dels anys seixanta, aprofitant la restrictiva legislació franquista, es fiquen per les excletxes del sistema i posen en evidencia tots els seus desajustos" (9) [throughout the sixties, taking advantage of restrictive Francoist legislation, slip through the system's cracks and make manifest its breakdown]. Using the alignment of this organic democracy based on family or municipality, the protests championed by neighbourhood associations will become the first to publicly wage war against Francoism, alongside university students and other professional groups.

On the other hand, however, Candel already pointed out a clear failure: neighbourhood associations would be absorbed by new political forces in the 1980s (although they would return towards the end of the 1990s, albeit with diminished relevance) and the city would become the unshaped mass that he saw in the Zona Franca. Vázquez Montalbán confirms this point of view: the dissent that had initially impelled this notably participatory form of democracy eroded and disappeared, partially due to the rules imposed by the Transition, which became the moment when anti-establishment social movements lost most of their steam (La lluïta" 9). That is to say, in the wake of the dictatorship, the city continued to be mired in the same conundrum that we have seen in these chapters: the imposition of an urbanistic directive that ignores the needs of those who actually live there. Barcelona becomes impersonal, with its residents' identity once again dissolving into the unformed mass of reforms that imply, as Delgado will say about a later Barcelona, "la deportación de clases populares para asentar, en lo que fueron sus escenarios de vida, vecindarios más solventes o para someterlos a la colonización turística" ("Todas" 330) [the deportation of popular classes in order to settle more solvent residents in what was the backdrop for their lives, or to submit them to touristic colonization]. The absolute space of the dictatorship never fully disappears, and indeed continues to reappear forcefully in the obsession over coherency and legibility that, in this case, serve speculation and spectacle.

To that end, Manuel Delgado explains that "no hay ruptura tajante entre el tardofranquismo y la etapa llamada democrática, cuanto menos en materia de concepción y organización urbanística" (La ciudad 22) [there is no definitive break between late Francoism and the stage called democracy, much less so in terms of urbanistic conception or organization], but rather the city follows the trends undertaken by the Francoist administration,[1] whose objective is "poner la ciudad a disposición de los intereses del capitalismo inmobiliario y financiero internacional" (33) [to put the city at the disposal of the interests of real estate and international financial capitalism]. But in the same way that this conundrum never really goes away, so do Candel, Colom, and Colita come back again, due to the relevance of their discourses and practices.[2] The conflict and happenstance that they capture in the movement of their characters, the stubborn resistance and transgression that they portray in their works, bring us back to an earlier Barcelona fraught with a critical and participatory conscious that is crucial to our understanding of the construction of the city and the importance of spaces for subversion and noise, lest we forget that the triumph of the city comes from disorder and conflict, not harmony and the suppression of difference.

When neighbourhood associations give way to the representative political system that makes them irrelevant, the whole popular, marginal history that undergirds the identity of Barcelona disappears with them. It is not until the beginning of the twenty-first century that this history is reconsidered by exhibitions and, more recently still, the work of the inhabitants of the old slums and their suburban proxies, who make the case for their role in the construction of Barcelona in the form of photographic exhibits and oral chronicles, subjective experiences that reconstruct the city's intra-history. Exhibits like "Barraques: La Barcelona informal del segle XX" (Museu d'Història de Barcelona, 2009) [Slums: The informal Barcelona of the twentieth century], documentaries like *Barraques: La ciutat oblidada* (TV3, 2010) [Slums: The forgotten city], or projects like the Observatori de la Vida Quotidiana (OVQ) [Observatory of Everyday Life], a multidisciplinary collective that researches and creates content on the dynamics of contemporary social life, all seek to make a case for the importance of the spaces that laid the foundation and then gave way to the Barcelona of today. "Memòries visuals de barris (Sant Genís, La Teixonera, Trinitat Vella)" (OVQ, 1999) [Visual neighbourhood memories (Sant Genís, La Teixonera, Trinitat Vella)] is an example of the recovery of the popular memory of those neighbourhoods through the testimony of the neighbours who lived there. The most prominent feature of these works is how they recover the organized, associative character of the neighbourhoods and the city's cultural institutions, reinserting them into the history of Barcelona as active constitutive elements in its make-up.[3]

And here lies the importance of the margins, how they signal the limits of the city, not as a neutral referent but as a point of resistance that points to other meanings, to the possibility and coexistence of other structures. Hence, the city is composed not of the urbanistic structure of the official order, but rather of a series of micro-stories of those displaced by the overarching narrative of the regime, challenging the cultural connections through unexpected times and spaces. Thus, the everyday life that underlines the space of the margins becomes moments of crises, of rupture, with the potential to overturn or radically alter any univocal narrative. The margin becomes then the negotiating arena for political interests and ideas that, through the emphasis on the visual, which functions as a substitute for political discourses and practices, heralds not only the possibility of a democratic political system, but also the contradictions that will shape the construction of contemporary Barcelona.

Candel, Colom, and Colita remind us of the necessity and importance of recovering the elusive Barcelona that lies beyond officialdom's reach. They open a breach in that "urbanismo que pretende ser ciencia y técnica, mostrándolo una vez más como discurso" (Delgado, "Todas" 336) [urbanism that pretends to be science and technique, revealing it yet again as a discourse]. The chaos of the experiences that they relate, their potential for making noise, gives back to us a Barcelona of margins.

Notes

Introduction

1 Essential studies in this field include *Thinking Barcelona* by Edgar Illas, *The Global Cultural Capital* by Mari Paz Balibrea, *Urban Change and the European Left* by Donald McNeill, *Sensing Cities* by Mónica Degen and, although focused on the Barcelona of the 1920s and 1930s, *Jazz Age Barcelona* by Robert A. Davidson.

2 Here I am echoing various theories that distinguish between two essential elements in any given city's structure: Michel de Certeau's differentiation between space and place; Henri Lefebvre's and Manuel Delgado's notions of the urban and the city; and Merleau-Ponty's geometric and anthropological space.

3 Here this break is not defined in terms of the problematic space referred to by Henri Lefebvre when he connects social and mental space (*Production* 413), but rather, by emphasizing physical elements and the importance of urbanistic organization, in terms of the creation of a spatial practice that ends up deposited as sediment underneath a public space of presence. As Lefebvre explains, spatial practice "is observed, described and analyzed on a wide range of levels: in architecture, in city planning ... in the organization of everyday life, and, naturally, in urban reality" (413–14). Here we return yet again to not just the distinction between geometric and anthropological space, but also to the practice that connects the two.

4 Mónica Degen analyses in detail the meaning of senses in the (re)configuration of contemporary public space and life in *Sensing Cities*. Although her focus is on contemporary Barcelona, her insistence on the creation of public space through our senses establishes a connection to Gil de Biedma's poem, since it is on his walk, in his sensorial experience of space (sound, touch), that he reimagines the monumentalization of Barcelona. In both cases, we are talking about the regeneration of public space through

a sensuous prism, the goal of which is the renewal of a public space annulled by an economic structure or totalitarian regime, which emphasizes how space, as a social process – here in keeping with Henri Lefebvre – "is something made and re-made" (Degen, *Sensing* 20). In this book, I turn to this idea of (re)construction to examine how the formation of a public space characterized by presence becomes a first step towards the (re)construction of democratic society during the Franco dictatorship. The multisensorial creation of a space for living out day-to-day existence will be revisited in Francisco Candel's work.

5 What we do not see in this poem, however, is how these voices acquire agency, which is why Gil de Biedma's poem is useful to us here only insofar as it serves as an anecdote to show how the margin is constituted and contains within itself the potential for change. Because Gil de Biedma continues to speak from his own place, social order is upheld, and we only see a desire for change that does not grant those voices the power to shape their own destiny. The margins that I seek to expose and analyse in this book are not the product of an imposed mediation but rather are predicated upon an authority that becomes radical potentiality.

6 We employ this analogy carefully: we are not stating that the city is the only linguistic system given that, as Henri Lefebvre claims, this assumption would imply accepting "the ideology of organized consumption" (*Writings* 115). When we refer to "language," we recognize the possibilities of a system of multiple levels and dimensions (115), which is what the margin seeks to denote.

7 For a detailed analysis of the role played by tourism in the construction and development of the economy under Francoism, see *The Mobile Nation* by Tatjina Pavlović, *Destination Dictatorship* by Justin Crumbaugh, and *Spain Is (Still) Different* by Eugenia Afinoguénova and Jaume Marti-Olivella.

8 Foucault employs an analysis of sexuality to show us the construction of a new language that, through the death of God, uncovers excesses that reveal and transgress limits. In this relationship, limit and transgression do not mutually depend upon one another, and therefore limits are not destroyed. Rather, they form an infinite relationship in which identities may be reformulated. It is important to note that theirs is not a black and white relationship between opposites, but rather it is a relationship that reformulates spaces, affirming "the limitlessness into which it leaps as it opens this zone to existence for the first time" ("Preface" 35).

9 Photography is largely overlooked both by detailed studies of Barcelona such as those already mentioned here, as well as by more general introductory volumes such as Ernic Bou and Jaume Subirana's *The Barcelona Reader* or Dominic Kewon's *A Companion to Catalan Culture*. The exception that

confirms the rule is *Barcelona: La metròpoli en l'era de la fotografia, 1860–2004* (2016) [The metropolis in the era of photography], based on the exposition of the same name, which lays out a history of the urbanistic development of Barcelona and its popularity using photography. However, this book, although it offers a historical contextualization of the urban development of the city, is more a book of photography than a critical essay about the construction of the city.

1 A Change of Pace: The Spatial Dimensions of the Franco Dictatorship

1 We are referring here to Hayden White's concept of fiction in history that he presents in "The Historical Text as Literary Artifact," where the historian interprets history as a narrative construct.

2 The concept of power applied here is linked to the appearance of a society organized in a spatial matrix, as described by Michel Foucault in *Folie et Déraison: Histoire de la Folie à l'âge Classique* (1961) [*History of Madness* (2009)] and further developed in later works. That is to say, the gaze, a gaze with multiple origins that generates order (e.g., demographic, economic, political, etc.), imposes a spatial distribution of bodies that organizes and controls them, giving shape to structures of power or knowledge that produce a social domain. For Lefebvre, this organizing power is capital, which is one of the most important forces in the construction of space in Barcelona in this period, as indicated by Benjamin Fraser's analysis in *Henri Lefebvre and the Spanish Urban Experience*. In spite of the fact that we are in total agreement with this approach, here we would like to maintain a more flexible notion of power, that is, remain aware the possibility of multiple power relations that can act simultaneously upon a given space.

3 It is true that in recent years in the field of cultural studies there has been talk of an urban turn – although not necessarily using that terminology – to refer to the analyses of the construction of the city (for the most prominent example, see Benjamin Fraser). However, this book intends to go a step further: more than a mode of analysis, it is a question of how the regime perceives the creation of the nation in a material turn that affects not only the demographic and economic constitution of Spain, but also the creation of a social fabric that will encourage the creation and strengthening of urban movements.

4 Manuel Delgado's work is mainly centred on the development of public space in the post-dictatorship; however, in his analysis he develops a theory about the construction of the urban that serves us here to explain the creation of the margin and of a space for dissidence under the dictatorship. Indirectly, this connection underscores certain commonalities in the perception and understanding of public space through the adoption of a

neoliberal economy and of the effects of the dictatorship on the space of the post-dictatorship.

5 Manuel Castells identifies neighbourhood associations as the space that stimulates the creation and development of a "prolific social tissue" in a context in which civil society "had been so shunned by the State" (*City* 215). These associations maintained a close connection to democratic political objectives and even socialism, "as well as to specific interests of underground left wing parties who realized that the neighbourhood associations could provide a marvellous opportunity to reach people while allowing the parties to remain less exposed to police repression" (215). This close connection between neighbourhood associations and democratic political objectives reinforced the link between urbanism and dissent underscored in this book, where we trace the creation of this social fabric before the formation of these groups.

6 Following a decade of famine and widespread poverty, Franco's government liberalized residence laws, allowing Spaniards to move freely throughout the state. This change in the law unleashed a chain of migration towards the principle Spanish cities that increased exponentially from the end of the 1940s until Franco's death and shifted the geography of the country. For a more detailed description of the changes in demographic patterns among the Spanish population under the dictatorship, see the works of Adrian Shubert and Borja de Riquer i Permanyer. For a detailed explanation of the creation of a technocratic cabinet and the modernization of Francoist economy, see the works of Paul Preston and Tatjiana Pavlović.

7 Books like Tatjiana Pavlović's *The Mobile Nation* or Justin Crumbaugh's *Destination Dictatorship* refer to Francoism's ideological turn, substituting the regime's metaphysical self-justification with a more material one that makes the nation more profitable. In *The Mobile Nation*, which shares several points with Crumbaugh's *Destination Dicatorship* (including the links between Francoism and industrialization, and a variety of theoretical sources), Pavlović does not focus on urban or urbanistic aspects in play, choosing instead to explain the idea of a shift in national identity as a result of the adoption of neoliberal policies and economic models derived therein, with urbanistic changes largely viewed as lesser consequences of said political and economic turn.

In this context, the urban turn that I propose in this book reinforces and underscores the relevance of this political change through an emphasis on the city as a symbol of the progress and aperture promoted by the regime on a material, physical, and social level, and the unexpected consequences of this opening, one of which was the creation of social movements, as Manuel Castells proposes. The urban turn, then, is a consequence of this shift in Francoist politics and economics, but it is not just another facet of the evolving dictatorship. Rather, it is an essential feature to be taken into consideration.

Along these lines, what is a casual point of reference in these two sources, "the investment in urbanization," becomes the sticking point in the development of an identity not just at the level of Francoist representation, but also, and especially, at the street level. In both of these books, urbanism becomes part of the mythology of Francoism, as we will see forthwith; however, neither book analyses in detail to what degree this new urbanistic mythology is what enables the creation of dissent that will lead to the development of more popular democratic objectives.

In her study on how to define the relationship between culture and city in a contemporary context, Mari Paz Balibrea, following in the footsteps of Pavlović and Crumbaugh, refers to the urban transformation that has made cities into consumer goods, which can be read as the continuation of the urban policies of Francoism. This continuation can also be read in the creation of the global city as demonstrated in Edgar Illas's book, *Thinking Barcelona*, and we can likewise read Mónica Degen's *Sensing Cities* along these same lines. Like in these other sources, Degen uses the "urban turn" to stress the relevance of cities, especially Barcelona, in the development of political and cultural discourses and practices.

In this book, we trace the existence of these practices under the dictatorship, underscoring the relevance of urbanistic matters in the creation of identity-based discourses and practices, whether on the part of the regime or oppositional social and urban movements that are not necessarily directly related to the sphere of politics, as we will explain later.

8 As Nathan Richardson has already noted in *Constructing Spain*, the regime saw in the city the origins of a Marxist revolution backed by a proletariat that was corrupted by the depravity of the city, creating the oversimplification of the goodness of country life versus the wickedness of the city, a position made untenable by the urban turn of large swaths of the population in the 1950s (5–10).

9 The development of cities during Franco's dictatorship has been viewed in relation to subjects such as tourism or economics; for different perspectives, see Crumbaugh and Pavlović. For an approach to the construction of the city as cultural capital, see Balibrea and Illas.

10 As Richardson indicates, this year saw a change in the make-up of the Francoist ranks, in which ministers were technocrats, professionals chosen more for their educational and work experience than for their ideological allegiance. This shift leaves out the popular discourse of the first decade of Francoism and gives way to a material reality rooted in an economic revolution (52). For more on this shift in the make-up of the government, see Preston; Castells, *The City and the Grassroots*; Crumbaugh; and Pavlović.

11 Francoist urbanism was characterized by, in the words of Manuel Castells, "the right of the state to decide on the use of most land, channeling speculation through the patronage system of Franquist bureaucracy" (*City* 218). Keeping with this nepotistic policy, Porcioles "constantly favored the ruling classes through underhanded policies, provided total immunity to real estate speculators, and administered the municipal government with autocratic rule" (Illas 46). This period of nepotistic abuse that took shape mainly in the destruction of the urban and social fabric of Barcelona is known as *porciolisme*, which was characterized by anarchic capitalism that destroyed the city with "high-rise housing and expressways which snaked around and over any attempts to submit it to rational planning criteria," favouring the elite of Barcelona, who grew richer with the help of a "city counsil completely removed from any democratic supervision, the rotten underbelly of Franco's morality crusade" (McNeill 115).

In the face of this critical discourse, Robert Hughes makes the following claim: "It is de rigueur today to blame Porcioles and, through him, Franquism itself for everything that went wrong with the urban structure and services of Barcelona between the end of the war and 1975, as though the Caudillo's ideology had some unique power to degrade a city that other political systems did not possess. But the truth is that neither the capitalist nations ... nor the Marxists regimes ... did much better than the ritually loathed Porcioles in the domain of urbanism" (14). While this claim is accurate albeit incomplete, given that urbanistic exploitation is rooted in the adoption of a capitalistic economic system, the connection between the regime and the urbanistic development of Barcelona by a state-directed closed circle of power, in addition to the use of cities as the focal point for the development of a national identity that oppressed its citizens through its use of space, justifies this correspondence between urbanistic failure and Francoism in the context that presently concerns us.

For a detailed description of the abusive urbanism of these decades, see McNeill (114–17), or the studies by Martín Perán and Dolors Genovès.

12 What Barthes describes here corresponds to the image with which Michel de Certeau opens his chapter in *The Practice of Everyday Life* titled "Walking in the City," where he describes the view from the top of the World Trade Center. Like in Barthes' text, this view contrasts with what is happening below on the street, "A wave of verticals. Its agitation is momentarily arrested. The gigantic mass is immobilized before the eyes" (91). The gaze becomes important not just for the direct observation that it enables, but also, returning to Foucault, because it collects and organizes information through which structures of power or knowledge create the modern individual. It is the fiction of knowledge that de Certeau spoke about and which contrasts with the unpredictable movement of passersby.

Building upon the theories developed by Henri Lefebvre, Richard Sennett, and Jane Jabobs among others, this contrast allows Manuel Delgado to differentiate between the city – the material disposition of stable constructions – and the urban – the uncontrollable movement that generates the speech of the city's inhabitants in such a way that they infiltrate actions unplanned and unanticipated by urban policies (*Sociedades* 11 and *El animal* 23). Although Manuel Vázquez Montalbán constructs his "Barcelonas" from a more urbanistic than urban point of view, he also recognizes the contrast between these two ways of seeing/constructing the city and announces "el desordre legítim de la vida, al marge de codis hipòcrites – admirables, això sí – de la bellesa" (*Barcelones* 319) [the legitimate disorder of life, apart from hypocritical – but of course admirable – codes of beauty]. In our case, both points of view will be essential and the idea of the margin proposed here comes, as we have seen, from the conjunction of both structures.

13 See also Delgado, *Sociedades* 11–12. When Cerdà designed the Eixample, he had in mind the implications of movement and kept transit and circulation at the centre of his project. Nevertheless, he reduced it to a simple physical structure. For more on Cerdà's project, see the works of Fraser; Joan Ramon Resina; and Brad Epps.

14 Morcillo's thesis is based on the concept of the neo-baroque, used to establish a direct relationship between the baroque and the present that made National Catholicism into the ideological substrate of the dictatorship following the Allies' victory in the Second World War, thus establishing the notion of a mystic body resulting from the symbolic union of the national body and the state with the blessing of Spanish Catholic traditions. Like in the baroque period, National Catholicism made Franco the head of the state – a role assigned to the king in the early modern period – which made him an important ally of the Catholic Church during the Counter-Reformation. In exchange, the Church granted legitimacy to the regime, making a bodily whole in which the Church is the heart and soul, and Franco was able to silence internal critiques by referencing tradition and religion in order to demonstrate that Spain was special, that it had its own destiny to pursue separate from the rest of Western Europe (16–26).

15 Eduard Moreno explains how the organization of the territory by parts benefits land speculation: "La planificación es el enemigo del especulador y del estraperlista, porque no les interesa el espacio planificado previamente, sino la revalorización constante del territorio mediante su intervención en la clasificación del suelo" (Vázquez Montalbán and Moreno 44) [planning is the enemy of the speculator and black marketeer, because they are not interested in previously planned space, but rather the constant revaluation of territory by their intervention in the classification of land"]. As we will

see, attempts at general urbanistic planning are subordinate to a perception of absolute space that depends on new capitalist interests, leading the general plans to failure or reshaping into piecemeal plans.

16 Although Santiáñez acknowledges that Francoism is founded on this conception of absolute space, he emphasizes that, in regard to the fascist politics of space, relative space-time (a function of movement and behaviour that establishes the discursivity of place through its usage) and relational space-time (performativity, the space and time produced by human and social processes) were more dominant. For the fascists, relative space-time meant the space of the political tactics used to complete certain objectives and the strategic plans that aimed to create an absolute space. That is, these two types of spaces were often functions of an absolute space whose stability could only be achieved by the instability that they provided.

17 The Francoist utopia of the countryside as the origin of the true Spanish nation was expressly declared in the Falange's twenty-seven-point manifesto: "vivero permanente de España" (point 17) [Spain's permanent breeding ground]. Vázquez Montalbán explains it in the following way: "el campo es donde se ha refugiado la España verdadera, y en cambio la ciudad ha sido el infierno, el lugar donde enraizaban las ideas que han disuelto la idea de nación, la idea de Estado, la idea de patria" (Vázquez Montalbán and Moreno 28) [the countryside is where the true Spain has taken refuge, whereas the city has become hell, the place where ideas that have dissolved the idea of nation, State, and homeland have taken root]. This discursive issue also has a material and practical reason for being: "Además, ha de pensarse que la ciudad es laberíntica, y es muy difícil de controlar ideológicamente, mientras que el campo es mucho más fácil, y lo han hecho a través de la Iglesia y de la Guardia Civil" (29) [Besides, it should be noted that the city is labyrinthine, and very difficult to control ideologically, whereas in the countryside it is much easier, and they have taken control with the Church and the Civil Guard]. This notion of the city as a labyrinth is precisely what substantiates the rationale of the urban centre and its margins, although at the same time it will be what enables concealment and secrecy through spatial movements.

18 The General Proposal for Urban Planning only affected Madrid and its outskirts; however, it serves us here to point out the discursive turn reflected in urbanistic practice. In Barcelona, because it is not the capital, we do not find a monumentalizing urbanism, although the city did undergo an "aggrandizement" on a symbolic level, with the imposition of monuments or nomenclature aimed at ideological reconstruction. The city was "punished" for its Republican affiliation and no improvements were made to it until the 1950s, leaving ruins as material witnesses of the ideological and cultural sins of the vanquished (Richardson 33). Reforms, when made,

were to be "ejemplo de urbanismo dedicado a la vivienda, irracional y especulativo" (Moreno and Vázquez Montalbán 49) [an example of irrational and speculative urbanism devoted to housing]. The Regional Plan of 1953 was the first attempt to confront the new urbanistic reality of Barcelona, although it was preceded by the creation of services such as the Servicio de Represión del Barraquismo (1949) [Service for the Repression of Slums], enacted by the city hall of Barcelona in order to tamp down on the expansion of slums.

19 In 1959, in his speech during the plenary session of the courts where the Plan de Urgencia Social [Plan on Social Needs] was presented, Arrese said: "el hombre, cuando no tiene hogar, se apodera de la calle y, empujado por su mal humor, se hace subversivo, agrio, violento …" (qtd. in Naredo 19) [man, when he does not have a home, takes over the street and, driven by his foul mood, becomes subversive, bitter, violent …]. This comment allows us to see the direct relationship between space and social problems.

20 In 1949 the Servicio de Represión del Barraquismo [Service for the Repression of Slums] was created in order to combat the increase in the number of slums; it exercised its mandate by counting and placing identification plaques on extant slums, which allowed it to identify and then demolish any new ones that cropped up (although it did also establish the right of transfer for sanctioned slums). In spite of their illegality, slums held a sort of ambiguous status: even when their presence was undesirable, they paid taxes when they were built on municipally owned land or fees when built on private land, which in a certain way acknowledged the need for the workforce that they housed.

21 During the 1940s, the regime was ambivalent with regard to prostitution. On the one hand, it saw prostitution as a necessary evil, "a healthy outlet for natural male desires" (Morcillo 92), but with the other hand it demonized prostitutes, whose bodies were seen to debase the pure and chaste bodies of "True Catholic Women and the future mothers of the New Spain" (92).

22 As Morcillo explains, "by decree of March 3, 1956, the regime moved officially from tolerance to the abolition of prostitution … The law made prostitution illegal. Article 1, if you read its justification, was enacted to 'ensure women's dignity and the interest of social morality,'" which highlights the creation of a legal framework tied to Catholic values to give shape to an absolute space of unquestionable truth.

23 During the Republic, the discourse on marginal zones was similar to what we have seen with Franco or Arrese. The GATCPAC (Grup d'Arquitectes i Tècnics Catalans per al Progrés de l'Arquitectura Contemporània) [Group of Catalonian Architects and Technicians for the Progress of Contemporary Architecture] was charged with elaborating a plan for the renewal

of the Raval, which was known as the Pla Macià and conceived of as a collaboration between Le Corbusier and Josep Lluís Sert, who called this neighbourhood a "cáncer barcelonés" (Fernández González 107) [a cancer on Barcelona]. The answers they came up with continued to be based on sanitization and reducing the density of buildings in the neighbourhood, "destruyendo trama urbana y patrimonio habitacional" [destroying urban cohesiveness and housing patrimony] based on a proposal that "[esta-blecía] como premisas la socialización del suelo" (109) [established as its premise the socialization of land].

Le Corbusier's maxim, "Arquitectura o revolución. La revolución puede evitarse" [Architecture or revolution. Revolution can be avoided], reminds us of the premises behind Barón Haussman's project in Paris or Ildefons Cerdà's in Barcelona, premises that are resumed under Franco's regime (Fernández González 109 and Richardson 11) by recurring, as Harvey explains, to an organization of social and physical space favourable to the accumulation of capital (*Urban* 29). The same happens with the construction of housing complexes far from the city centre: already during the 1930s there was a saturated housing market, in which supply could not keep up with demand and the traditional housing market separated from working-class housing, creating a form of substandard housing that eventually led to an increase in slums. One of the solutions proffered was the destruction of the slums and the construction of socially urgent housing in the form of *polígonos* [public housing complexes], such as the Casas Baratas, which housed metro and Exposition of 1929 workers who lived in the slums of Montjuïc and would soon be characterized by some politicians as "barracas de cemento" [cement slums] (Tatjer 46). These same characteristics will be seen in practices of the regime that, on various occasions, even take up the reform plans initiated during the Republic, which emphasizes the perception of urbanism as a tool bereft of political connotations.

24 We have already mentioned the urbanistic continuity between projects undertaken by the Republic and Francoism. Aesthetically and urbanistically speaking, we see an opening and connection with European trends conceived of as politically neutral and, therefore, ripe for importation into the Spain of that time. Prime examples of the urbanism developed under the dictatorship include the aforementioned urbanistic influence of the Republic's projects, as is the case with the Pla Macià, or European projects in neighbourhoods in Berlin and Paris. Xavier Subias, the architect who designed Barcelona's city hall and in 1956 developed the Plan Comarcal [Regional Plan] and the Plan de la Diagonal Norte [Diagonal North Plan], acknowledged the influence of the Pla Macià in the development of these projects. To design city hall, he travelled to Berlin to see the Hansa district, although it would prove very difficult to adapt to Barcelona: "But we had

the forerunner of what is, for me, Le Corbusier's best work in urban planning: the plan for this area, drawn up together with Sert, part of the Macià Plan" (181). Possible political connotations of these concepts are eliminated by the insistence upon a supposedly neutral discourse and practice based on social needs.

25 For more on the influence of artistic trends, in particular in the editorial world and the figure of Castellet, on the social make-up of Francoist Spain, see Pavlović.

26 For more on this connection, see Castells, *The City and the Grassroots*.

27 For more on this connection, see Castells' "The Making of an Urban Social Movement" in *The City and the Grassroots*.

28 Phillip E. Wegner, in "Spatial Criticism: Critical Geography, Space, Place, and Textuality," has observed that Lefebvre's theory differs from other theoretical traditions on space in that "space is itself never constituted [as] a singularity," but that it is polyvalent and constituted by a "dialectally interwoven matrix" of human interactions (qtd. in Tally 118). Here the urban element is emphasized in how space is constituted not by material but rather by the action that unfolds within that materiality.

29 This link between public space and art is relevant if we keep in mind that the margin becomes visible due to the application of an artistic form, whether literature or photography. It is especially interesting in this case because it reveals the essential connections between space and practice, space and everyday life, and space and body, and it also reveals a city that is constituted, as Deutsche explains, following Raymond Ledrut, by "la interacción e integración de diferentes prácticas" ("Uneven" 128) [the interaction and integration of different practices].

2 Breaking the Silence: The Cultural Mobilization of Francisco Candel

1 For a detailed description of the Regional Plan, see Fernando de Terán; Ferrer ("El Pla"); and Joan Busquets.

2 Torres Clavé is referring to one of the groups of "cases barates" [cheap houses] built during the first great wave of immigration to Barcelona to house workers that moved to the city to work on the World's Fair of 1929 and the construction of the subway. The rationale for mentioning this example, in spite of it not coinciding chronologically, is to show how this type of construction is part of the history of material and geographical precariousness that precedes it.

3 As Manuel Vázquez Montalbán explains, while the Regional Plan sought to create a city of services by reassessing certain areas, completing unfinished features, creating thoroughfares, and moving industry into the metropolitan area, subsequent assessments in the 1960s and 1970s took a

different track, characterized by taking over previously restricted green areas, building over areas designated as gardens or other features, increasing urban congestion, and destroying the internal logic of the city with the construction of high speed thoroughfares (*Barcelones* 249).

4 For example, the Obra Sindical del Hogar [House Trade Union], a state entity that managed the construction of "unidades vecinales de absorción" [neighbourhood units of absorption] explicitly allocated for the absorption of slums, demarcated the needed land in marginal zones that were located far from the city, unsuitable for building and urbanization because of humidity, steep slopes, and inconsistent earth, and almost always not for sale because they were designated green areas or open terrain. None of these reasons were impediments to construction, which consequently led to the urban and social isolation of the complexes (Ferrer, "Barraques" 70–1).

5 In fact, the Regional Plan of 1953 attempted to regulate the advent and construction of housing complexes, but even still it was overrun by rampant speculation that sought to maximize the land that makes a city a lucrative investment (Borja, "Ciudadanía"). Only with the General Metropolitan Plan (1976) do we find attempts to regulate speculation and create a coordinated urban policy of intervention in urban space that goes beyond the centralized control and social assistance of the 1950s and abandons the tentative rhetoric of the urbanistic development of the 1960s that, apart from the legitimization of existing chaos, had little or no effect (193). This plan would result in part from the consolidation of the interventions of neighbourhood associations (Calavita and Ferrer 798), in whose make-up Francisco Candel would find an essential protagonist.

6 Fabre and Huertas Calvería explain how the Church would send students from well-to-do families to catechize immigrants (354), and Genís Sinca talks about the "señoritas de las conferencias" [young ladies of the conferences], "senyores d'alt standing que en un moment donat van voler baixar al suburbi per ocupar-se dels pobres ... per a elles, era com anar a civilitzar una colla de salvatges, i es prenien com a missió el fet d'assegurar l'assitència dels immgrants i treballadors a missa, o apropar a l'Església les ovelles esgarriades, com a únic camí plausible ... per a la salvació divina" (86–7) [high-ranking ladies who at one time wanted to go down to the suburbs to take care of the poor ... for them it was like going to civilize a group of savages, and they took as their mission assuring the attendance of immigrants and workers at mass, or drawing the devastated sheep into the Church, as the only plausible path ... to divine salvation].

In spite of this claim, the role of the Church is much more complex. It is true that its initial role, especially in the early years of the dictatorship, was to impose a moral code on the city's inhabitants; however, isolated figures that break from this trend would begin to appear. Fabre and Huertas

Clavería talk about an emerging young and progressive clergy who will go to the suburbs to support the workers, not with a paternalistic spirit but rather as part of a collective awareness that was taking shape at that moment (354). For his part, in *Donde la ciudad cambia su nombre* (1957) [Where the city changes its name] Candel highlights the figure of Mosen Jaume Cuspinera (Mosen Lloveras) whose actions contrast, for example, with those of the Hermandad Obrera de Acción Católica (HOAC) [Brotherhood of Workers of Catholic Action], showing the independent spirit of these young people towards the regulations imposed on them by the Church.

7 This article was originally published in *Solidaridad Nacional* on 27 January 1957. Although the source cited here is in Catalan, it was originally published in Spanish.

8 As Tatjer explains, in spite of this critique, years later Bohigas would allow himself to be seduced by the optics of the functionalist urbanism heavily suffused with a sanitizing and modernizing discourse that began to pervade Porcioles's city, driven by the initiative of new real estate agents – large agencies connected to foreign capital – and the special plan for organizing the southwest zone of Montjuïc (1964). In this plan, Bohigas no longer spoke of keeping "las alegres barracas de hojalata y ladrillo" [the cheerful tin and brick slums], but rather opted for their eradication and the transfer of their inhabitants to remote and poorly designed housing complexes that were nothing like the "zonas residenciales entre cuyos verdes vayan a jugar nuestros hijos" (Tatjer 58) [residential zones among whose greenery our children will play].

9 Vázquez Montalbán mentions the work of architects and urban planners such as Salvador Tarragó, Helio Piñón, and Ignasi Solà-Morales, the journalism of local correspondents in the late 1960s in *El Correo Catalán*, with critics like Josep Maria Huertas Clavería, Rafael Padras, Jaume Fabre, and Josep Martí Gómez, and architecture schools that express their critiques through publications such as *CAU (Construcción, Arquitectura y Urbanismo)* or *Cuadernos de Arquitectura (Barcelones* 250–51).

10 *La providència es diu Paco* is the title of the biography of Candel that Genís Sinca published in 2008, in which he refers to the indispensability of the figure of Candel "per fer de mitjancer de conflictes entre ambdues comunitats" (181) [to become a mediator of conflicts between the two communities].

11 Candel's bibliography is vast. For a detailed list, see Sinca.

12 For more on this reading of Candel, see, for example, Resina, the works of Joan Gilabert, or Najat El Hachmi's introduction to *Els altres*.

13 Here Candel is talking about the article, "Els altres catalans," which was published in the magazine *La jirafa* in 1958 under the same title as his future book.

14 Candel's marginality also extends to what Joan Gilabert describes as "in-
dependencia ideológica" [ideological independence] – "que en los años
cincuenta también lo era estética" [which in the 1950s was also aesthetic] –
that prevents him from "comulgar con los preceptos del realismo social,
sobre todo en lo referente a la idealización de las clases oprimidas" ("La
obra" 101) [communing with the precepts of social realism, especially in
regards to the idealization of the oppressed classes]. For a reflection on the
particulars of Candel's social realism, see Gilabert, "Aspectos peculiares."
15 It is an intrusion also because it is a gaze that breaks the pact of coexistence accepted among neighbours. In *¡Dios, la que se armó!*, Candel explains
the problems he had following the publication of *Donde la ciudad cambia su
nombre* with the neighbours of Casa Antúnez, who threatened and sued
him for portraying them in his novel. As he acknowledges in that book, he
limited himself to "contar unos hechos que eran del dominio público y no
particulares, unos hechos de los que todo el vecindario decía que en una
novela estarían bien y tendrían mucha gracia ... el Candel se sintió como
cronista oficial de la ciudad" (11) [telling events that were part of the public domain and not at all specific, events that everyone in the neighbourhood said would be okay in a novel and would be very funny ...
Candel felt like the official chronicler of the city]. However, "uno de los
defectos básicos del Candel fue que escribió este libro más de cara a los
plutócratas que a los miserables, olvidándose por completo de que éstos
también tienen su corazoncito, su amor propio y su honrilla. El libro sobre
ellos no era para ellos" (12) [one of Candel's basic flaws was that he wrote
this book for plutocrats rather than the poor, completely forgetting that
the latter also have a heart, self-love, and pride. This book about them was
not for them]. Here Candel disclosed intimate details of the private life of
the neighbourhood when he exposed it to the city, breaking an implicit
contract agreed upon by the residents of Casa Atúnez, which emphasizes
the voyeuristic characterization that we were mentioning, bringing us to
another element to take into consideration: the imposition Candel's voice
over the neighbourhood.
16 Joan Gilabert, Rosa Rull, and Manuel Abellán agree that Candel was one of
the writers "más victimizados y censurados durante los años de la dictadura franquista ... no sólo por no ser propagador de 'buenas costumbres'
sino por otras razones que se confabularon para que así fuera" (Gilabert,
"La obra" 100) [most victimized and censored during the years of Franco's
dictatorship ... not only for not propagating "good habits" but for other
reasons that they invented to keep him down]. Candel himself acknowledged as much in an interview where he said that "con Alfonso Sastre, yo
fui, dicen, el escritor más censurado ... De una novela envió la censura la
siguiente recomendación: 'suprímase de la página 1 a la 200'. ¡Y la novela

tenía 200 páginas!" ("El escritor") [together with Alfonso Sastre, I was, so they say, the most censored writer ... Regarding one novel, the censor's office sent the following recommendation: "delete pages 1–200." The novel was 200 pages long!].

All of Candel's works published during the dictatorship were censored, and some of them, like *Ser obrero no es ninguna ganga* (1964) [Being working class is no bargain], were seized and not published until the 1970s (Fabre and Huertas Clavería 17). He was censored as much for his social critique as for his political commentary: in *Han matado*, along with his depiction of police actions, all mention of living conditions and the slums were deleted. The suppression of this information allows us to see the connection between urban/urbanistic space and political discourse, especially in how the former plays a key role in the formation and application of the latter over the populace.

Apart from *Ser obrero no es ninguna ganga*, where the urbanistic is not as prominent as in earlier works, this connection between space and discourse stands out for the importance of the urban in the constitution of space and a social class that will later be the base for the resurgence of social movements and political parties that will be key during the Transition. The regime was all too aware of this connection, and thus suppressed details related to the suburbs in Candel's writing.

17 Here Candel is making a play on words with street names that, in their residents' speech, take on a sharply heightened tone, becoming insults. I have not been able to conceive of an English translation that captures this linguistic sinuosity.

18 Although *Els altres* is the book that made Candel famous and came to characterize critics' and the public's understanding of his work, his prior writings had already developed in great detail these same social themes that would be at the heart of these essays.

19 Already in *Han matado*, Candel describes the demolition of the slums, but it was deleted by the censor's office. Candel included it in *Els altres* years later (217–19), although it is difficult to determine if it appears in the first edition or not until the complete edition of 2008 (in any case, *Han matado* was published unabridged in 1984). I am interested in stressing, however, how in 1959 Candel was already elaborating this critique based on the humanization of the suburbs, even though he was always aware of the neutrality he needed to pursue in order to be able to publish:

> Ja sabem que són els necessaris tràmits burocràtics els qui no tenen cor, i no les persones competents. Que cal sacrificar l'individu i els seus sentimentes pel bé de la societat ... El món funciona així. Deixant de banda que no es respecti el sentimentalisme que pot haver-hi en el fet que cadascú hagi agafat afecte al barri on viu i li dolgui deixar-lo. (*Els altres* 219–20)

We already know that required bureaucratic procedures have no heart, not competent people. We know that we have to sacrifice the individual and his feelings for the good of society ... That's how the world works. Leaving aside the fact that we don't respect the sentimentality that can be found in our attachment to the neighbourhoods where we live and how much it hurts to leave them.

Be that as it may, Candel attempts to question that neutrality by emphasizing the daily living that informs the experience of the slum dwellers, carefully and subtlety criticizing the city's actions. In this way, precariousness becomes the point of contact between city and suburb: if the city imposes order and control through its urbanistic practice concerning the suburbs and the bodies that inhabit them, the only way to counteract that power is through that same language, placing it also at the core of its identity.

20 Ignasi Riera talks about a "pensament fluctuant, sempre provisional, basat en una comprensió, creixent però parcial, d'una realitat que evoluciona" (56) [fluctuating, always provisional thought, based on a growing but limited understanding, of an evolving reality]. The main issue in *Els altres*, whose genesis is in the article published in *La Jirafa* in 1958, continued to evolve in subsequent editions of the book (1963–2008), and in *Encara més sobre el altres catalans* (1973) [Even more about the other Catalans] and *Els altres catalans 20 anys després* (1985) [The other Catalans twenty years later]. Nevertheless, the topic dealt with in these essays was already being cultivated in *Donde la ciudad cambia su nombre* (1957) and *Han matado a un hombre, han roto un paisaje* (1959).

21 In a certain respect, this connection can be associated with the idea of "collective consumption" elaborated in *The Urban Question* by Manuel Castells, who claims it as the catalyst for social transformations in the city because it pushes citizens to fight for what they are due in terms of material structure. Castells elaborates this theory in order to challenge the concept of "urban struggle," which differentiates among urban problems using a conceptualization that ignores the political and economic specificity underlying urban concerns (376).

22 Candel did not just turn eyes away from the city and towards "el olvidado suburbio" (*Dios* 141) [the forgotten suburbs], but following the controversy with *Dios* he managed to acquire benefits for the Port clinic. As far as the creation of an identity is concerned, Candel became the point of articulation of voices emanating from the suburbs: he is the "personatge solució" [solution character], as Sinca explains (157), but above all, he is the one who records and documents the difficulties and will to live of those who live in these neighbourhoods.

23 It could be claimed that this humanistic turn is also found in the cycle of talks organized in Barcelona under the title *Los suburbios 1957: Compendio*

de las ponencias y coloquios desarrollados durante la "Semana" the same year
that *Donde* was published. The introduction to those talks explains that
"la importancia que dimos al urbanismo durante nuestra Semana, al con-
siderar que éste condiciona así mismo el problema de la vivienda, dice el
Papa: 'el problema de la vivienda, antes que técnico, es humano. La construcción de las casas y el trazado de las urbes no se pueden separar del
concepto de que el hombre y la familia son sus destinatarios'" (Duocastella
6) [the importance that we confer upon urbanism during our Week, by
considering how it conditions the housing problem, is explained by the
Pope: "the problem of housing is more a human problem than a technical one. The construction of houses and the layout of metropolitan areas
cannot be separated from the concept that men and their families are their
beneficiaries"].

    There are two key differences between Candel's approach and the one
developed in *Los suburbios 1957*. First, the latter upholds the legitimacy
of the dictatorship's discourse and practice of absolute space through the
evangelizing fervour of the church, which seeks to implement and impose
a lifestyle instead of analysing everyday practices to figure out what needs
are going unmet: "de no mediar una paciente y eficaz labor evangeliza-
dora de los suburbianos durante su proceso de transformación humana,
ésta se produciría en sentido negativo y dificultaría enormemente, para
lo sucesivo, 'su verdadera integración ciudadana en el Reino común de
todos los hijos de Dios'" (Duocastella 7) [if there is not a patient and effi-
cient evangelization of suburban residents during their process of human
transformation, this process will be carried out in an negative way and in
the future will greatly complicate "the true integration of citizens into the
common Kingdom of all God's children"]. Second, the latter ignores the
voice of the suburbs, since all of its analysis and conclusions are drawn
from elements unconnected to and outside of the suburbs, citing as its
principal source to resolve their problems "la caridad cristiana" (Jubany 9)
[Christian charity], which only reinforces the dissolution of agency mentioned by Candel in *Els altres*. Nevertheless, we would be remiss not to acknowledge the analytical contribution made by this conference as an early
effort to acknowledge the suburbs and increase their visibility.

24 The comparison to this journal is revealing for what it tells us about
Candel and how he gets inserted as a crucial step in the logical evolution
of this matter. In the 1940s, *CAU*'s content was mainly architectural, focused on project memoirs. As Amparo Bernal López-Sanvicente describes,
the journal privileged photographs and graphic documentation of blueprints over critical analysis (16). This approach makes sense if we keep in
mind that it is not until the 1950s that we begin to see the appearance of
urbanistically influenced projects in the form of housing complexes, which

is to say, until that moment they were thinking in terms of architectural interventions rather than in urbanistic concerns. Developments rushed due to scarcity of resources and rampant speculation led to the disillusionment of architects and a change in the journal's editorial slant, as it turned to critical analysis. It was not until the 1960s that the journal begin to consider the human element in these construction projects. Be that as it may, if we consider Candel's writings, we can see how the author takes the initiative both in instituting a critical approach specifically to the complexes and also in considering the human element at play in their construction, ignored by professionals until the 1960s. It is not until Candel opens the door to the suburbs that they really start to be considered by approaches that differ from the urbanistic proposals of the time.

25 As we can already see in Elke Sturm-Trigonakis's study, *Barcelona: La novela urbana 1944–1988* – to mention only one among many (gathered by Carles Carreras Verdaguer in *La Barcelona literaria*) – Candel is not the first to have Barcelona as a protagonist. However, the novels analysed by these types of critical studies are centred on the city, not the suburbs, and focus more on the urban rather than the urbanistic, and, although there is no doubt that they contain a critique of the system, in them the limits of the nineteenth-century city remain intact.

26 It should be mentioned that the Special Plan for Montjuïc did not go anywhere: "nunca fue aprobado por el Ayuntamiento y chocaba con la oposición del Servicio de Parques y Jardines, que defendía el carácter de parque y de zona verde de la montaña" [it was never approved by City Hall and was met with the opposition of the Park and Garden Service, which defended Montjuïc as a park and green area on the mountain], while also clashing with the "propuestas vecinales para mejorar los barrios de barracas que se habían desarrollado durante esas fechas" (Tatjer 58–9) [neighbourhood proposals to improve the slums that had flourished at that time]. Apart from the humanistic turn of Bohigas, who no longer defended "las alegres barracas" [the happy slums], in the attempt to reclassify the area from green zone to construction zone we can see evidence of the speculative tendencies that prevailed during Porcioles' term as mayor.

27 Resina explains how the appearance of new technology, the train in this case, modifies the way in which the city is visualized: "But from mid-century on, the train ride made it possible to bring the nation's concrete totality into the visual field. The nation is not so much an imagined community, in Benedict Anderson's catchy turn of phrase, as the community contemplated from an inclusive horizon whose ultimate metaphor is the bird's-eye view. The moment is liminal" (*Barcelona's* 12).

In Candel's case, this modification is produced by the interaction between both ways of creating collectivity, a result of the urban turn already in progress when *Donde* is published. Additionally, with Candel we find a proximity that we do not see in that trip on the train and which corresponds to the epistemological turn that we will see later in photography: the insertion of authors in the world surrounding them, which displaces liminality to the lens and, by extension, the body.

As Ignasi Riera explains in his brief biography of Candel: "Home que escriu, home que xerra, home que medita. I, per damunt de tot, home que passeja. Com sabia també Josep Pla ... un país no pot ser conegut en cotxe, sinó a peu. El 'vol gallinaci' dels cotxes, expressió de Josep Pla que ha fet seva C.J. Cela, ofereix únicament una realitat superficial, sense el contacte dels cinc sentits amb l'espai concret" (14) [A man who writes, a man who talks, a man who thinks. And, above all, a man who walks. Just like Josep Pla knew ... you can't get to know a country by car, only on foot. The "chicken flight" of cars, an expression of Josep Pla's that C.J. Cela has made his own, only offers a superficial reality without the contact of the five senses in concrete space].

28 Apart from the censorship office's action taken against Candel's work, there are many examples that brand his literary production as vulgar or inadequate for the reading public of that time. It suffices to cite as an example the journal *Ecclesia*, which declared the novel *Han matado* "no recomendable y contraria a los preceptos morales del catolicismo" (qtd. in Riera 90) [not recommendable and against the moral precepts of Catholicism"].

29 To cite one example among many, this quotation will suffice: "El Candel, un día que paseando por las Casas Baratas entró en casa del Paquirri, encontró a su padre el Flamenco con el libro en la mano desternillándose de risa, esto es: rompiéndose las ternillas. 'Pero si todo esto es verdad, ¡cla, cla! Pero si todo lo que cuentas aquí es la pura verdad, ¡cla, cla! Pero si esto es la monda, ¡cla, cla! El Candel, que siempre quiso hacer una literatura sencilla y fácil de entender, de cara al pueblo, entonces hubiera deseado escribir en chino ...'" (*Dios* 25) [One day walking through the Casas Baratas, Candel went into Paquirri's house and found his father Flamenco book in hand cracking up with laughter, really splitting his sides. "But all this is true, sure, sure! But everything you tell here is the pure truth, sure, sure! But this is a riot, sure, sure! Candel always wanted to write literature that was simple and easy to understand, for the people, so he would have liked to write in Chinese ..."] (*Dios* 25).

30 Candel conceived of his second novel already from the title as a world that disclosed the heterogeneity and difference of the suburb with respect to the city: "*Donde la ciudad cambia su nombre*, al principio no se llamó *Donde la ciudad cambia su nombre*, sino *El Dado* ... [que] eran diversas caras del azar de un mundo abigarrado y confuso, o una martingala, así" (*Dios* 14) [*Where the City Changes Its Name* at first wasn't called *Where the City Changes Its*

Name, it was called *Dice* … they were the different faces of chance in a jumbled and confusing world, or a trick, something like that"]. The lack of order and linearity, but also the idea of presence, are stressed here.

31 In his quarrel with historian Antoni Jutglar, who accused him of reducing the problem of immigration to Barcelona as a question of "culture" and not class, Candel had this to say: "Let's not confuse the right to a culture, a language, certain forms of collective life, which are local and rooted rights, with the right to absolute equality and the defense of the working class, international rights that here [in Spain] are national rights and only if Catalonia enjoyed some form of autonomy would then be Catalan rights, but only then" (*Encara més* 241, trans. and qtd. in Resina, *Barcelona's* 159). In this warning, we can see how the identity question is immersed in an urban dialectic in which the construction of a local environment enables the formation of a civil society.

32 It is true that Costa and Ros locate the origin of this identity in the actions that resulted from neighbourhood protests and mobilizations against municipal indifference and ineffectiveness in the Franco era, invigorating social life. However, in order to instigate these actions, first the residents of these neighbourhoods needed to become united by an identity that grouped them under a singular collective conscience that energized them. This is where Candel comes into play.

33 Candel's exceptionalism is manifestly expressed in this anecdote told by Vázquez Montalbán:

> [Q]uan Porcioles arriba a l'alcaldia, substuint alcaldes per fer bonic o de compromís, Barcelona no té moviments socials i quan algun periodista com Luis Marsillach gosa criticar les "cases barates" que formen part de l'obra social de l'habitatge protegida pel règim, el mateix governador civil, Acedo Colunga, el crida a capítol i el maltracta de paraula i obra. Aquesta lamentable arquitectura d'urgència, destinada a un client que agraïa qualsevol sostre i no estava en condicions culturals d'oposar-hi objeccions estètiques, forma part de les ruïnes contemporànies de la ciutat." (*Barcelones* 251).

> [W]hen Porcioles became mayor, replacing mayors to play nice or because he had committed to it, Barcelona had no social movements, and when a journalist like Luis Marsillach dared to criticize the "Cheap Houses" that were part of the regime's social program to protect housing, the same civil governor, Acedo Colunga, scolded him and mistreated him in word and deed. This lamentable emergency architecture, destined for a customer who would be grateful for any roof over his head and was in no position to make aesthetic objections, is part of the contemporary ruins of the city.

Here Vázquez Montalbán is referring to the brief article published by Luis Marsillach in *Solidaridad Nacional*, "Las casas de papel" [Paper houses]. In this article, Marsillach criticizes speculation and the resulting low quality of the houses built in the Verdún neighbourhood. This anecdote is revealing because in it we can see Candel's exceptionalism: Marsillach directly criticizes the regime, while Candel, also a critic of speculation and thus indirectly the actions taken and approved by the city, bases his critique on the needs of the suburbs, again, on the alleged neutrality of urbanism. As we have already mentioned before, this does not make him immune to censorship, but it does create a path for inclusion and critique from the suburbs, using the same discourse being developed by the city.

34 For a detailed analysis of how this search for integration works in Candel's texts, see Resina and the articles written by Joan Gilabert, who together with Rosa Rull is the only critic that has analysed the author's work in detail.

3 The Quiet Revolution of Photography: The Barcelona of Joan Colom

1 *Barcelona, ¿a dónde vas?* was in fact the first book published by the Dirosa publishing house, which fomented political debate along different fronts in order to promote free thought in Spain as it was coming out of Francoism. Created in 1974, Dirosa issued this first volume to criticize municipal corruption and urbanistic speculation in Porcioles' Barcelona. This debate fed into the discourse of plurality in Spain, which is indicative of the close relationship between urban space, identity, and social and political dissidence. The publication of this book unleashed a long battle over publishing and politics, with intense pressure exerted by Arias Navarro's government.

2 Two notable books on these subjects are, respectively, *Tots els barris de Barcelona* [All of Barcelona's neighbourhoods], which he co-authored with Jaume Fabre, and *Barcelona en lluïta* [*Disputed Barcelona*], although these represent only a fraction of the author's writing on Barcelona. For a detailed bibliography, see *Josep M. Huertas Clavería i els barris de Barcelona* [Josep M. Huertas Clavería and the neighbourhoods of Barcelona].

3 In Marsé's *Últimas tardes con Teresa* [Last afternoons with Teresa], panoramic views split Barcelona in two, and the mobility of its characters between these two spaces is connected to their place of origin, such that Pijoaparte's mobility is only transitory while he is with Teresa, and in the end he is detained for having left his space. On the other hand, in Goytisolo's *Señas de identidad* [Marks of identity], the protagonist stresses the difference between the official Spain open to tourists and the authentic Spain of terror and oppression, a contrast that culminates in the form of the city. The flight of the narrator reinforces, similar to Pijoaparte, the impossibility of modifying space and its social designation. This impossibility of change, in spite of critique, is what we mean by staticity.

4 We have already mentioned how Candel was one of the most censored
authors, together with Alfonso Sastre. Although never arrested, he was
constantly reported and assiduously did battle with censors. See the works
of Gilabert and Sinca.

5 Xavier Miserachs (1937–98) began his professional studies in medicine,
which he abandoned for photography when he won the Lluís Navarro
prize in 1954. He is considered the most precocious of his generation
(Formiguera, "La segunda" 164). In 1960 he opened his own photography
studio in Barcelona, where he worked in the fields of publishing and book
illustration. For a general overview of Miserachs's work, see Formiguera
or López Mondéjar.

6 In this regard, on the signifying possibilities of photography, John Berger
says that photography "cita las apariencias pero no las interpreta" (qtd. in
Castellote 27) [cites appearances but does not interpret them] and, as Alejandro Castellote explains, images must be translated, heeding temporal,
cultural, and ideological concerns (27). Both cases insinuate what Kathrin
Yacavone calls the singularity of the image, an idea born of her comparative
analysis of the work of Walter Benjamin and Roland Barthes. Her notion of
the singularity of the image emphasizes precisely the interrelation between
subject/spectator and the existential and historical contexts in which images are embedded: "Los escritos de Benjamin y Barthes sugieren que en el
espacio figurado de la singularidad se abre la relación entre la fotografía, su
referente o modelo y el observador de la imagen" (34) [The writings of
Benjamin and Barthes suggest that the relationship between photography,
its referent or model, and the observer of the image, the figurative space of
singularity is opened]. We are interested in pointing out this approach
because here we can perceive the encounter with otherness, the absent other
who becomes visible through the interaction that comes from observation.

7 As López Mondéjar explains, in Barcelona, photographers like Ramón Masats, Oriol Maspons, Xavier Miserachs, Leopoldo Pomés, Ricard Terré, and
Julio Ubiña abandoned the AFC because the organization was incapable of
accepting the new trends that were arriving from Europe and the United
States (*Photography* 78).

8 Oriol Maspons (1928–2013) began his career in the AFC. His work took
him to Paris, where he came into contact with photographic groups such
as Club 30x40, in which artists like Cartier Bresson, among others, were
active. Maspons became the critical voice of the new generation of Catalan
photographers (Formiguera, "La segunda" 162). His professional work un-
folded in advertising and publishing, working jointly with Julio Ubiña. For
his part, Ubiña (1921–88), although undeservedly relegated to the background behind Maspons, with whom he shared a studio and more than
one professional project (Formiguera, "La segunda" 164), was an essential

protagonist in the documentary revival of the 1960s. His photography is best characterized as "irónica y burlona" [ironic and sardonic] and for employing a documentary style "sin complejidades contextuales, con un lenguaje directo y de una gran eficacia narrativa" (López Mondéjar, *Historia* 233) [without contextual complexities, with direct language and great narrative efficacy]. He was a prominent member of AFAL and also worked for magazines like *Stern* and *Paris Match*.

9 In 1962, the publisher Lumen launched a collection under this title, "Palabra e Imagen," based on the collaboration between a writer and a photographer, an idea conceived by Esther Tusquets. Some of the collaborations and titles include *Neutral Corner* (text by Ignacio Aldecoa and photographs by Ramón Masats); *La caza de la perdiz roja* [The hunt for the red partridge] (Delibes/Maspons); and, later, *Luces y sombras del flamenco* [Lights and shadows of flamenco] (J.M. Caballero Bonald/Colita). The publisher found its first success with *Izas*, which showed exceedingly direct content in a still highly repressive era. Later in the chapter, we will speak in greater detail on the scandal that emerged from the publication of this book and the relevance of AFAL.

10 David Balsells and Jorge Ribalta trace Colom's photographic production after 1964 using the archive of his negatives. There is scant evidence of his work between 1964 and 1988, and only in 1990 does he reinitiate his production, introducing colour in 1993. However, we cannot rule out the possibility of phases not represented in this archive, given the quantity of material that Colom acknowledged having discarded (Balsells and Ribalta 31). For a detailed description of his later work, see Balsells and Ribalta (31–3).

11 The history of the Raval has been linked to the development of the working classes since the neighbourhood's inception, given that it was the location where Catalonian industrialization originated. However, from the 1920s onward, social groups and commentators began to call it the Barrio Chino ("Chinatown"), an iconography imagined with negative connotations that would go on to influence its image even nowadays (Ealham, "Imagined" 374). This conceptualization is rooted in the expansion of illegal activities during and immediately following the First World War, during the course of which the criminal underworld became intimately connected to the bourgeoisie that existed beyond the boundaries of the Raval (Ealham, "Imagined" 380). For a more detailed explanation of the construction of exoticism in the Barrio Chino, see Chris Ealham's "An Imagined Geography," Gary McDonogh's "The Geography of Evil," and Paco Villar's *Historia y leyenda del Barrio Chino*.

12 As we will see in the following chapter, there are limits to this way of perceiving the city; however, the confluence of perspectives also opens the door to other possibilities not considered in Colom's discourse.

13 Although the role of social movements in the transition to democracy have been recognized, when we speak about protest and rupture during the dictatorship, critics seem to limit themselves to literature and cinema – that is, to an elitist discourse that defines cultural and social domains connected to youth who did not live through the Civil War and who rejected the environment they inherited (see, for example, Gracia García and Ruiz Carnicer). We are not denying the role of these young people in either literature, cinema, or later social and political changes, but rather proposing that their interventions should be complemented by a consideration of the previous generation's presence and action in diverse cultural fields.

14 Photographic *salonismo* refers to a style indebted to the aesthetic propositions of late-Pictorialism, and by extension landscape art, which is directly linked to painting by both theme and technique. This type of photography was intimately connected to the photography associations and salon exhibits that arose during the dictatorship. As Castellote explains, Pictorialism decouples photography from its social functionality and directly links it to artistic circles that are removed from direct documentary photography (48), which will be the prevailing form taken by the photography of the Nova Avantguarda.

15 As Publio López Mondéjar explains, censorship took care of every artistic representation from the time of the Serrano Law of 1938. Censorship on photography fell to the Photographic Division of the Ministry of Press and Propaganda, which "in years of the National-Catholic orthodoxy was obsessive in its upholding of morality" and was most preoccupied in hiding the harsh reality of the country (*Historia* 19).

16 This was a brief moment and was used to make reference to photography from 1957 – the year when Ricard Terré, Xavier Miserachs, and Ramon Masats had their exhibits, and when the Sala Aixelà was opened, although Ribalta explains that date could be moved up to 1954 with the publication of Català Roca's book, *Barcelona* ("La dictadura" 110) – to 1965, with the publication of Miserachs's book *Barcelona: Blanc i negre*, and a change in the attitude of these photographers:

> Ben aviat, però ... l'actitud d'autors joves com Maspons, com Masats, o com el mateix Colom ja no responen tant a la posició iconoclasta i revolucionària de tota avantguarda, sinó més aviat a un intent d'adaptació a la realitat circumdant ... cercant la qualitat dins unes exigències comercials inevitables, frenadores al cap i a la fi de l'autèntica recerca personal i expressiva. (Casademont qtd. in Ribalta and Balcells, *El carrer* 23).

> Quite early, but ... the attitude of young authors like Maspons, Masats, or even Colom himself no longer respond as much to the iconoclastic and revolutionary position of all avant-garde, but rather to an attempt to adapt to their

surrounding reality ... seeking quality within unavoidable commercial demands, that put the brakes on authentic personal and expressive inquiry.

17 Maspons would be expelled from the AFC in 1958 because of formal disagreements expressed in that article. His expulsion could be read as a victory for traditional canons, a trend exemplified in what Ignacio Barceló, who founded *Arte Fotográfico* in 1952, says in that same magazine: "hay quien se empeña en seguir practicando en la creencia de que aquello, la miseria, la tristeza, la cochambre es fotografía moderna" (545) [there are those who endeavour to keep practicing in the belief that that – misery, sadness, filth – is modern photography]. In spite of this criticism, what Maspons managed to do was open the door to a new type of photography separate from the official associations, also opening the door to the outside world with his interviews with Cartier-Bresson, Brassaï, Sudre, and Sougez, among others, which he published in the pages of *Arte Fotográfico*.

18 Here we see the establishment of the distinction between art and technique; that is, the development of rigid archetypical themes and repetitive formulas, and a formal freedom more closely tied to humanist photography that favours capturing movement and eschews artificial composition in order to let "reality" permeate the execution of the photograph. This does not mean, however, that there is no formal technique or that there is not a search for innovative rhetoric in the language of photography.

19 These connections have been noted by critics such as Pere Formiguera ("Ricard"), Joan Fontcuberta ("De la posguerra"), Jorge Ribalta (*Paradigmas*), and Laura Terré (*Historia*). However, it is necessary to revisit them here in order to stress the connection of this photography with not just cities, but also a question of rhythm and emphasis on bodies that reconnects with what we have already seen in Candel and the development of a specific form of dissent.

20 It is true that Steichen's exhibit was criticized for the ideological and propagandistic charge evident in the construction of a simplistic and homogenizing Cold War era humanism (see, for example, Sekula "Traffic"); however, on this occasion, we are not out to emphasize the subject matter or content of the photographs, but rather a widespread tendency that accentuates a temporal and routine everyday gaze.

21 We are not referring to whether or not the photographers who were part of the Nova Avantguarda backed the regime. We are interested in examining how their characterization through their photographic work breaks with the narrative constructed by the regime by recovering, in a certain respect, elements that had been eliminated from the country's artistic history. Let us recall, once again, that the idea of dissent does not entail a clear, organized, and direct protest like what we see in the 1970s; rather, it is a critique that, clear as it may be, is rooted in the daily struggles of everyday life,

through the formation of a community that can become politically and socially organized.

22 We are referring here to photographers such as Pepe Encinas, Francesca Vintró, Kim Manresa, Marta Povo, and Pilar Aymerich. In a parallel fashion, in the 1970s we find a line of more creative photography associated with the magazine *Nueva Lente* [New Lens] (1971–9).

23 Such is the case, to mention two notable examples, of Joan Colom and Ignasi Marroyo, whose work was rediscovered in the 1980s and 1990s. This lack of prominence can also be attributed to one of the basic tenets of El Mussol, the group that gathered these photographers under one umbrella, according to which photojournalism was a group effort, shunning the spotlight conferred by authors' signatures. Examples include the exhibit commissioned by Pere Formiguera in 1992, *Temps de silenci*, and another organized by Jorge Ribalta and David Balsells on Joan Colom, *Joan Colom: Fotografías de Barcelona, 1958–1964*, which put the photographer's work back in the spotlight and would later become part of a larger exhibit, *Jo faig el carrer: Joan Colom, fotografies 1957–2010*, which also included some of his work from the 1990s.

24 On this matter, Cánovas says: "Les instàncies oficials que, en fotografia … van ignorar-ho sempre quasi tot, estaven més ocupades a controlar els canvis que se'ls tiraven al damunt – la situació política i social del país sofria tremendes convulsions – que no pas a fer ni tan sols un mínim toc d'atenció a problemes tan 'minsos'" (24) [The official instances that, in photography … they always ignored almost everything, they were more occupied with controlling the changes that were coming at them – the political and social situation of the country underwent tremendous convultions – than with paying the slightest bit of attention to "trifling" problems]. Nevertheless, photography and Candel's literature were what gave shape to a social identity that, combined with certain political elements, will serve as the basis for the political and social changes of the Transition.

25 Jorge Ribalta, in his article "AFAL como síntoma" [AFAL as symptom], established this same relationship through the format of photography at the time: photography's dependence on the printed page connected the authors of this decade to later photojournalism and reporting, which distanced them from exhibit-driven creative photography (82).

26 Ramón Masats (1931) was the first photographer of the Barcelona School (we should not confuse here the denomination used by López Mondéjar with the cinematographic school of the same name) to follow the path of pure reporting, influenced by Català Roca's documentary style, French humanism, and Italian neorealism (López Mondéjar, *Historia* 230). He came to be known after winning the Lluís Navarro prize in 1956, the year that he became a profesional photographer after publishing in the magazine *La*

Gaceta Ilustrada. Masats settled in Madrid, where he alternated photography with cinema and television. For a general overview of Masats' work, see the works of Formiguera or López Mondéjar.

27 The housing complexes were also photographed by people like Maspons and Ubiña, but, as Isabel Segura Soriano explains, the circulation of these images was restricted to memoirs or the internally distributed documents of institutions that promoted the construction of these buildings and funded the pictures ("Polígonos" 130).

28 See, for example, the sequence of images titled "Rètols en diversos indrets de la ciutat" (photos 208–20) or "Detall de cases i torres a la part alta de la ciutat: Horta, Guinardó, Carmel i Mare de Déu del Coll" (photos 185–93) in *Barcelona: Blanc i negre*.

29 Català Roca (1922–98) is considered the most important photographer of the Nova Avantguarda, and of photography in the 1950s in general (López Mondéjar, *Historia* 200). His profesional formation ocurred alongside his father, Pere Català Pic, from whom he "heredó su destreza técnica" [inherited his technical skill] and "audacia formal" (200) [formal audacity]. His work is especially relevant for how it spearheads a renovation in form, distancing itself from pictorialism – or *salonismo*, to return to the term coined by Maspons – and guiding a whole new generation of photographers in the 1950s and 1960s.

30 Eugeni Forcano (1926–2018) joined the AFC in 1949 and was an active member throughout his career, although he did not practice photography professionally until 1960, after winning the *Destino* photography prize. His work engaged in documentary photography and, in the 1970s, included fashion and advertising. The work of Leopoldo Pomés (1931–2019), on the other hand, developed outside the confines of photographic associations. He was affiliated with the independent work group Dau al Set and, after 1960, worked in film and advertising.

31 Apart from a general thematic correspondence to neorealism, which seeks to construct the image of a popular subject in the wake of the Second World War and in doing so links this style to the objectives of humanist photography described here, Fontcuberta places special emphasis on Nova Avantguarda relationship to Italian neorealism, particularly the Gruppo Friulano (Gianno Bergno-Gardin, Fulvio Roiter, Nino Migliore, Italo Zanier), because of a confluence of both historical circumstances as well as attitude, "la amargura e impotencia fruto de unas circunstancias históricas recibidas como herencia de la generación anterior" ("De la posguerra" 417) [the bitterness and impotence born of historical circumstances inherited from the previous generation]. However, the connection to neorealism as practiced in Spain is challenged: on the one hand, both neorealism and humanist photography highlight the tension between centre and periphery, a

tension that arises from the rapid industrialization of urban areas and consequent migration and that seeks to observe, in part, "el fenómeno de la emergencia de una clase popular desenraizada en las periferias urbanas" (Ribalta, *Paradigmas* 31) [the phenomenon of the emergence of a rootless popular class in the urban periphery]; on the other hand, in Spain we notice "una profunda ambivalencia en las condiciones poéticas neorrealistas" [a profound ambivalence in neorealist poetic conditions] since we find "una relativa coincidencia formal de tal vanguardia con las imágenes promovidas desde los organismos estatales de promoción del turismo" (32) [a relative formal coincidence between this avant-garde and the images promoted by organisms of the state that promote tourism]. How should we differentiate one set of images from the other? This correspondence of form and content will become the jumping off point for the controversy between Laura Terré, Joan Fontcuberta, and Jorge Ribalta, as we will describe forthwith.

32 With this commentary, we are not trying to strip Català Roca's work of its value or contributions. He is the first to fill the void between avant-garde and the new documentary production of the 1950s and 1960s through creativity and a technique reaffirmed in how he was perceived. "Català Roca," wrote Alexandre Cirici, "is a typical Catalan whose sense of reality is firmly rooted in pragmatism and who bases the value of pictures on the communication of ideas, elevating particular or ephemeral scenes to the status of meaningful archetypes" (qtd. in López Mondéjar, *Photography* 28). This emphasis on perception proper is what, according to López Mondéjar, influenced the work of the photographers of the Nova Avantguarda (28). Be that as it may, Català Roca's black and white Barcelona is not characterized by dissent. He is always on the sidelines; he does not move into and through areas that could be problematic, like Candel and Colom do.

33 Ricard Terré (1928–2009) took up photography in 1955, and that same year became a regular at the AFC, where he met Maspons, Masats, and Miserachs. His photography follows the directives of European humanism formally and thematically, but his deeply personal style makes it somewhat difficult to categorize.

34 In regards to photography, these authors open a channel of communication with the outside world through their own exhibits and publications, among which *AFAL*'s stand out, as they break with the state's paradigm already through their cultural content. AFAL begins to introduce the work of American and European photographers that will influence the Nova Avantguarda, setting off artistic debates that will extend to social issues through the image/urbanism connection that can be seen in publications like *CAU*. Specialized journals enable a field of expression that is wider if not more open, and they also encourage a break from the academicism

that defines art following the Civil War, distancing themselves from officialdom.

35 Here we are referring to the work that Colom developed on Somorrostro, together with Ignasi Marroyo, for the journal *El Correo Catalán*. The objective of that article, as we will see shortly, was to praise the construction of the boardwalk and the razing of that group of shanties; however, there is much more to be read in those images that can reveal the function of Colom's photography in that context.

36 In fact, in Henri Cartier-Bresson's description of the "decisive moment," we can discern the characteristics encapsulated in this movement of Lefebvre's rhythm: "La fotografía es para mí el reconocimiento en la realidad de un ritmo de superficies, líneas o valores ... En fotografía hay una plástica nueva, función de líneas instantáneas; trabajamos en el movimiento, una especie de presentimiento de la vida, y la fotografía tiene que atrapar en el movimiento el equilibrio expresivo" (Cartier-Bresson 24) [For me photography is the acknowledgment of a rhythm of surfaces, lines, or values in reality ... In photography, there is a new plastic, the product of instantaneous lines; we work on movement, a type of premonition of life, and photography has to trap expressive equilibrium in motion]. Movement, rhythm, life, instantaneousness are all elements at the core of everyday experience, which is what in the end gives form to urban place and the margin, whatever its previous intention may have been.

37 Here I am employing the language used by Jean-François Lyotard to explain the concept of matrix. Although Lyotard is referencing a matrix that opens in an individual's psychological subconscious, I believe that this same language can be useful to describe this margin that, in its own way, operates similar to a matrix, as if it were a matter of the subconscious buried in the middle of place: "If the matrix is invisible, it is not because it arises from the intelligible, but because it resides in a space that is beyond the intelligible, is in radical rupture with the rules of opposition ... It is its characteristic to have many places in one place, and they block together what is not compossible. This is the secret: the transgression of the constitutive intervals of discourse, and the transgression of the constitutive distances of representation" (339).

38 Another example of beautification and ennobling will be found in the residences of the Casas del Gobernador. Due to the naval manoeuvres that were going to take place in the summer of 1966 before Franco, the Somorrostro slums were demolished and their inhabitants transferred to temporary shelters.

39 Jordi Borja describes public space as "un espacio sometido a una regulación específica por parte de la administración pública, propietaria o que posee la facultad de dominio del suelo y que garantiza su accesibilidad

a todos y fija las condiciones de su utilización y de instalación de activi-
dades" ("Ciudadanía") [a space subjected to specific regulation on the part
of public administration, owners, or whoever possesses the land rights
and guarantees its accessibility to everyone and determines the conditions
for its use and the activities to take place therein"]. It is obvious that this
type of space, regulated by the administration, existed in dictatorship-era
Barcelona, but in order to see how the space photographed by Colom corresponds to the space opened up by the return to democracy, we must go
a step further and look for other aspects that fit more closely with the way
public space functioned at that time.

40 Even though we are talking about a more selective repression, political
repression did not disappear, but rarther changed shape, centred on the
idea of public image. For example, in 1963 the Tribunal de Orden Público
[Court of Public Order] was created with the charge of controlling and
punishing dissidence and protest (Ortiz Heras 15), which in itself was an
indication of the consolidation of the actions of social movements.

41 We have to add to this the Law of Public Order of 1959, "que ampliaba de
forma considerable el espectro sancionador hasta incluir a cualquier dete-
nido en una huelga, manifestación o por destrozar bienes públicos" (Ortiz
Heras 22) [which considerably expanded the spectrum of sanctions even
including anyone detained in a strike, protest, of for destroying public
property] and the Decree on Banditry and Terrorism of 21 September 1960.
These changes do not imply a weakening of the control of social order
and public space, but rather a shift in the practices and discourse of the
regime that reveals, first, the separation of crime into political and social
categories and, second, the implementation of a bourgeois morality that
connects class status and social stability, making room for dissidence in
the social domain. Of course, these two domains, the social and the political, are always united, as the creep of politics into the social domain (and
crimes) will clearly show. Nevertheless, there seems to be an apparent separation in the search for an image of consensus and social accord during
Francoism.

42 The Raval was an independent administrative district until the 1980s. Now,
however, it forms part of the area known as Ciutat Vella [Old City]. The
southern part of the Raval is what was known as the Barrio Chino due to
the prostitution and crime that was associated with it. Workers and bourgeois families inhabited the northern part (McDonogh, "Discourses" 45).

43 Laura Terré justifies the articles published in AFAL with the pretext of
eluding censorship; however, there is no commentary or article that leads
us to think the same. In fact, the selections from other newspapers and
magazines that AFAL includes in the section dedicated to commentaries
on Colom's photos (see Querol) seem to indicate that a more open opinion

on his exhibition was indeed possible. In the case of the article published in the *Diario de Tarrasa*, "Exposición Colom," the author, although continuing to reference charity, highlights the dialectic of the photographs taken by Colom, "poniendo los hombres al descubierto a través de un agudo, sincero, a veces optimista, a veces pesimista, pero siempre caritativo objetivo" (qtd. in Querol 14) [putting the men in the open through a sharp, sometimes optimistic, sometimes pessimistic but always charitable lens]. The second article, published in *Destino*, accentuates the relationship of the images to everyday life: because "elige a sus modelos entre la gente feliz ... Colom refleja el mundo como es ... [sus fotografías] captan el paso del hombre a lo largo de las intrincadas calles de una gran ciudad" (qtd. Querol 15) [he selects his models from among happy people ... Colom reflects the world as it is ... his photographs capture the passage of man along the intricate streets of a grand city]. These commentaries emphasize the complexity of city life and the possibility of another way of being in the world, even if it does not jibe with the parameters of place.

44 Colom's photography became known through expositions in different centres and art galleries. While it is true that he won popular acclaim through the book *Izas, rabizas y colipoterras* (1964), Colom played no role in its creation, nor do I believe that it represents the author's intentions for how his work should be seen and considered. In an interview published in *El carrer. Joan Colom a la sala Aixelà, 1961* (MNAC, 1999), Colom himself speaks in some detail about his experience with *Izas, rabizas y colipoterras*:

> El projecte d'aquest llibre va ser instigat per Oriol Maspons, qui tenia molta amistat amb Esther Tusquets. Ell coneixia el meu treball del "Xino" i altres coses. Les hi vaig deixar. Vaig conèixer Cela en algun moment d'aquella època ... La meva sorpresa va venir després, en veure la selecció que havien fet de les meves fotografies, que s'havia centrat només en les prostitutes. (40)

> This book project was instigated by Oriol Maspons, who was a close friend of Esther Tusquets. He was familiar with my work in "Xino" and other things. I gave them to him. I met Cela at some point in that time period ... My surprise came later, upon seeing the selection they made of my photographs, which was focused only on prostitutes.

This disconnect between how Colom sought to present his work and the intentions of Tusquets and Cela is emphasized thematically by the process in which the book started out, as Jorge Ribalta explains in that same interview:

> Maspons s'ha referit a aquesta col·lecció i al teu llibre dient: "Esther Tusquets va tenir la idea de fer un llibre i vam pensar en Camilo José Cela. A ell li va encantar la idea. Deia que ja tenia el llibre fet, en fitxes ... Les fotografies ja estaven totes fetes i després Cela les va il·lustrar amb el text." (40)

Maspons has referred to this collection and your book saying, "Esther Tusquets had the idea of making a book and we thought of Camilo José Cela. He loved the idea. He said that he already had the book done, on cards ... The photographs were already all done and then Cela added the text.

To this Colom responded as follows: "Jo sempre havia cregut que el text estava totalment inspirat en les imatges, com una mena de comentari de cadascuna. Jo només sé que no vaig treballar per encàrrec de ningú." (40) [I had always believed that the text was totally inspired by the images, as a type of commentary on each one. I only know that I didn't work on commission].

Colom did not participate in the design of the book either, including its photographic composition:

En general, l'enquadrament original del negatiu sempre tenia algun problema perquè jo disparava sense mirar. Això vol dir que, en general, en fer les còpies m'havia de plantejar l'enquadrament bo de la imatge. Però, excepte això, jo no vaig participar en el disseny del llibre, i els reenquadraments quadrats, adequats al format del llibre, no són meus. (40)

In general, the original framing of the negative always had some problem, because I snapped photos without looking. This means that, in general, when I made copies I had to find a good frame for the image. But, except for this, I didn't participate in the design of the book and the square reframing, tailored to the book, is not mine.

As a result of the commercial success of the book, Colom had a conflict with one of the photographed women, who filed a legal complaint against him, although it never went to trial (Fontcuberta, "Izas" 45). As a result, Colom abandoned his photography for many years. However, because he had nothing to do with the composition and publication of the book and because it was published years after his expositions, which he personally organized, the consequences laid out here do not affect, in my opinion, the original intentions that can be gleaned from the approach to his work as a whole.

As his work in the Raval proves, "el propio Colom no está satisfecho con esa simplificación que limita su trabajo al entorno de la prostitución y está constantemente reivindicando que su interés no eran las prostitutas sino la vida de la calle en un sentido más amplio" (Balsells and Ribalta 19) [Colom himself is not satisfied with that simplification that limits his work to the world of prostitution, and he is constantly defending that his interest was not in prostitutes but street life in a broader sense].

45 Even the discursive ambivalence present in contemporary critics falls into this limited view of Colom's work; for them, the possible critique of the regime is based on the lack of a solution to the problem of social injustice –

the other side of this critique being the paternalism and social victim-hood of humanist politics, which we also see in Francoist urban planners (Balsells and Ribalta 34) – a social injustice based on these same principles of bourgeois morality evident in its emphasis on prostitution, which to a degree shows a limited understanding of Colom's work. Nevertheless, faced with this approach, we should keep in mind that this discourse of dissidence is made possible by the urban, the difference that urban space brings to bear on place and its inhabitants.

46 The execution of this work coincides with the peak of the Nova Avant-guarda, which corresponds with the periodization of Casademont, who lists *Izas* as the conclusion of the Nova Avantguarda due to the abandon-ment of formal concerns in favour of a social discourse (see Ribalta, "La dictadura" 110). Nevertheless, form continues to be essential in Colom's work in spite of the emphasis that *AFAL* and Casademont put on social concerns.

47 Here we are following Henri Lefebvre's reading of what he calls a "blind field": "these [fields] are not merely dark and uncertain … but blind in the sense that there is a blind spot in the retina, the center – and negation – of vision … The urban remains unseen … [I]t is not a question of lack of ed-ucation, but of occlusion. We see things incompletely" (*Urban* 29). These fields become regions of force and conflict.

48 Colom explains how his photographs are inserted in a narration that shapes his idea of the city constructed through the multiplicity of its innumerable and unpredictable relationships: "Siento intensamente el reportaje, pero no a retazos deslavazados captados allá y acullá sin hi-lación entre sí. Antes, al contrario, creo en las grandes posibilidades de la fotografía dentro de una continuidad temática, como medio de expresar, relatar o divulgar cualquier aspecto de la vida, de las personas y de las cosas" (8) [I feel reporting intensely, but not as disconnected fragments captured here and there without connection between them. Rather, to the contrary, I believe in the great possibilities of photography within a the-matic continuity, as a medium for expressing, relating, or divulging any aspect of life, people, and things].

49 In order to appreciate this difference in styles, I recommend comparing Català Roca's photography, "Gitaneta de Montjuïc" (159), and Joan Co-lom's "La Calle" (78), where the documentary style of the former and the street photography style of the latter can be noted.

50 Here we can perceive a connection to the "blind field" that Lefebvre de-scribed (*Urban* 29): a break with the order established by the official city enlightens precisely that "elsewhere," that region that remains in the shad-ows, thus shattering the limits of the bourgeois gaze. In this definition we also see a connection with the "blind field" described to us by Scott.

51 But at the same time, it also confirms this narrative, as we will see shortly, since the objectification of the woman delineates the heterotopic and exotic discourse attributed to the Raval. Nevertheless, we should keep in mind that this reading is made possible, above all, by observing the photographs in isolation, which breaks with the discourse created by considering them together as a whole. As Balsells and Ribalta explain, in this moment "el trabajo del fotógrafo es concebido como un conjunto de imágenes, no como imágenes aisladas, rompiendo los hábitos que dominaban en ese momento" (22) [the work of the photographer is conceived as a group of images, not as isolated images, breaking the prevailing customs of that time]. This statement, together with Colom's idea of photographic narrations, instructs us to read the photographs inserted in the story of "The Street" as a whole, rather than as separate images.

52 One solution to reduce the density of the Raval and accommodate the residents of the shantytowns was the creation of the previously mentioned housing complexes on the outskirts of the city. As we saw in Candel, this new construction ignored the needs of its inhabitants and led to what became known as "barraquismo vertical," mainly due to the lack of services and the poor quality of the materials that were used because of the rampant speculation of the 1960s. For more, see Busquets or Ramoneda.

4 A Female City: Colita and the Conceptualization of Barcelona

1 Photography in this case offers us a privileged gaze. As Marsha Meskimmon explains (viii), since its inception photography has been considered a medium that is more open to all kinds of creators, as opposed to "fine art," not because it has a more egalitarian approach, but because its uncertain status as "art" and its definition according to a set of "ill-defined" rules have made for a more democratic access to it as a practice. Its status as a popular and amateur practice has made it into a medium that is accessible to women, especially in moments when artistic practice for women was restricted. These contradictions and ambiguities of the medium are, therefore, what allow us to access a new perspective on the use of urban space under the dictatorship.

2 It is not our intention to approach the work of these photographers under the general label of "women photographers," as if we were dealing with a utopic community that emerges from a collective undertaking, although that appears to be what the genealogies that separate them into a parallel history apart from the History of the canon do. Rather, we are going to consider female photographers whose work in relation to Barcelona implies the development of a type of dissent that changes the urban landscape.

3 Del Valle explains how social memory is elaborated from the present, which underscores the notions of selection and fiction at work in an operation reminiscent of Hayden White's concept of fiction in history in "The Histori-cal Text as Literary Artifact." Here we see the drafting of narrative constella-tions that Henri Lefebvre lays out in his concept of the urban matrix.

4 This conceptualization of space imagined by del Valle, specifically as tied to the question of gender, is intimately tied, as we have seen, to the defini-tions of urban space postulated by Lefebvre and Michel de Certeau.

5 López Mondéjar notes, when speaking about Català Roca's photogra-phy, that in his work "parece primar el puro instinto visual y la certera percepción de lo real" (*Historia* 200) [he seems to prioritize pure visual instinct and the accurate perception of the real], which emphasizes pre-cisely this connection between masculine perspective and unique and true narrativity.

6 As Annette Kuhn notes, "where photography takes women as its subject matter, it constructs 'woman' as a set of meanings, which become stand-ards by which images of women are read" (qtd. in Leet 163). Women are considered inside the masculine structure that defines them in social space.

7 Alejandro Cirici wrote in 1958: "Dentro de la misma fotografía, cuántas veces fotos absolutamente incorrectas resultan de una vida extraordinaria, ayudándonos a conocer el mundo y hasta a conocernos a nosotros mis-mos. Y cuántas veces, por el contrario, vemos esas fotografías de concurso, impecablemente realizadas según la técnica, pero que no tienen la más mínima trascendencia" (qtd. in López Mondéjar, *Historia* 198) [Within the same photography, how many times do absolutely incorrect photos result from an extraordinary life, helping us to know the world and even know ourselves. And how many times, to the contrary, do we see these contest photographs, impeccably executed in terms of technique, but which do not have the least bit of transcendence], a comment that explains the percep-tion of contest photography. Although we do not necessarily disagree with this claim, in the context that we are examining, we should keep in mind the social limitations that are applied to photography shot by women.

8 In all of the photographic anthologies that have passed through my hands, the presence of women during the dictatorship has been relegated to the background. López Mondéjar briefly mentions Colita, and although he acknowledges her role in the Nova Avantguarda (*Historia* 234), he does not acknowledge others such as Juana Biarnés or Montserrat Sagarra. Fontcu-berta mentions the presence of women in photography during Francoism ("De la posguerra" 429), however his references also amount to little more than brief mentions, and he does not stop to comment on any of their pho-tographs, nor the relevance of their contributions. The question of visibil-ity and relevance is, again, a matter of masculine vision and presence.

Of course, things begin to change and we find exhibits such as *Fotò-grafes pioneres a Catalunya* (2005), or more recent publications, like the chapters in *La mirada mecánica* (2016) or *Joana Biarnés: Disparando con el corazón* (2017), *Carme García: Des del terrat* (2018) or *Barcelona fotògrafes/fotógrafas* (2020), which intend to fill this void. These two extremes have been accompanied by more or less detailed exhibits (*Es de mujeres*, Instituto de la Mujer, Madrid, 1986; *Miradas de Mujer*, Museo Esteban Vicente, 2005) and a theoretical corpus that has begun to take shape in the last few years (see Vega 731). Nevertheless, women continue to be excluded from genealogies that are considered to be canon-building and are subjected to a gendered condition of "femininity" – as we can see, for example, in the title of the book on Biarnés – that keeps them subject to a masculine narrative. When they are included, they are also put in separate chapters instead of included in the main narrations; an exception is the case of the recent *Fotografía en España* by Carmelo Vega, who, in spite of separating them out from his main narration, is the first to acknowledge the value of their work and later studies that have tackled this subject and includes the name of Colita as one important figure throughout his study. Of course, many authors, like Fontcuberta or Horacio Fernández in his *Variaciones en España*, are conscious of the process of selection implied by writing a genealogy of photography and each has their own criteria, although that does nothing to mitigate the predominance of male figures in this field.

9   André Malraux explains how from the museum, together with the ample photographic reproduction of multiple objects, "a Babylonian style seems to emerge as a real entity, not a mere classification – as something resembling, rather the life-story of a great creator. Nothing conveys more vividly and compellingly the notion of a destiny shaping human ends than do the great styles, whose evolutions and transformations seem like long scars that Fate has left, in passing, on the face of the earth" (46). Narration is constructed a posteriori, in a search for causality that, in reality, lacks the spontaneity that it attempts to grant. Here in this case, space in the museum is what gives narration this air of inevitability.

10 In this sense, and reminiscent of what Malraux states regarding museums, we should turn to Griselda Pollock's definition of the image in her article "Missing Women." According to Pollock, this concept is problematic within the framework of a "woman's image" because it assumes a fully formed, defined, and meaningful world in which images are judged relative to the world they reflect, reproduce, or distort – although such an analysis could be applied to any type of context if we are mindful of how any given construct is the result of a discursive practice. The *real* is always present as a criterion by which images are valued and is itself never

questioned as a product of representation. The image is true or false as a reflection of the *real* and, in this way, positioned in a hierarchical relationship where the *real* precedes and determines the image (203). Nevertheless, the *real* is neither beyond scrutiny, fixed nor unique; rather, it is also a construct and therefore is as malleable as the image since it is itself also an image (204). The images of male and female photographers are constructs; they result as much from material, social, and ethical practices as the social, cultural, and political narratives or discourses of the space of the city and the female body. I hope this clarifies the title of this chapter.

11 Of course, the chronology developed in this book, as well as its being centred on the marginal, is also but one discourse among many; however, this new imagining hopes to reveal a new way of perceiving space, place, and the photographic canon that has reigned until now. Consequently, this book is not constructing a detailed genealogy of all the female photographers that undertook their work from the 1950s to the 1970s, but rather it will highlight those cases that create and initiate dissent and examine how they dialogue with a masculine canon by both creating and deconstructing new corporal geographies.

12 As Di Febo explains, towards the end of the 1960s women began to orchestrate protests on social situations, like the struggle of the miners in Asturias (1968–9), and the occupation of churches to appeal for amnesty for political prisoners or the end of mistreatment in prisons (*Resistencia* 156–7). Through these protests, women utilized the Francoist legal structure, thanks to their obligations as spouses, to become messengers for things that were illegal (Abad Buil 246); at the same time, they came out from behind the closed doors of their private world and were in the public eye, showing that open participation in society was possible and becoming an important part of the anti-Francoist struggle in the process.

13 Mary Nash explains that although the Jornadas Catalanas de la Dona (May 1976) initiated a historic point of reference in the awakening of this new feminism and the visibilization of women as protagonists in the Transition, antecedents can be found starting in 1970. At this point "grupos de autoconciencia feminista que denuncian la opresión doméstica y cuestionan el arquetipo femenino sometido del franquismo" [feminist groups that denounce domestic oppression and challenge the subjugated woman archetype of Francoism] already exist (10). The peripheral neighbourhoods are, once again, centres for organizing this type of group, mixing daily experience with space and politics, since the anonymous women of these neighbourhoods are the ones who in the 1970s begin to take to the streets since they experience firsthand the direct consequences of the lack of basic needs and services in their day-to-day lives (60). However, already in the 1960s, we can see signs of the creation of this identity and collectivity, as

we show in this chapter. The intersection of gender and city helps us to see how what Nash calls a "ciudadanía en femenino" (11) [female version of citizenship] begins to take shape.

14 Together with Colita and Joana Biarnés, Pilar Aymerich is one of the most important names in Spanish photojournalism. She captured the activist conscience and social movements of the 1970s, and her photographs are taken to be the most representative portrait of the civil society that impelled the Transition (Carabias and García, "Ojos de mujer" 153). The sphere of culture – theatre and literature – and women are the predominant themes in her work. She has published in magazines and newspapers including *Triunfo*, *Cambio 16*, *El Mundo*, and *El País*, among others.

15 Di Febo ("La lucha") refers to the dissemination of feminist texts like *The Feminine Mystique* by Betty Friedan and *The Second Sex* by Simone de Beauvoir in intellectual circles, and the creation of the Sección de Derechos de la Mujer [Section of Women's Rights] in Barcelona in 1968 and the Asociación Española de Mujeres Juristas [Spanish Association of Women Jurists] in Madrid in 1967, which sought to fight juridical inequality.

16 This shift in the role of women in the feminist and anti-Francoist struggle takes place simultaneously in different social, cultural, and political fields. In the field of art, for example, Esther Boix, María Dapena, and Ana Peters develop their work in tandem with feminist discourse and practice in Spain; that is, first as part of the anti-Francoist struggle, and then dealing with questions focused on the situation of women. For a detailed description, see, for example, Juan Vicente Aliaga and Patricia Mayayo's *Genealogías feministas en el arte español: 1960–2010*.

The same happens in literature and cultural criticism, where, as we have already mentioned, we begin to find anti-Francoist tendencies related to feminism following the 1950s, where Maria Aurèlia Capmany stands out. Our path leads us towards photography with a more popular and urban approach, in search of connections to the spaces where daily life happens. It should be emphasized here that what characterized the architecture and urbanism of this period is the lack of female voices.

17 The rationale for highlighting Candel as an example of this erasure of women is the contradiction that he presents in his work: while ostensibly representing those who were excluded from the centre of power, his approach to the presence of women in social and urban construction clashes with his goal of representing those without representation, precisely because he ignores women and resists granting them a voice. We believe that this contradiction makes him a representative example of processes at work more generally in the social, cultural, and political environment of Spain at that time.

18 Sinca dedicates a chapter to Maruja, Candel's wife, where she is described as an illiterate woman, a gambling addict, and crude, "una creu que, malgrat tot, Candel va saber arrossegar amb resignació" (131) [a cross that, in spite of everything, Candel knew how to bear with resignation], which could explain her absence and reduced role in Candel's books. However, we could find many objections to this argument, especially if we keep in mind his opinion on the feminism of the 1970s. In a context where the role of women was narrowly defined, we see the emergence of a feminism that is

virulent ... Hi havia dones que no eren ni carn ni peix. Fumaven i bevien i cridaven com també feien alguns homes, com si això fos signe de més llibertat ... Després, més cap a la transició, les feministes van caure a sobre dels barris i la veritat és que anaven tan exaltades que no tenien sentit de l'equilibri ... En els temps en què jo vaig començar a escriure, el feminisme era una cosa inexistent, encara que ja n'hi havia, de feministes, però més endavant, la cosa es va anar fent una mica més esperpèntica. Hi havia dones, com la Lidia Falcón, la Carmen Alcalde i unes quantes més que ... semblaven pollastres asexuats. (Candel qtd in Sinca 213)

virulent ... There were women that were neither meat nor fish. They smoked and drank and shouted like some men did, as if that were a sign of greater freedom ... Later, more toward the Transition, feminists invaded the neighbourhoods and it's definitely true that they were so overexcited that they had no sense of balance ... At the time when I was starting to write, feminism did not exist, although there already were feminists, but later on, things got crazier. There were women, like Lidia Falcón, Carmen Alcalde, and a few others that ... seemed like asexual chickens.

In spite of recognizing the need for greater freedom, Candel continues to be invested in a limited reading of what it means to be a woman and continues to subject their actions to his masculine gaze.

19 The most notable example is Custodia Moreno, who led the protest and neighbourhood struggle in the neighbourhoods of Torre Baró and El Carmel, but to hers we could add many silenced female voices in the struggles of neighbourhood associations. For more information, see Nash.

20 Due to our objective and focus in this book, I have selected women photographers whose work evinces the development of dissent, takes place in Barcelona, and is, in one way or another, urban. It is not at all a complete list of photographers who satisfy these criteria; for an expanded list, consult Nash and Colita's book, *Fotògrafes pioneres a Catalunya*.

21 The selection of these two examples is not made at random; through a comparison of the contexts of their production, we can see how in spite of their being contemporaries their gazes construct, limit, objectify, create, and maintain distance in a different way. The dictatorship formally

differentiates between men and women, completely eliminating, as we mentioned, the equal rights attained by the latter in the years of the Second Republic, which can be seen in the photographic production of this period. For a detailed study of the social roles of women in the first half of the twentieth century and under the dictatorship, consult Mary Nash's *Dones en Transició* and María Teresa Gallego Méndez's *Mujer, falange y franquismo.*

22 The information on Milagros Caturla referenced here was researched and published by Begoña Fernández Díez on the internet (accessed 25 June 2017). Since then some of her work and biography has been gathered in Carmelo Vega's *Fotografía en España.*

23 In 1958 Caturla won third place in a contest among members of a course given by the AFC, which included both male and female participants; José Tomás won first place and Andrés Basté placed second. In August of 1961 she won second place with her photo "Maternal" in the IV Salón Nacional de Fotografía Artística "Fiesta Mayor de Gracia," another mixed contest where first prize went to Eugeni Forcano and second to Ramón Vilalta. On 3 August 1961 she won fifth place with her work "Recela" in the XVII Salón Nacional de Arte Fotográfico (Vilanova i la Geltrú). In April of 1962, she took fourth in the IV Concurso fotográfico de la sección femenina, and on 11 August 1962 she won third place with her work "Faces" in the XVIII Salón Nacional de Arte Fotográfico (Vilanova i la Geltrú).

24 Caturla's work owes its reappearance to sheer coincidence. Tom Sponheim, an American tourist visiting Barcelona in 2001, bought some negatives in the Encants market. When he developed the photographs, he was astonished by their quality and set out to find the photographer using social media. Following his lead, Begoña Fernández Díez took up the search and wound up uncovering the photographer's identity in 2017. Since then, Caturla's photographs have been exhibited in the festival of analogue photography *Revela't* under the title "Las fotos perdidas de Barcelona" (Vilassar de Dalt, May 2017).

25 As Mónica Carabias and Francisco José García explain ("Los ojos visibles"), it will not be until the 1970s that we begin to see a professionalization of photographic language on the part of women, coinciding with a crucial moment in their development and independence.

26 Here we are not trying to affirm that the intention behind Colom's photographs was to make all women out to be prostitutes, but his work does depend on a male gaze that cannot be surrendered and that gives him the amnesty necessary to walk unseen through the Raval. We have seen his work through the construction of public space; here, however, I am interested in the construction of his male gaze and how it shapes spaces in the Raval in order to link this narrative with Colita's work later.

27 The starting point for this reflection is Henri Lefebvre (1970), who proposes to reconceptualize "the city" as "the urban" in order to acknowledge
the contingency that is part and parcel of "the real." Once again, we come
back to Pollock's definition of the image ("Missing Women").

28 Caturla's work's first characterization within this context gives us a clue
as to the limited scope available to female photographers, although the
technique and themes in some of her photos push back against the limits
of this type of photography. That said, it is true that some of her images,
mainly photography contest winners such as "Fervor," can be characterized under this conceptualization.

29 This lack of change in social structure persists even today. In the description included with Caturla's work in the *Revela't* festival in 2017, Daniel
Venteo ("Las fotos") explains that "[d]e profesión maestra, funcionaria de
la Diputación de Barcelona, *murió de Alzheimer, soltera y sin descendencia*"
(emphasis added) [a teacher by profession, a public servant in Barcelona's
city council, *she died of Alzheimer's, unmarried and without children*]. In no
other case is personal information about the photographer included, and
here we see how a woman's identity is tied to her domestic roles.

30 For a selection of Caturla's photographs, see Silvia García and Daniel
Venteo ("Milagros").

31 This photographer's name appears in two distinct formats: as Carme
Garcia de Ferrando, with the second last name being her husband's, and as
Carme Garcia Padrosa. Although we have opted for Carme Garcia, following the style of the book edited by Segura Soriano, it is important to point
out the difference in order to show the limitations on the female body and
this photographer's propriety in an exclusively male world, as we can
already see through her name alone. It is also significant that only in the
latest compilation of her work is her original name used, leaving out her
husband's last name, which indicates the acceptance of conventionalism
and the place of women in an "aside."

32 Carme Garcia got her start in photography as a hobby in the 1930s, although
few of her photographs from that period remain. Due to the war and family
obligations, Garcia did not resume her photography until the 1950s, when
she signed up for a course exclusively for women that the AFC organized.
She shot photos actively until 1985, during which time she participated in
exhibits and contests, both in Spain and abroad, despite her work being
excluded from the art world, which in the 1950s and 1960s did not include
women (Segura Soriano, "Carme" 11). In spite of her recognition in contests,
her work was relegated to the women's scene, where women and their creations were excluded from the public art sphere outside the AFC.

33 Carme Garcia's work was recognized nationally and internationally. In 1963
she won the prestigious Luis Navarro Award, in 1973 the Nikon, and in 1966

the l'Interpress-Photo de Moscou, among others. Her photographs have been published in the Fédération Internationale de l'Art Photographique's *Photo-amateur* (1967) and in *Photography Year Book* (1973). For more information, see Nash and Colita (106) and Segura Soriano ("Carme" 6).

34 Journalism will be essential for the development of the Spanish documentary form and will also offer a field where women photographers can work in photography, even before the Civil War. In the world of professional photography, there is only one known antecedent that predates 1939, Anna Maria Martínez Sagi (1907–2000), "únic testimoni gràfic en femení a la premsa barcelonina entre 1900 i 1939. En un ofici dominat pels homes, la primera signatura d'una dona no s'ha trobat fins a l'esclat de la Guerra Civil" (González Morandi et al. 158) [the only female graphic witness in the press in Barcelona between 1900 and 1939. In a field dominated by men, the first female signature was not found until the outbreak of the Civil War]. In the 1960s and 1970s, in addition to Colita we see photographers such as Joana Biarnés (1935–2018) – although her work differs from Colita's for how it is primarily journalistic in nature and not centred in the city of Barcelona - and Pilar Aymerich. Following the dictatorship, the sweeping changes in the political, social, and cultural panorama gives way to a new series of female photographers that will evolve the documentary genre towards "documentalismo intimista" (Carabias and García, "Ojos de mujer" 154) [intimist documtentary]. However, our focus on the dictatorship and the creation of dissent puts our limits on the figures that we analyse in this book.

35 Colita's work has been recognized with prestigious awards on multiple occasions: in 1998, the city government of Barcelona awarded her a gold medal for artistic merit alongside Oriol Maspons and Leopoldo Pomés; in 2004, she was given the Creu de Sant Jordi by the Generalitat de Catalunya; and the FAD prize of honour in 2014. Also, in 2014, she was granted the National Prize in Photography, which she rejected in protest of the state of culture and education in Spain. Her work has been exhibited since 1965 and published in numerous books. Her work figures in the collections of the Museu Nacional d'Art de Catalunya, Museo Nacional de Arte Reina Sofía, and Fundación Elsa Peretti, among others.

36 With this commentary, I wish to draw attention not to the characterization of these photographers' work, but towards an external characterization that responds to the "mythological" division – following Bourdieu in *La dominación masculina* – the male/female binary that persists in the historicization of culture. For more on this subject, see also Griselda Pollock's text "Historia y política."

37 As Rosón Villena explains, the "destape" let the naked or semi-naked female body take centre stage, which, on the one hand, defied censorship

and the moral dictates regarding the body in Spanish society during late Francoism, and, on the other, was based on hypervisibilization and the objectification of women's bodies (66). The female body, then, becomes a space for the negotiation of political ideas and interests, but while the male gaze reads it as a sign of tolerance, democracy, and repression, as, for example, Vázquez Montalbán defends in articles like "Los desnudos y los muertos" (Marí, "El Umbral" 245–6), in practice women continue to be reduced to the same place of oppression and submission to which the regime limited them, so that, as Maite Garbayo Maeztu claims, the "destape" "terminó tapando la ausencia real de libertades" (13) [ends up concealing the real absence of freedom]. For more on the conflict over the "destape," see also Jorge Marí, "Desnudos, vivos y muertos."

38 Francesc Català Roca has a similar photograph, "Señoritas en la Gran Vía de Madrid" (1955), in which six women walk arm in arm down the famous boulevard. They are shot from behind, but at a distance. In spite of the similarities between the two photos, the space occupied by the bodies in Català Roca's is one socially ascribed to them – they are out shopping – which strips them of the strength and agency we see in Colita's. Indeed, any comparison between the two photos necessarily becomes a critique, albeit an involuntary one, of Català Roca's. Furthermore, the fact that the women in Colita's photo are prostitutes gives her a platform for making a powerful and much more relevant social critique of space and the "consumption" of the female body.

39 This intersection of spaces can also be seen in the work of Pilar Aymerich, who explicitly conjures in her images the questioning of women in public space and the social limitations imposed upon them by the male gaze in her reports on the feminist movement in Barcelona (see Laura Terré, *Pilar Aymerich*), which looks at demonstrations and protests during the final years of the dictatorship and then the Transition). This photographer challenges oppressive discourse using its own words and space against it, uncovering and criticizing the limitations imposed by the gaze on body and space, in a move reminiscent of Colita. In the work of these two photographers, distance is translated into proximity: the switch of perspective grants the body a new materiality and, in the process, attempts to redefine space through the centrifugal force emitted by the images.

40 Again, we have a similar image from Català Roca, "Marineros en el Barrio Chino" (1953), in which we see two sailors entering the Raval accompanied by two women. In this case, the bodies of the women are subjugated and read by the fact that they are subject to the male body and gaze. The neighbourhood, like the city, is always masculine. It is important to note that Català Roca always seems to stay at the entrance to the Raval (another similar image is "Calle Arco del teatro" [1950], where we see a man

leaving the Raval combing his hair); he is always at the limits of what is considered legal/illegal, insinuating but never daring to say what.

41 Ignasi Marroyo (1928–2017) was, together with Colom, one of the members of the photographic group El Mussol that collaborated with AFAL. Keeping with the collaborative spirit of the Catalan group, he photographed the Somorrostro neighbourhood with Colom for *El Correo Catalán* (1964). As a professional, he specialized in industrial photography – factories, warehouses, machinery, and the like – although he did continue to practice documentary photography in the 1960s and 1970s.

Conclusion

1 Delgado goes on to say that the urban policy of the post-Franco democratic period is staunchly characterized as technocratic and interventionist, a policy foreshadowed in the Plan of 1953 and its revision in 1964, and the General Metropolitan Plan of 1974 (*La ciudad* 22). In this context, neighbourhood opposition to these initiatives cannot compare to the resistance put forth to city hall in late Francoism (26). Protest under the dictatorship was reinforced by the hope for change in the political order: it was not simply a matter of protest, but the right to protest (26). Once that right was granted, neighbourhood associations were enshrined in city hall, which thus managed to domesticate "a sus críticos, convirtiéndolos en cómplices dependientes de la prebenda y la subvención" (26) [its critics, making them into accomplices dependent on privileges and subsidies].

   For more information on the decline of neighbourhood associations, see Domingo and Rosa Bonet. For more on the continuation of Francoism's urbanistic policies under democracy, see Laura García's book, *El Carmel, ferida oberta* (2005) [El Carmel, open wound] or Rosa Tello's article, "Barcelona post-olímpica."

2 In fact, Candel would continue to write until 2006, when he published *Primera historia, primera memoria* [First history, first memory]. His work is always connected to the urban memory of Barcelona and its inhabitants. Likewise, we see the same continuity in Colita, whose work will be inextricably linked to feminism whether directly or indirectly.

3 This list is a brief sample of the exhibitions and activities that have begun to pop up. We could add to this list books like Esteve Lucerón's *La Perona, 1980–1989*.

Works Cited

Abad Buil, Irene. "Movimiento democrático de mujeres: Un vehículo para la búsqueda de una nueva ciudadanía femenina en la transición española." *Actes del congrés la transició de la dictadura franquista a la democràcia.* Barcelona: Centre d'estudis sobre les èpoques franquista i democràtica, 2005, pp. 245–53.

Abellán, Manuel L. *Censura y creación literaria en España (1939–1976).* Ediciones Península, 1980.

Afinoguénova, Eugenia, and Jaume Martí-Olivella, editors. *Spain Is (Still) Different: Tourism and Discourse in Spanish Identity.* Lexington Books, 2008.

Agamben, Giorgio. *Potentialities.* Stanford UP, 1999.

Alfeo Álvarez, Luis, and Juan Carlos Deltell Escolar, editors. *La mirada mecánica: 17 ensayos sobre la imagen fotográfica.* Editorial Fragua, 2016.

Aliaga, Juan Vicente, and Patricia Mayayo, editors. *Genealogías feministas en el arte español: 1960–2010.* This Side Up, 2013.

Amin, Ash, and Nigel Thrift. *Cities: Reimagining the Urban.* Polity Press, 2008.

Anderson, Benedict. *Imagined Communities: Reflections on the Origin and Spread of Nationalism.* Verso, 2006.

Ansón, Antonio. *Novelas como álbumes: Fotografía y literatura.* Mestizo, 2000.

Antich, Xavier. "Barccelona, periferias urbanas." *La Vanguardia, Cultura/s,* 18 Dec. 2013, pp. 3–5.

Arendt, Hannah. *The Human Condition.* U of Chicago P, 1958.

– *On Violence.* A Harvest Book, 1970.

Aricó, Giuseppe. "De proletarios a propietarios, o los orígenes de la lógica espacial del urbanismo neoliberal." *Observatori d'Antropologia del Conflicte Urbà,* 23 May 2016, https://observatoriconflicteurba.org/2016/05/23/de-proletarios-a-propietarios-o-los-origines-de-la-logica-espacial-del-urbanismo-neoliberal/.

Balibrea, Mari Paz. *The Global Cultural Capital: Addressing the Citizen and Producing the City in Barcelona.* Palgrave Macmillan, 2017.

Balsells, David, and Jorge Ribalta. "Introducció." *Jo faig el carrer: Joan Colom, fotografies 1957–2010*, edited by Jorge Ribalta and David Balsells, La Fábrica/MNAC, 2013, pp. 13–35.

Barceló, Ignacio. "Nota del editor." *Arte Fotográfico*, vol. 79, July 1958, pp. 545–6.

Barcelona fotògrafes/fotógrafas, edited by Isabel Segura, Ajuntament de Barcelona, 2020.

Barcelona: La metròpolis en la era de la fotografia, 1860–2004. Editorial RM, 2016.

Barraques: La Barcelona informal del segle XX. 18 July 2008–22 Feb. 2009, Museu d'Història de Barcelona, Barcelona.

Barraques: La ciutat oblidada. Directed by Alonso Carnicer and Sara Grimal, "Sense Ficció" TV3, 2010, https://www.ccma.cat/tv3/alacarta/urbanisme-a-barcelona/barraques-la-ciutat-oblidada/coleccio/2850/2333059/.

Barthes, Roland. *Camera Lucida: Reflections on Photography*. Translated by Richard Howard, Hill and Wang, 1981.

– *Empire of Signs*. Translated by Richard Howard, Hill and Wang, 1982.

– "La Torre Eiffel." *La Torre Eiffel*, translated by Enrique Folch González, Paidós, 2001, pp. 55–79.

Benjamin, Walter. "Pequeña historia de la fotografía." *Sobre la fotografía*, translated by José Muñoz Millanes, Pre-Textos, 2007.

Berger, John. *Another Way of Telling*. Pantheon, 1982.

Bernal López-Sanvicente, Amparo. *Las revistas Arquitectura y Cuadernos de Arquitectura, 1960–1970*. 2011. U de Valladolid, PhD dissertation.

Biarnés, Joana. *Disparando con el corazón*. Art Blume, 2017.

Bohigas, Oriol. "Elogi de la barraca." *Entre el Pla Cerdà i el Barraquisme*, Edicions 62, 1963, pp. 149–55.

– "El polígono de Montbau." *CAU*, vol. 60, 1965, pp. 23–33.

Bordetas Jiménez, Ivan. "De la supervivència a la resistència: La gestació del moviment veïnal a la Catalunya franquista." *Construint la ciutat democràtica: El moviment veïnal durant el tradofranquisme i la transició*, edited by Carme Molinero and Pere Ysàs, Icària, 2010, pp. 35–112.

Borja, Jordi. "Ciudadanía y espacio público." *Ciutat real, ciutat ideal: Significat i funció a l'espai urbà modern*. Barcelona: CCCB, 1998, http://www.cccb.org/rcs_gene/ciudadania_espacio_publico_cast.pdf.

– *Movimientos sociales urbanos*. Ediciones SIAP, 1975.

– "La promoción pública del hábitat marginal: Las viviendas de la Obra Sindical del Hogar." *La Gran Barcelona*, Alberto Corazón, 1972, pp. 59–60.

Bou, Enric, and Jaume Subirana, editors. *The Barcelona Reader: Cultural Readings of a City*. Liverpool UP, 2017.

Bourdieu, Pierre. *La dominación masculina*. Translated by Joaquín Jordá, Anagrama, 2000.

– "Introduction." *Photography: A Middle-Brow Art*, translated by Shaun Whiteside, Polity Press, 1990, pp. 1–10.

Brangulí, Josep. *Brangulí: Barcelona 1909–1945*. Barcelona: CCCB, 2010.

Busquets, Joan. *Barcelona: Evolución urbanística de una capital compacta*. Editorial Mapfre, 1992.

Caballé, Anna. *El feminismo en España: La lenta conquista de un derecho*. Cátedra, 2013.

Calavita, Nico, and Amador Ferrer. "Behind Barcelona's Success Story: Citizen Movements and Planners' Power." *Journal of Urban History*, vol. 26, no. 6, Sept. 2000, pp. 793–807.

Cambril Soriano, Bibiana. *Las viviendas del Congreso Eucarístico*. 2013. U Politècnica de Catalunya, MA thesis. *Treballs Acadèmics UPC*, http://hdl .handle.net/2099.1/11017.

Candel, Francisco. *Els altres catalans*. 1964. Edicions 62, 2008.

– "El amazacotamiento." *CAU*, vol. 60, 1965, pp. 5–8.

– "De cuando *Donde la ciudad cambia su nombre* cambió la indiferencia hacia la ciudad suburbial." *Donde la ciudad cambia su nombre*, La Busca, 1998, pp. 15–25.

– *¡Dios, la que se armó!* Ediciones Marte, 1964.

– *Donde la ciudad cambia su nombre*. Janés, 1957.

– *Encara més sobre els altres catalans*. Curial, 1973.

– "El escritor del proletariado." Interview by Juan Cruz. *El País*, 11 Sept. 2005, https://elpais.com/diario/2005/09/11/eps/1126420016_850215.html.

– *Han matado a un hombre, han roto un paisaje*. Ediciones G.P., 1967.

– *Primera historia, primera memoria*. Edicions 62, 2006.

– *Ser obrero no es ninguna ganga*. Ariel, 1968.

– "La vida catalana: Barraques de la riera Comtal: Uns veïns als quals ningú no fa cas." *Serra d'Or*, vol. 5, May 1965, pp. 71–3.

Cánovas, Carlos. "Entre dues ruptures." *Temps de silenci: Panorama de la fotografia espanyola dels anys 50*, Fundació la Caixa, 1992, pp. 9–24.

Carabias, Mónica, and Francisco José García. "Ojos de mujer: Aproximación a medio siglo de creación fotográfica en España." *La Mirada mecánica: 17 ensayos sobre la imagen fotográfica*, edited by Luis Alfeo Álvarez and Juan Carlos Deltell Escolar, Editorial Fragua, 2016, pp. 147–66.

– "Los ojos visibles de Juana Biarnés: Historia de un comienzo (1950–1963)." *ASRI*, vol. 7, Oct. 2014.

Carminal, Miquel. "Presentació." *Construint la ciutat democràtica: El moviment veïnal durant el tardofranquisme i la transició*, edited by Carme Molinero and Pere Ysàs, Icària, 2010, pp. 7–11.

Carrera, Judit. "El Raval: La ciudad sin puertas." *El País*, 7 Oct. 2010, p. 2.

Carreras Verdaguer, Carles. *La Barcelona literària: Una introducció geogràfica*. Proa, 2003.

Cartier-Bresson, Henri. *Fotografiar del natural*. Editorial Gustavo Gili, 2003.

Casademont, Josep M. "La fotografia." *L'art català contemporani*, edited by Enric Jardí, Proa, 1972, pp. 431–55.

Castellet, Josep Maria. "De l'arquitectura a l'humanisme." *Serra d'Or*, vol. 6, no. 1, Jan. 1964, pp. 26–7.

– *La hora del lector: Notas para una iniciación a la literatura narrativa de nuestros días*. Seix Barral, 1957.

Castellote, Alejandro. "España: Fragmentos propios y ajenos de nuestro imaginario visual." *España a través de la fotografía, 1839–2010*, Taurus, 2013, pp. 27–93.

Castells, Manuel. *The City and the Grassroots: A Cross-Cultural Theory of Urban Social Movements*. U of California P, 1983.

– *The Urban Question: A Marxist Approach*. Translated by Alan Sheridan, MIT P, 1979.

Cela, Camilo José. *Izas, rabizas y colipoterras*. Lumen, 1964.

Certeau, Michel de. *The Practice of Everyday Life*. U of California P, 1984.

Chambers, Ross. *Room for Maneuver: Reading (the) Oppositional (in) Narrative*. U of Chicago P, 1991.

Chevrier, Jean François. "The Adventures of the Picture Form in the History of Photography." *The Last Picture Show: Artists Using Photography 1960–1982*, edited by Douglas Fogle. Minneapolis: Walker Art Center, 2003, pp. 113–28.

Colita. *Antifémina*. Text by Maria Aurèlia Capmany, Editora Nacional, 1977.

– *Colita, ¡Porque sí!* Edited by Laura Terré, Editorial RM, 2014.

– *Luces y sombras del flamenco*. Text by J.M. Bonald, Lumen, 1975.

Colom, Joan. "Autobiografía." *AFAL*, vol. 34, Jan./Feb. 1962, pp. 8–9.

Costa, Joan, and Adela Ros. "Diversitat dels fluxos migratoris, integració social i multicultural a Barcelona: Els darrers vint anys." *L'articulació social de la Barcelona contemporània*, edited by Joan Roca Albert. Barcelona: Proa i Institut Municipal d'Història, 1997, pp. 227–40.

Crumbaugh, J. *Destination Dictatorship: The Spectacle of Spain's Tourist Boom and the Reinvention of Difference*. State U of New York P, 2009.

Davidov, Judith Fryer. *Women's Camera Work: Self/Body/Other in American Visual Culture*. Duke UP, 1998.

Davidson, Robert A. *Jazz Age Barcelona*. U of Toronto P, 2009.

Dawidoff, Nicholas. "The Man Who Saw America." *New York Times Magazine*, 2 July 2015, https://www.nytimes.com/2015/07/05/magazine/robert -franks-america.html.

Debord, Guy. *Society of the Spectacle*. AK Press, 2005.

Degen, Mónica Montserrat. *Sensing Cities: Regenerating Public Life in Barcelona and Manchester*. Routledge, 2008.

Delgado, Manuel. *El animal público: Hacia una antropología de los espacios urbanos*. Anagrama, 1999.

- "La ciudad levantada: La barricada y otras transformaciones radicales del espacio urbano." *Arquitectonics: Mind, Land & Society*, vol. 19–20, Mar. 2010, pp. 137–53.
- *La ciudad mentirosa: Fraude y miseria del "Modelo Barcelona."* Catarata, 2010.
- *Elogi del vianant: Del "model Barcelona" a la Barcelona real.* Edicions de 1984, 2005.
- "Elogio y rescate de Henri Lefebvre: La usurpación de 'El derecho a la ciudad' por las nuevas políticas urbanas." *El País*, 19 Mar. 2018.
- *El espacio público como ideología.* Catarata, 2011.
- *Memoria y lugar: El espacio público como crisis de significado.* Ediciones Generales de la Construcción, 2001.
- *Sociedades movedizas: Pasos hacia una antropología de las calles.* Anagrama, 2007.
- "Todas las ciudades están poseídas." *Matar al Chino: Entre la revolución urbanística y el asedio urbano en el barrio del Raval de Barcelona* by Miquel Fernández González, Virus Editorial, 2014, pp. 329–36.
- Del Valle, Teresa. *Andamios para una nueva ciudad: Lecturas desde la antropología.* Cátedra, 1997.
- Deutsche, Rosalyn. *Agorafobia.* Quaderns portàtils, 2008.
- "Uneven Development: Public Art in New York City." *Out There: Marginalization and Contemporary Cultures*, edited by Russell Ferguson et al., MIT P, 1990, pp. 107–30.
- Di Febo, Giuliana. "La lucha de las mujeres en los barrios en los últimos años del franquismo: Un ejemplo de utilización de la 'historia de género.'" *La oposición al régimen de Franco: Estado de la cuestión y metodología de la investigación. Actas del Congreso Internacional del Departamento de Historia Contemporánea de la UNED*, vol. 1, no. 2. Madrid: UNED, 1988, pp. 251–69.
- *Resistencia y movimiento de mujeres en España, 1936–1976.* Icaria, 1979.
- Domingo, Miquel, and Maria Rosa Bonet. *Barcelona i el moviments socials urbans.* Barcelona: Fundació Jaume Bofill y Edicions Mediterrània, 1998.
- Donato, José E. "Barrios altos de San Andrés." *CAU* vol. 60, 1965, pp. 19–40.
- Duocastella, R. "Prefacio." *Los suburbios 1957: Compendio de las ponencias y coloquios desarrollados durante la "Semana," seguido de gráficas y estadísticas.* Gráf. Levante, 1957, pp. 5–7.
- Ealham, Chris. "An Imagined Geography: Ideology, Urban Space, and Protest in the Creation of Barcelona's Chinatown." *International Review of Social History*, vol. 50, no. 3, 2005, pp. 373–97.
- *La lucha por Barcelona: Clase, cultura y conflicto (1898–1937).* Alianza, 2005.
- Elden, Stuart. "Rhythmanalysis: An Introduction." *Rhythmanalysis: Space, Time and Everyday Life* by Henri Lefebvre, Continuum, 2007, pp. vii–xv.
- El Hachmi, Najat. "Pròleg." *Els altres catalans* by Francisco Candel, Edicions 62, 2008, pp. 7–11.

"El programa de la Falange Española de las J.O.N.S." *ABC Diario Ilustrado*, 30 Nov. 1934, pp. 32–4.

Epps, Brad. "Els llocs d'enlloc: Aspiracions utòpiques i limitacions materials del Pla Cerdà." *Treballs de la Societat Catalana de Geografia*, vol. 63, 2007, pp. 105–19.

Fabre, Jaume, and Josep M. Huertas Clavería. *Tots els barris de Barcelona: La Verneda I La Pau, els Barris del Besòs, els tres "lumpen-barris," els Nou Barris, el Districte V*. Edicions 62, 1977.

Fernández, Horacio. *Variaciones en España: Fotografía y arte, 1900–1980*. La Fábrica, 2004.

Fernández de Alba, Francisco. *Sex, Drugs, and Fashion in 1970s Madrid*. U of Toronto P, 2020.

Fernández Díez, Begoña. "Photographic Research." *Emilbeat Photography*, https://emilbeatphotography.com/photographic-research. Accessed 25 June 2017.

Fernández González, Miquel. *Matar al Chino: Entre la revolución urbanística y el asedio urbano en el barrio del Raval de Barcelona*. Virus Editorial, 2014.

Ferrer, Amador. "Barraques i polígons d'habitatges en la Barcelona del segle XX." *La Barcelona informal del segle XX*, Museu d'Història de Barcelona, Institut de Cultura, 2010, pp. 61–79.

– "El Pla comarcal de 1953 i la codificació de les formes urbanes." *1856–1999 Barcelona Contemporània*. Barcelona: CCCB, 1996, pp. 132–3.

Fontcuberta, Joan. "Barcelona: Nuevo documentalismo." *Historias de la fotografía española: Escritos 1977–2004*, Gustavo Gili, 2008, pp. 77–85.

– "Izas, rabizas y colipoterras: Un álbum furtivo." *Joan Colom: Fotografías de Barcelona, 1958–1964*, edited by Jorge Ribalta and David Balsells, Lunwerg, 2004, pp. 45–51.

– "De la posguerra al siglo XXI." *La fotografía en España: De los orígenes al siglo XXI*, edited by Juan Miguel Sánchez Vigil, Espasa-Calpe, 2001, pp. 387–472.

Formiguera, Pere. "Ricard Terré: Donde no llega la mirada." *Ricard Terré*, http://www.ricardterre.com/crterre.html. Accessed 11 July 2018.

– "La segunda ruptura: La fotografía catalana de los años cincuenta y sesenta." *Introducción a la historia de la fotografía en Cataluña*, Lunwerg, 2000, pp. 149–212.

– *Temps de silenci: Panorama de la fotografia espanyola del anys 50 i 60*. Barcelona: Fundació Caixa de Catalunya, 1992.

Foucault, Michel. *History of Madness*. Routledge, 2009.

– "A Preface to Transgression." *Language, Counter-Memory, Practice: Selected Essays and Interviews by Michel Foucault*, edited by Donald F. Bouchard, Cornell UP, 1977, pp. 29–52.

Fraser, Benjamin. *Henri Lefebvre and the Spanish Urban Experience: Reading the Mobile City*. Bucknell UP, 2011.

– *Toward an Urban Cultural Studies: Henri Lefebvre and the Humanities*. Plagrave McMillian, 2015.

Gallego Méndez, María Teresa. *Mujer, falange y franquismo*. Taurus, 1983.

Garbayo Maeztu, Maite. *Cuerpos que aparecen: Performance y feminismos en el tardofranquismo*. Consonni, 2016.

Garcia, Carme. *Carme Garcia: Des del terrat*. El cep i la nansa, 2018.

García, Laura. *El Carmel, ferida oberta: De l'esvoranc al 3%*. Mina, 2005.

García, Silvia. "Milagros Caturla era la enigmática autora de las fotos perdidas de Barcelona." *Cultura Inquieta*, 29 Mar. 2017, https://culturainquieta.com/es/foto/item/11806-milagros-caturla-era-la-enigmatica-autora-de-las-fotos-perdidas-de-barcelona.html.

Gardiner, Michael E. "The 'Dictatorship of the Eye': Henri Lefebvre on Vision, Space and Modernity." *The Handbook of Visual Culture*, edited by Ian Heywood and Barry Sandywell, Bloomsbury, 2017, pp. 342–60.

Genovès, Dolors. *Les Barcelones de Porcioles: Un abecedari*. Proa, 2005.

Gilabert, Joan. "Aspectos peculiares del realismo social en la obra de Candel." Prologue to *El perro que nunca existió y el anciano padre que tampoco*, by Francisco Candel, Laia, 1973, pp. 7–22.

– "La obra de Francisco Candel ante el poder y la censura." *La Chispa' 93, Selected Proceedings*, edited by Gilbert Paolini, Tulane U, 1993, pp. 98–108.

Gilbert, Sandra, and Susan Gubar. *The Madwoman in the Attic: The Woman Writer and the Nineteenth-Century Literary Imagination*. Yale UP, 2000.

Gil de Biedma, Jaime. "Barcelona ja no és bona, o mi paseo solitario en primavera." *Las personas del verbo*, Lumen, 1999, pp. 85–8.

González Morandi, Pablo, et al., editors. *Repòrters Gràfics: Barcelona, 1900–1939*. Ajuntament de Barcelona, 2015.

Goytisolo, Juan. *Fiestas*. Destino, 1969.

– *Señas de identidad*. Alianza Editorial, 2007.

Gracia García, Jordi. *La resistencia silenciosa: Fascismo y cultura en España*. Anagrama, 2004.

Gracia García, Jordi, and Miguel Ángel Ruiz Carnicer. *La España de Franco (1939–1975): Cultura y vida cotidiana*. Editorial Síntesis, 2001.

Hall, Jacqueline. "La bena i la mordassa: Els catalans davant la immigració de l'època franquista." *Treballs de sociolingüística catalana*, vol. 5, 1983, pp. 71–92.

Haraway, Donna J. "A Cyborg Manifesto: Science, Technology, and Socialist-Feminism in the Late Twentieth Century." *Manifestly Haraway*, U of Minnesota P, 2016, pp. 3–90.

Harvey, David. *Ciudades rebeldes: Del derecho de la ciudad a la revolución urbana*. Translated by Juanmari Madariaga, Akal, 2013.

– *The Condition of Postmodernity: An Enquiry into the Origins of Cultural Change*. Blackwell, 1990.

– *Cosmopolitanism and the Geographies of Freedom*. Columbia UP, 2009.

– "The New Urbanism and the Communitarian Trap." *Harvard Design Magazine*, Winter/Spring 1997, pp. 1–3.

– *The Urban Experience*. Johns Hopkins UP, 1989.

Heidegger, Martin. "The Age of the World Picture." *The Question Concerning Technology and Other Essays*, Harper and Row, 1977, pp. 143–87.

Hollander, Jocelyn A., and Rachel L. Einwohner. "Conceptualizing Resistance." *Sociological Forum*, vol. 19, Dec. 2004, pp. 470–85.

Holston, James, and Arjun Appadurai. "Introduction: Cities and Citizenship." *Cities and Citizenship*, edited by James Holston, Duke UP, 1999, pp. 1–20.

Homberger, Eric. "Transcending the Agendas: Gender and Photography." *Word & Image: A Jounal of Verbal/Visual Enquiry*, vol. 7, no. 4, 1991, pp. 377–82.

Huertas Clavería, Josep M. *Barcelona en lluita: El moviment urbà 1965–1996*. Federació d'Associacions de Veïns de Barcelona, 1996.

– "Han roto un paisaje." *Donde la ciudad cambia su nombre*, La Busca Edicions, 1998, pp. 5–8.

Hughes, Robert. *Barcelona*. Alfred A. Knopf, 1992.

Illas, Edgar. *Thinking Barcelona: Ideologies of a Global City*. Liverpool UP, 2012.

Irigaray, Luce. "Interview." *Les Femmes, la pornographie, l'erotisme*, edited by Marie-Françoise Hans and Gilles Lapouge, Seuil, 1978, pp. 43–58.

Jacobs, Jane. *The Death and Life of Great American Cities*. 1961. Vintage Books, 1992.

Jay, Martin. "Scopic Regimes of Modernity Revisited." *The Handbook of Visual Culture*, edited by Ian Heywood and Barry Sandywell, Bloomsbury, 2017, pp. 102–14.

Josep M. Huertas Clavería i els barris de Barcelona: Antologia de reportatges (1964–1975). Federació d'Associacions de Veïns i Veïnes de Barcelona, 2013.

Jubany, Narciso. "Presentación de la Semana del Suburbio." *Los suburbios 1957: Compendio de las ponencias y coloquios desarrollados durante la "Semana," seguido de gráficas y estadísticas*. Gráf. Levante, 1957, p. 9.

Jutglar, Antoni. "A propósito de *Els altres catalans*: Carta abierta a Francisco Candel." *Cuadernos para el diálogo*, vol. 15, 1964, pp. 13–14.

Keown, Dominic, editor. *A Companion to Catalan Culture*. Tamesis, 2011.

Klein, William. *New York 1954–55*. Lunwerg, 1995.

Laclau, Ernesto, and Chantal Mouffe. *Hegemony and Socialist Strategy: Toward a Radical Democratic Politics*. Verso, 1985.

Langer, Susanne K. *Feeling and Form: A Theory of Art*. Charles Scribner's Sons, 1953.

Larrea, Cristina, and Mercè Tatjer. "L'estudi interdisciplinari del barraquisme." *Barraques: La Barcelona informal del segle XX*, Museu d'Història de Barcelona, Institut de Cultura, 2010, pp. 15–19.

Ledrut, Raymond. "Speech and the Silence of the City." *The City and the Sign: An Introduction to Urban Semiotics*, edited by M. Gottdiener and Alexandros Ph. Lagopoulos, Columbia UP, 1986, pp. 114–34.

Leet, Sri-Kartini. *Reading Photography: A Sourcebook of Critical Texts, 1921–2000.* Lund Humphries, 2011.

Lefebvre, Henri. *The Production of Space.* Translated by Donad Nicholson-Smith, Blackwell, 1991.

– *Le retour de la dialectique: 12 mots clés.* Messidor Éditions Sociales, 1986.

– *Rhythmanalysis: Space, Time and Everyday Life.* Translated by Gerald Moore and Stuart Elden, Continuum, 2007.

– "The Right to the City." *Writings on Cities*, edited and translated by Eleonor Kofman and Elizabeth Lebas, Blackwell, 1996, pp. 63–181.

– *The Urban Revolution.* Translated by Robert Bononno, U of Minnesota P, 2003.

– *Writings on Cities.* Edited and translated by Eleonore Kofman and Elizabeth Lebas, Blackwell, 1996.

"La liberación de Barcelona continúa. El Paseo Marítimo, una gran obra urbanística con proyección social." *El Correo Catalán. Suplemento Gráfico*, 24 Jan. 1964, pp. 34–5.

López Mondéjar, Publio. *Historia de la fotografía en España.* Lunwerg, 1997.

– *Photography in Franco's Spain.* Lunwerg, 1996.

Lucerón, Esteve. *La Perona, 1980–1989.* Barcelona: Produccions Editorials de la Imatge, 2010.

Lyotard, Jean François. *Discours, Figure.* Editions Klincksieck, 1971.

Mackay, David. "Viviendas del Congreso Eucarístico." *CAU*, vol. 60, 1965, pp. 17–21.

Malraux, André. "Museums without Walls." *The Voices of Silence*, translated by Stuart Gilbert, Princeton UP, 1978.

Marí, Jorge. "Desnudos, vivos y muertos: La transición erótico-política y/en la crítica cultural de Vázquez Montalbán." *Manuel Vázquez Montalbán: El compromiso con la memoria*, edited by José F. Colmeiro, Tamesis, 2007, pp. 129–42.

– "El Umbral del destape." *Valoración de Francisco Umbral: Ensayos críticos entorno a su obra*, edited by Carlos X. Ardavín, Libros del Pexe, 2003.

Marsé, Juan. *Últimas tardes con Teresa.* Seix Barral, 2005.

Marsillach, Luis. "Las casas de papel." *Solidaridad Nacional*, 17 July 1953. Rpt. in "Abans d'Ara," *ARA*, 16 May 2014, https://www.ara.cat/premium/las-casas-papel_1_2099555.html.

Masats, Ramón. *Neutral Corner.* Text by Ignacio Aldecoa, Lumen, 1962.

Maspons, Oriol. *La caza de la perdiz roja.* Text by Miguel Delibes, Lumen, 1963.

— "Salonismo." *Arte fotográfico*, vol. 61, Jan. 1957.

Massey, Doreen B. "Cities in the World." *City Worlds*, edited by Doreen Massey et al., Routledge, 1999, pp. 93–150.

— "The Conceptualization of Place." *A Place in the World? Places, Culture and Globalization*, edited by Doreen B. Massey and Pat Jess, Oxford UP, 1995, pp. 45–85.

— "On Space and the City." *City Worlds*, edited by Doreen Massey et al., Routledge, 1999, pp. 151–74.

Mateos, Abdón. "Los decisivos años cincuenta." *La España de los cincuenta*, edited by Abdón Mateos, Editorial Eneida, 2008, pp. 9–11.

McDonogh, Gary W. "Discourses of the City: Policy and Response in Post-Transitional Barcelona." *City & Society*, vol. 5, no. 1, June 1991, pp. 40–63.

— "The Geography of Evil: Barcelona's Barrio Chino." *Anthropological Quaterly*, vol. 60, no. 4, 1987, pp. 174–84.

McNeill, Donald. *Urban Change and the European Left: Tales from the New Barcelona*. Routledge, 1999.

"Memòries visuals de barri." Observatori de la Vida Quotidiana, http://ovq .cat/portfolio/memories-visuals-de-barri/. Accessed July 2018.

Mendoza, Eduardo, and Leopoldo Pomés. "Aquí no se borra nada: Conversación entre Leopoldo Pomés y Eduardo Mendoza." *Barcelona 1957*, La Fábrica, 2012, pp. 21–30.

Merleau-Ponty, Maurice. *Phenomenology of Perception*. Translated by Colin Smith, Taylor & Francis, 2002.

Meskimmon, Marsha. *Engendering the City: Women Artists and Urban Space*. Scarlet, 1997.

Metz, Christian. *The Imaginary Signifier: Psychoanalysis and the Cinema*. Indiana UP, 1982.

Miserachs, Xavier. *Barcelona: Blanc i negre*. Electa, 2003.

Molinero, Carme, and Pere Ysàs, editors. *Construint la ciutat democràtica: El moviment veïnal durant el tardofranquisme i la transició*. Icària, 2010.

— "Introducció." *Construint la ciutat democràtica: El moviment veïnal durant el tardofranquisme i la transició*, edited by Carme Molinero and Pere Ysàs, Icària, 2010, pp. 17–31.

Morcillo, Aurora G. *The Seduction of Modern Spain: The Female Body and the Francoist Body Politic*. Bucknell UP, 2010.

Moreno, Eduard, and Manuel Vázquez Montalbán. *Barcelona, ¿a dónde vas? Diálogos para otra Barcelona*. Ediciones de la Tempestad, 1991.

Nadal Oller, Luis. "Reflexiones en torno a La Guineueta." *CAU*, vol. 60, 1965, pp. 35–9.

Naredo, José Manuel. "El modelo inmobiliario español y sus consecuencias." *Boletín CF+S*, vol. 44, Mar. 2010, pp. 1–27, http://habitat.aq.upm.es/boletin /n44/n44-ajnar.pdf.

Nash, Mary. *Dones en Transició: De la resistència política a la legitimitat feminista, les dones en la Barcelona de la Transició*. Ajuntament de Barcelona, 2007.

Nash, Mary, and Colita, editors. *Fotògrafes pioneres a Catalunya*. Barcelona: Institut Català de les Dones, 2005.

"No queremos una España de proletarios, sino una de propietarios." *ABC*, 2 May 1959, pp. 41–2.

"Nota de la dirección." *AFAL*, vol. 34, Jan./Feb. 1962, p. 9.

Ortiz Heras, Manuel. "Control social y represión en la dictadura franquista (1951–1962)." *La España de los cincuenta*, edited by Abdón Mateos, Editorial Eneida, 2008, pp. 15–43.

Pavlović, Tatjiana. *The Mobile Nation: España Cambia de Piel (1954–1964)*. Intellect, 2011.

Perán, Martín. *Barcelona–Madrid, 1898–1998: Sintonies i distàncies*. Barcelona: CCCB, 1997.

Pollock, Griselda. "Historia y política. ¿Puede la historia del arte sobrevivir al feminismo?" *Feminisme, art et histoire de l'art*, edited by Yves Michaud, Espaces de l'art, 1995.

– "Missing Women: Rethinking Early Thoughts on Images of Women." *The Critical Image: Essays on Contemporary Photography*, edited by Carol Squiers, Bay Press, 1990, pp. 202–19.

Pomés, Leopoldo. *Barcelona 1957*. La Fábrica, 2012.

Porcioles, Josep Maria de. "Transformación del suburbio en barrio." *Los suburbios 1957: Compendio de las ponencias y coloquios desarrollados durante la "Semana," seguido de gráficas y estadísticas*. Gráf. Levante, 1957, pp. 96–100.

Preston, Paul. *Franco: A Biography*. Basic Books, 1994.

Querol, G. "La fotografía testimonio. El implacable realismo de Joan Colom." *AFAL*, enero/febrero 34, 1962, pp. 12–20.

Ramoneda, Josep et al. *1856–1999: Barcelona Contemporània*. Barcelona: CCCB, 1996.

Rancière, Jacques. *Dissensus: On Politics and Aesthetics*. Translated by Steven Corcoran, Continuum, 2010.

Relph, Edward. *Place and Placelessness*. Pion, 1976.

Resina, Joan Ramon. *Barcelona's Vocation of Modernity*. Stanford UP, 2008.

Ribalta, Jorge. "AFAL como síntoma: La ambivalencia de la vanguardia fotográfica española." *Revista El viejo topo*, vol. 228, 2007, pp. 78–87.

– "La dictadura de Franco, 1940–1970." *Barcelona: La metròpolis en la era de la fotografia, 1860–2004*, Ajuntament de Barcelona, 2016.

– "Entrevista a Joan Colom." *El carrer. Joan Colom a la Sala Aixelà, 1961*, edited by David Balsells and Jorge Ribalta, MNAC, 1999, pp. 35–41.

– *Paradigmas fotográficos en Barcelona, 1860–2004*. Quaderns 22, 2009.

Ribalta, Jorge, and David Balsells, editors. *El carrer. Joan Colom a la Sala Aixelà, 1961*. MNAC, 1999.

– *Joan Colom: Fotografías de Barcelona, 1958–1964*. Lunwerg, 2004.

– *Jo faig el carrer: Joan Colom, fotografies 1957–2010*. La Fábrica/MNAC, 2014.
Richardson, Nathan. *Constructing Spain: The Re-Imagination of Space and Place in Fiction and Film, 1953–2003*. Bucknell UP, 2012.
Riera, Ignasi. *Candel, Paco o Francesc: Apunts per a un retrat*. Barcelona: Xarxa Cultural, 1988.
Riquer i Permanyer, Borja de. "Social and Economic Change in a Climate of Political Immobilism," *Spanish Cultural Studies: An Introduction: The Struggle for Modernity*, edited by Helen Graham and Jo Labanyi, Oxford UP, 1995, pp. 259–70.
Roberts, John Michael. "Public Spaces of Dissent." *Sociology Compass*, vol. 2, no. 2, Mar. 2008, pp. 654–74.
Roca i Albert, Joan. "La ciutat informal." *Barraques: La Barcelona informal del segle XX*, Museu d'Història de Barcelona, Institut de Cultura, 2010, pp. 11–19.
Rosler, Martha. *Decoys and Disruptions: Selected Writings, 1975–2001*. October Books, 2004.
– *Imágenes públicas: La función política de la imagen*. Barcelona: Gustavo Gili, 2007.
Rosón Villena, María. "Colita en contexto: Fotografía y feminismo durante la transición." *Arte y políticas de identidad*, vol. 16, June 2017, pp. 55–74.
Rull, Rosa. "Candel, el cronista de la Barcelona marginal." *La nueva literatura hispánica*, vol. 5–7, 2001–3, pp. 123–38.
Salvadó, Ton, and Josep M. Miró. "Els apèndixs de la ciutat dels ronyons," *1856–1999 Barcelona Contemporània*. Barcelona: CCCB, 1996, pp. 134–49.
Santiáñez, Nil. *Topographies of Fascism: Habitus, Space, and Writing in Twentieth-Century Spain*. U of Toronto P, 2013.
Scarry, Elaine. *The Body in Pain: The Making and Unmaking of the World*. Oxford UP, 1985.
Schmalriede, Manfred. "*Subjektive Fotografie* and its Relation to the Twenties." *Subjektive Fotografie: Images of the 50s*, Museum Folkwang, 1984, p. 22.
Scott, Clive. *Street Photography: From Atget to Cartier-Bresson*. Palgrave Macmillan, 2007.
Segura Soriano, Isabel. "Carme Garcia: Des del terrat." *Carme Garcia: Des del terrat*, El cep i la nansa, 2018, pp. 4–11.
– "Polígonos: Tan lejos, tan cerca." *Barcelona: La metrópolis en la era de la fotografía, 1860–2004*. Instituto de Cultura del Ayuntamiento de Barcelona/Editorial RM, 2016, pp. 129–31.
Sekula, Alan. "Desmantelar la modernidad, reinventar el documental: Notas sobre la política de la representación." *Aún no: Sobre la reinvención del documental y la crítica de la modernidad. Ensayos y documentos [1972–1991]*. Madrid: Museo Nacional Centro de Arte Reina Sofía, 2015, pp. 153–68.
– "The Traffic in Photographs." *Art Journal*, vol. 41, no. 1, Spring 1981, pp. 15–25.

Sennett, Richard. *The Conscience of the Eye: The Design and Social Life of Cities.* Norton, 1990.

Shubert, Adrian. *A Social History of Modern Spain.* Routledge, 1990.

Simmel, Georg. "Bridge and Door." Translated by Mark Ritter. *Theory, Culture & Society*, vol. 11, no .1, 1994, pp. 5–10.

– "The Stranger." Translated by Kurt H. Wolff. *The Sociology of Georg Simmel*, edited by Kurt H. Wolff, Free Press, pp. 402–8.

Sinca, Genís. *La providència es diu Paco: Biografia de Francesc Candel.* La Magrana, 2008.

Sontag, Susan. *On Photography.* Picador, 1997.

Sturm-Trigonakis, Elke. *Barcelona: La novela urbana 1944–1988.* Kassel: Kurt and Roswitha Reichenberger, 1996.

Subias, Xavier. "L'urbanisme del 1953 al 1970." *1856–1999 Barcelona Contemporània.* Barcelona: CCCB, 1996, pp. 180–1.

Los suburbios 1957: Compendio de las ponencias y coloquios desarrollados durante la "Semana," seguido de gráficas y estadísticas. Gráf. Levante, 1957.

Tagg, John. *The Burden of Representation: Essays on Photographies and Histories.* U of Minnesota P, 1993.

Tally, Robert T., Jr. *Spatiality.* Routledge, 2013.

Tatjer, Mercè. "Barraques i projectes de remodelació urbana a Barcelona, de l'Eixample al litoral (1922–1966)." *La Barcelona informal del segle XX*, Museu d'Història de Barcelona, Institut de Cultura, 2010, pp. 37–60.

Tello, Rosa. "Barcelona post-olímpica: De ciudad industrial a escenario de consumo." *Estudios Geográficos*, vol. 54, no. 212, July 1993, pp. 507–22.

Terán, Fernando de. "Notas para la historia del planeamiento de Barcelona: La era de Franco." *Ciudad y Territorio* vol. 2, no. 77, 1971, pp. 73–86.

Terré, Laura. *Historia del grupo fotográfico AFAL: 1956/1963.* Photovision, 2006.

– *Pilar Aymerich, el goig i la revolta.* Fundació Privada Vila Casas, 2012.

Thompson, Jerry L. *Why Photography Matters.* MIT P, 2016.

Torres Clavé, Josep. "L'organització col·lectiva de l'habitació." *Arquitectura i Urbanisme*, June 1936, p. 82.

Tuan, Yi-Fu. *Space and Place: The Perspective of Experience.* U of Minnesota P, 2014.

Tubau, Iván. "Un catalán de los 'otros', Candel." *Índice*, vol. 186, no. 17, 1964, pp. 9–10.

Vázquez Montalbán, Manuel. "Barcelona és una puta." *La providència es diu Paco: Biografia de Francesc Candel*, edited by Genís Sinca Algue, La Magrana, 2008, pp. 382–93.

– *Barcelones.* Editorial Empúries, 1990.

– "Los desnudos y los muertos." *Interviú*, May 2001, p. 394.

– *La literatura en la construcción de la ciudad democrática.* Mondadori, 2001.

– "La lluïta necessària." *Barcelona en Lluita (el moviment urbà 1965–1996),* edited by Josep M. Huertas Clavería and Marc Andreu, Federació d'associacions de veïns de Barcelona, 1996, p. 9.

Vega, Carmelo. *Fotografía en España (1839–2015): Historia, tendencias, estéticas.* Cátedra, 2017.

Venteo, Daniel. "Las fotos perdidas de BCN, de Tom Sponheim." REVELA'T 2017, http://revela-t.cat/2017/fotosperdidasbcn/. Accessed 18 July 2017.

– "Milagros Caturla: the Catalan Vivian Maier?" Alabern. Fotografia a Catalunya, https://www.fotografiacatalunya.cat/en/blog/milagros-caturla. Accessed 12 July 2021.

Villar, Paco. *Historia y leyenda del Barrio Chino, 1900–1992: Crónica y documentos de los bajos fondos de Barcelona.* Edicions la Campana, 1996.

Wegner, Phillip E. "Spatial Criticism: Critical Geography, Space, Place, and Textuality." *Introducing Criticism at the 21st Century,* edited by Julian Wolfreys, Edinburgh UP, 2002, pp. 179–201.

White, Hayden. "The Historical Text as Literary Artifact." *Tropics of Discourse: Essays in Cultural Criticism,* Johns Hopkins UP, 1986, pp. 81–100.

Wilson, Elizabeth. "The Invisible Flâneur." *New Left Review,* vol. 191, 1992, pp. 90–110.

Yacavone, Kathrin. *Benjamin, Barthes y la singularidad de la fotografía.* Translated by Núria Molines, Alpha Decay, 2017.

Index

Page numbers that appear in italics refer to photographs.

171, 173; photography and, 154; public sphere and, 171; urban space and construction of, 144. *See also* male bodies; women; women's bodies

General Metropolitan Plan, 206n5

General Proposal for Urban Planning/Plan General de Ordenación Urbana, 31, 202n18

geometric/anthropological space, 195n2

Gilabert, Joan, 208n14, 210n16, 215n34

Gilbert, Sandra, 157

Gil de Biedma, Jaime: "Barcelona ja no és bona" (poem), 4, 5; body in, 6; Degen compared to, 195n4; margin in, 7–9, 12; voice of, 196n5

Goytisolo, Juan, 52, 215n3

Gracia García, Jordi: on apolitical populations, 110; on Francoism's social structure, 106; Ruiz Carnicer and, 122, 218n13

graphic journalism, 36, 100

grassroots citizenship, 75

grassroots democracy, 39–40, 77

the grid, 35, 58

grid-based cities, 27–9, 33, 43, 58

Grup d'Arquitectes i Tècnics Catalans per al Progrés de l'Arquitectura Contemporània (GATCPAC), 203n23

Grupo R, 26, 91

Gubar, Susan, 157

gypsies, 58, 67

Han matado (Candel), 66, 67

Haraway, Donna J., 173

Harvey, David, 24, 30, 34, 75, 191, 203n23

Heidegger, Martin, 119

hierarchy and place-making, 187

Holston, James, 22, 23, 24

Homberger, Eric, 154

House Trade Union/Obra Sindical del Hogar (OSH), 206n4

housing: complexes, 48, 57, 66, 69, 206n5, 221n27; construction of, 47, 203n23; ownership, 32, 39; shortages, 26, 32; subsidized, 47; zoning, 32–3. *See also* public housing

Huertas Clavería, Josep M., 45, 206n6, 207n9

Hughes, Robert, 200n11

human capital, 32

humanist photography, 104, 106, 219n18, 221n31

ideal city, 45–6

image (concept), the, 216n6, 230n10

imagined community, 84, 212n27

immigration/immigrants, 74, 117, 206n6, 214n31. *See also* migrants/migration

inequality and spatial organization, 29

inside/outside dichotomy: Caturla and, 158–9; Garcia and, 161–3, 170; interior/exterior, 167; noise/chaos, 63; urban space and the present, 179

Instituto Nacional de la Vivienda/National Institute of Housing, 26

Irigaray, Luce, 145

irony, 173, 174

Italian neorealism, 106, 221n31

Izas, rabizas y colipoterras (Cela/Colom): about, 95, 110; Colom's involvement in, 225n44; publication/reception of, 217n9, 227n46; the regime and, 128–30; women in, 148, 153

Jacobs, Jane: on city/urban dichotomy, 39, 41; on community/citizenship, 43; on conflict/

Toronto Iberic